OLD ENGLISH

AND

MEDIEVAL LITERATURE

OLD ENGLISH
AND
MEDIEVAL LITERATURE

Selected and Edited by
GORDON HALL GEROULD

 BOOKS FOR LIBRARIES PRESS
FREEPORT, NEW YORK

First Published 1929
Reprinted 1970

STANDARD BOOK NUMBER:
8369-5312-6

LIBRARY OF CONGRESS CATALOG CARD NUMBER:
70-114913

PRINTED IN THE UNITED STATES OF AMERICA

CONTENTS

PREFACE 7

BEOWULF 9

CYNEWULF 56
   An Advent Hymn 57
   Constantine's Vision and Battle with the
      Huns 58

THE WANDERER 63

THE VISION OF PIERS PLOWMAN 67

THE AUTHOR OF *The Pearl* AND *Sir Gawain* 79
   The Pearl 80
   Sir Gawain and the Green Knight . . . 85

GEOFFREY CHAUCER 152
   THE CANTERBURY TALES 154
      The Prologue 154
      The Nun's Priest's Tale 182
      The Pardoner's Tale 202
      The Franklin's Tale 221
      The Second Nun's Tale 250

LYRICS 269
   Song 269
   Lady Fortune 270

v

"Against my will I take my leave" . . . 270
Truth 272
Ballade 273
The Compleynt of Chaucer to His Purse . 274
Song 275
A Carol 275

MALORY'S MORTE D'ARTHUR 276
The Choosing of Arthur 277
Launcelot and the Grail Castle 283
Arthur's Last Battle and Death 289

POPULAR BALLADS 297
Babylon; or, The Bonnie Banks o Fordie 299
Edward 301
The Maid Freed from the Gallows . . . 303
Lord Randal 305
Johnie Cock 307
Thomas Rymer and the Queen of Elfland 310
The Wife of Usher's Well 313
The Dæmon Lover 314
The Three Ravens 317
Hugh of Lincoln 318
Childe Waters 320
Sir Patrick Spence 326
Young Waters 328
The Bonny Earl of Murray 330
Mary Hamilton 331
Chevy Chase 333
Robin Hood and Guy of Gisborne . . . 343
The Lochmaben Harper 351
Jock o the Side 354

The Braes of Yarrow 360
The Unquiet Grave 362
Lady Isabel and the Elf-Knight 363
The Twa Sisters 365
Allison Gross 367
Tam Lin 369
Saint Stephen and Herod 376
The Cherry-Tree Carol 377
Bonnie George Campbell 379

PREFACE

THE purpose of this volume is to illustrate the best things written in English from the eighth century to the fifteenth. Nothing has been included merely because it has historical interest. It goes without saying that such a selection can be illustrative only, for at no period has the English genius for writing completely failed. The reader should remember, in this connection, that between 1150 and 1350 Englishmen used French as their ordinary medium of expression, when they wrote in the vernacular at all. Yet despite this fact, and despite the loss of uncounted manuscripts, the body of interesting literature in Old and Middle English is amazingly large. The editor's effort has been to pick out what will serve as an introduction to treasures that the student may later explore. As far as possible, the selections are complete in themselves, since fragments are likely to give false notions and to lack interest. On this account, Old English is largely represented by passages from *Beowulf* that serve to tell the whole story, when read in connection with the summaries of the sections omitted. Except for Chaucer, the lyrics, Malory, and the ballads, everything is of necessity given in modern English; and Malory's spelling has not been preserved. The editor is responsible for all the translations in the volume, save the brilliant rendering of *The Wanderer,* which he owes to the kindness of his colleague, Professor J. Duncan Spaeth.

February 1, 1929.

BEOWULF

"*Beowulf* occupies a unique position in the literature of Western Europe as the earliest poem of importance in any vernacular after the collapse of Roman civilization. It is the herald of modern letters, as the *Iliad* and the *Odyssey* are of classical letters, and it is not unworthy of comparison with those earlier and greater epics. Like them, it reflects the manners and ideals of an age which may with some propriety be called 'heroic.' Its chief adventures are as fantastic as any in the wanderings of Ulysses, yet its historical background affords an unrivalled picture of the early life of our pagan ancestors. Political and social conditions are as vividly and as truthfully set forth as if there were no demons lurking in the mists at nightfall, no dragon watching on the windy heights. But the main importance of a great poem must lie in its poetry. As to this, no apologies for *Beowulf* are necessary. The tale itself and the traditions encircling it have all the authority of centuries of story-telling over ale-cups and by winter firesides. Then, in a happy hour, it became the theme of a gifted poet, and received its final epic form. Although it deals with the exploits of Scandinavian heroes, it is a thoroughly English poem, written in the English language, in a verse and style characteristically English, and infused with the spirit and ideals of English folk. There is every reason why we of to-day who have inherited those traditions should know *Beowulf,* and appreciate it as a work of art." (W. W. Lawrence, *Beowulf and Epic Tradition,* 1928, p. vii.)

Beowulf is thus not only the first great landmark in English literature, but the earliest representative of the new civilization that gradually emerged in Europe after the barbarian invaders from the North had begun to absorb what was left of Roman culture. To the best of our knowledge, it was written in the early years of the eighth century. During the previous hundred years the Anglo-Saxons had been christianized by missionaries from Rome and Ireland, and with the new religion had taken over such learning as had survived the collapse of the ancient

world. The author of *Beowulf* was a contemporary of
Bede, who was internationally famous as a scholar though
he lived in a monastery close to the northern border of
England. He was a contemporary also of poets who put
into verse very like his own, stories from the Old Testament. Both he and they, though Christians and probably
clerics, had not forgotten the barbarian traditions of their
race, which accounts for the strange but appealing mixture
in their work of elements from two widely different cultures.
All of them worshipped God, but they remembered Wyrd
as the shaper of man's destiny; they had learned to read
Latin poetry, as they had learned to write in Roman letters,
but they composed in a style and metre peculiar to themselves.

This style was one adapted to recitation or chanting. It
abounded in bold metaphors, called kennings, and did not
avoid stereotyped phrases, probably because the familiar
sounds echoed pleasantly in the ears of the listeners. For
the same reason, doubtless, there is a marked use of parallel-
ism, the repetition of the same thought in different words—
a device with which everyone is familiar in the *Book of
Psalms*. Each line of Old English verse has four strong
beats or accents, but the number of unstressed syllables
varies widely. One of the stressed syllables in the second
half of the line always alliterates with one or both of the
stressed syllables in the first half. By this means an echo
of sound is produced that serves somewhat the same purpose as rhyme. In the translation that follows, an effort
has been made to reproduce these characteristic features of
Old English poetry, though it is difficult to do this successfully because of changes in our language—notably the loss
of inflectional endings. The translator can only hope to give
the reader some inkling of the imaginative power that
makes *Beowulf* no mere historical document but a living
work of art.

The poem opens with the story of Scyld, the mythical
king of the Danes, or Scyldings. Of his line was born
Hrothgar. (w. 1—63)

To Hrothgar was given glory in battle,
acclaimed with such honor that his clansmen loyal
gladly obeyed him, and his band of youths
waxed great and mighty. Then grew his heart eager

to build for himself a hall that was worthy,
a mead-hall mightier than men had known,
a dwelling that fitted the fame he had won;
and there within to the old and the young
what God had allotted he would give as was right,
save the rule of men and the realm that he held.
I have heard that the work through the world was
    spread
among many a tribe to make the folk-hall
and adorn it fitly. It was done at his will,
10 and with speed was finished, spacious and lofty,
the greatest of halls. Hart he named it,
the ruler whose word so widely had power.
He forgot not his promise of giving out rings,
wealth at the feasting. Till the flames devoured it,
the high hall stood with horns on the gables,
towered lofty, for the time was not yet
when the direful hate of a daughter's spouse
should stir to malice and slaughter there.
    But the monster who lurked in the lowering
    shadows,
20 the mighty demon, endured it ill
when he heard each day the din and the revelry
that was loud in the hall. The harp resounded,
and the minstrel sang, reciting clearly
what well he had mastered of man's beginning,
how the All-Wielder had wrought the earth,
the smiling world which the sea surrounds,
in triumph had set the sun and the moon
as lights to illumine the landsmen's ways,
and every region of earth made fair
30 with limb and with leaf; life, too, had given
to all of mankind who have ever had birth.
    So the tribesmen lived long with rejoicing,
blessed and happy, till the hellish fiend
his crimes began, that creature damned.

The monster grim Grendel was named,
who kept to the moors and the murky fens,
defying all law. Long had he dwelt there,
the hapless creature in the haunt of demons,
condemned by the Lord and driven forth
for his kinship to Cain, who had killed his brother.
Avenged was Abel by the edict of God,
Who banished the slayer for the sin he had done
from the race of mankind, the Ruler of Heaven.
10 The sire he was, the source of all monsters,
the giants and elves and the goblins, too,
the fearsome tribes who fought for long
against God the Eternal. He gave them their due.
    In the murky night came the monster to spy
on the Ring-Danes left in the lofty house
after the feasting, and he found therein
the band of æthelings bound in slumber,
full fed and asleep, all sorrows forgotten,
all woes of mankind. The wight of destruction
20 stern and greedy, stayed not his hand,
savage and fierce, but seized at their rest
some thirty thanes, and thence returned,
exultant hastened to his haunt in the moors,
dragging the spoil of the slaughter home.
As the light of morning lifted slowly,
the vengeance of Grendel was revealed to men;
there was sorrow at dawn, the sound of weeping
where the feast had been. The famous prince
sat unhappy and suffered dire grief,
30 the ætheling good for the thanes who had gone,
when once they had traced the track of the enemy,
the trail of the damned. Dreadful and tedious
the hateful war! Nor was it longer
than the very next night that the villain returned,
the creature to ravage, in crime relentless
and the wicked feud, bound fast in them.

Then many escaped, the men who could,
and sought their repose apart from the hall
in beds that they found in the bowers outside,
since the monster's hate was manifest there
by a visible sign. The survivors, thus,
were safer afar, as it seemed to them.
   So wickedly ruled and unrighteously fought
one against all, until empty stood
the noblest of houses. And the havoc went on;
10 twelve winters' time the trusted Scylding
endured affliction and depth of woe,
encompassing sorrow, till it came to be known
to the children of men by means of their lays
that Grendel it was, grim and hostile,
who waged against Hrothgar a war relentless
bitter with hatred, a battle enduring
for many a season. With no man would he
of the Danish power make peace at all,
remove the menace, for money compound it;
20 nor could the elders in any wise hope
that compensation the slayer would pay.
A shadow dark, the death-dealing monster
lay ever in wait for age and for youth
from the lair that he held in the heavy dark
of the mist-laden moors. Men could not fathom
by what devious ways the demons would come.

   None of Hrothgar's councillors could devise any way to
rid the country of the monster (vv. 164-193).

Then heard in his home Hygelac's kinsman,
great among Geats, of Grendel's deeds.
Mighty he was, of men the brawniest,
30 of mortal heroes highest in power,
both strong and noble. 'Make ready a ship,'
he bade them, and said, a battle-king he
over the swan-road would seek out the prince,

the king so renowned who had need of men.
His prudent henchmen to hold him back
made little attempt, though beloved was he;
they praised the venture, and viewed the omens.
From the Geats the chieftain had chosen his warriors,
the keenest among them as comrades and friends.
With fourteen followers whom he found to his liking
he marched to the shore, to the ship that waited,
a mariner trained with his men behind him.

10   The hour had come; at the hill's base rode
the boat on the waves.   The warriors mounted
the prow of the ship, while the surf came splashing,
sea against sand; they stowed their gear,
their weapons bright in the breast of the vessel,
their war-gear splendid.   Then the warriors eager
pushed out the boat well-bound and sturdy.
Over the waters by the wind impelled
went the foamy-necked ship like a flying bird.
For a day it waded the deep unchecked,

20 the craft with its prow that was proudly uplifted,
until the sea-farers had sight of land,
the shore-cliffs steep, the shining nesses,
the mighty forelands.   They had found their haven,
the voyage had ended.   Then eagerly sprang
the folk of the Wethers forth on the land;
they moored the sea-wood; their stiff sarks rattled,
their garments of war; and God they thanked
for the prosperous faring they had found on the
          journey.
    From the cliff by the shore the Scylding's sentinel,

30 who guarded the sea-wall, saw them bearing
over the bulwarks the bright-bossed shields,
the well-made armor; he wondered and questioned,
being eager to know who these aliens were.
Came riding, then, the thane of Hrothgar
down to the shore, and doughtily shook

the spear in his hands, and spoke as was fitting.
'What warriors are ye, weapon-bearers,
dressed in your corslets, who a ship high-keeled
over the sea-ways, over the ocean,
have hither brought? Long here have I been,
as guard of the coast have kept my watch
lest a hostile host do harm by a raid
on the land of the Danes down from their ships.
None more openly ever came hither
10 bearing their shields, though ye sought no leave
from the Danish clan, nor have claimed the right
by consent of the kinsmen. Never saw I on earth
a greater warrior than is one of you,
a hero in armor; no hall-thane merely,
if his looks deceive not, his splendid weapons,
his noble mien. Now must you tell me
what tribe you are from ere you farther move
as spies mayhap on the home of the Danes,
in doubtful ways. Far-dwellers, hear,
20 sea-wanderers, hearken; my words are plain;
it is best that quickly you break your silence,
declaring your race and whence you have come.'
    To him the leader unlocked his word-store,
gave him an answer the guide of the band:
'We are clansmen of the kin of the Geats,
hearth-companions of Hygelac's tribe.
My father was known to the folk full widely,
a noble war-leader whose name was Ecgtheow.
He lived many winters ere away he was reft,
30 old from our dwelling; and doubtless the wise
remember him well widely through earth.
We have come seeking the son of Healfdene,
thy lord, with hearts that are loyal and true.
We beg for thy counsel, since we have come hither
on a weighty errand to thy widely famed lord.
I make it known, since we need not conceal it,

as it seems to me. Instruct us, I pray thee,
if the rumor be true that has reached our ears
of something harmful, of hurt to the Scyldings,
of dire crimes done in the darkness of night,
of horror revealed and hurt unexampled,
of shameful murders. It may be to Hrothgar
my counsel might serve as a comfort to help him
in conquering this terror, overcoming the fiend,
if ever he find an end of affliction,
10 if trouble at length be turned away,
and the hot waves of care be cooled of their heat.
If not, then forever he must eke out wretchedly
a miserable life, while remains yet standing
on its lofty height the noblest of houses.'
　　The guardian spoke, where he sat on his steed,
the sentinel bold: 'The sharp-visioned warrior
whose thought is just must judge as of right
between words that are said and works that are done.
I now believe this a loyal band
20 to the lord of the Scyldings, and leave you to bear
your armor and weapons; I shall guide you.
Upon my companions I place the care
of your vessel here against hostile men,
your fresh-caulked ship that you leave on the sands,
to give it honor, till again it may bear
its dear lord returning o'er the deeps of the sea,
sharp-prowed and good, to the realm of the Geats,
should no harm be wrought in the rush of the battle
to him who will do deeds that are valorous.'
30 　　Then went they forth, while fast at anchor
stood in the offing their ship wide-bosomed.
Boar-figures glittered on golden helmets,
above the cheek-guards brightened and shone;
tempered by fire, talismans were they,
and guarded the men who moved together
and marched in haste till the timbered hall,

splendid with gold, they saw before them.
Most of renown known to earth-dwellers
was the stately hall where the high king sat;
the light of it shone over many lands.
Far off the soldier showed them the hall,
the dwelling resplendent of daring warriors,
made plain the pathway, then paused and said,
as he turned his steed: 'It is time for parting.
I go with the prayer that God Almighty
10 may guard and protect you by His guidance and
        grace,
keep you safe in your ventures! To the sea I must go
against hostile hosts to hold my watch.'
The street they followed with stones was bright,
and bright on the warriors the war-gear shone,
the ringed mail hard, hand-linked and burnished;
it sang as they moved, marching in order,
forth to the hall in fearsome array.
Sea-weary they set their broad shields down,
their bucklers strong, by the side of the dwelling;
20 they sank to the bench, their byrnies clanking,
the gear of the warriors; together they stood
their ashen shafts grey-tipped and sharp,
the seamen bold, for the band was armed
with splendid weapons.

Beowulf was then approached by Wulfgar, a court official,
who asked his errand and entered the hall to ask audience
for the strangers. Hrothgar, knowing Beowulf's lineage
and renown, welcomed them gladly and bade admit them
at once (vv. 332-398).

The leader arose and round him his band,
of the splendid troop all save a few
whom the chief commanded to remain with the gear.
They hastened together with the guidance of Wulf-
        gar

under Heorot's roof till the hardy leader,
bold in his helmet, on the hearth-stone stood.
Beowulf spoke—and his byrny shone,
his mail well wrought by the might of the smith:
'Hail thou, Hrothgar! I am of Hygelac
a thane and a kinsman, accustomed from youth
to deeds of greatness. What Grendel has done
at home in my country came to my knowledge.
Sea-farers have it that this hall is standing
10 empty and idle, useless for all men,
though the noblest of buildings, after night has descended
and the evening light is lost from the firmament.
My people, therefore, the prudent and brave,
gave me the counsel that I should come,
Prince Hrothgar, and seek thee, having seen and known well
the strength of my might; remembering doubtless
what they themselves saw when, stained by my foes,
I came from the battle where five giants I bound,
destroyed their race, and slew in the waves
20 the shadowy dragons, enduring things dire
but avenging the Wethers who woe had suffered—
made an end of their enemy. And now against Grendel,
this monster alone I long to contend,
to finish the demon. Thus, lord of the Danes,
prince of Bright-Scyldings, one boon I would ask,
if any favor I find with thee,
that thou wilt not forbid me, protector of warriors,
friend of thy folk, since afar I have come,
but let me cleanse with my clansmen alone,
30 this band of the hardy, Heorot hall.
This, too, I have learned, that leaving all weapons
the monster contends; so truly will I,
that my lord Hygelac may be happy of heart.

I will bear neither sword nor sheltering shield,
no buckler of yellow when the battle I enter,
but by the grip of my hands I will grasp at the foe,
contending thus only and trying my fate.
He whom death takes his trust must repose
in the Lord Who judges with justice mankind.
The demon will try, I doubt not, to eat
the folk of the Geats as before he devoured
oft in the hall, hesitant never,
10 the best of thy clansmen.   No burial rites
needst thou give to my head, but he will have me
drenched with my gore if death shall be mine;
will make me a feast in the fen he inhabits,
will deluge with blood his den, and alone
ruthlessly eat me.   Reck not of rites
to be done for my body.   But if battle takes me,
send to Hygelac the sark I wear,
best of war-gear, of garments the choicest,
an heirloom of Hrethel, a work of Weland.
20 Wyrd moves ever as Wyrd decrees.'

Hrothgar replied to Beowulf at length, bidding him welcome and rehearsing the ravages of Grendel.   At the feast
that followed, Unferth, an important official of the court but
jealous, taunted Beowulf with having been beaten in a
swimming contest with Breca.   Beowulf made answer.
(vv. 456-529.)

'Lo, many things, my friend Unferth,
drunken with beer, thou hast said about Breca,
hast told of his journey!   I will tell but the truth,
that I have more strength in swimming than others,
more endurance in hardness, more daring and power.
We two had boasted, boy-like and braggarts—
as yet, as I say, we were youths and not wise—
said one to the other that in the wide ocean
we would venture our lives, and verily did so.
30 When we entered the sound, a sword each had

to wield at his will, for we were minded
against whales to protect us. Nor in any wise could
      he
farther or faster in the flood go than I,
and I would not from him: we were companions.
Thus in the sea we swam together
five nights till the floods flung us apart,
the whelming waters and weather cold,
the darkness of night. The north wind came,
fiercely assailed us, and rough was the sea.
10 Ocean-bred monsters were angered with me;
against them, only my armor of mail
strongly made by man's hand helped me and saved
      me,
the interlocked corslet that lay on my breast,
brightened with gold. To the bottom bore me
my terrible foe, for he had me fast
in his direful grip, yet was granted to me
to pierce the monster with the point of my sword.
The storm of battle destroyed the sea-beast,
despite his power, through my prowess of hand.
20 So often and often my enemies
pressed me sorely. I served them well
with my faithful sword as was befitting.
They were baulked of the joy of a generous feast
when me they'd have eaten, those evil-doers,
sitting about in the depths of the sea.
So in the morning by me wounded,
along by the shore they lay cast up,
slain by the sword, and since then never
have they hindered or stayed the sailors faring
30 on the ocean deep. From the east came a light,
God's own bright signal, and the waves subsided,
so that I saw sea-nesses shining
and wind-swept cliffs. Wyrd often preserves

the hero undoomed if his valor endure!
To me it was given to get with my sword
nine of the monsters; and never heard I
of a harder night-battle under heaven's dome
nor of man more beset in the streams of the sea;
but worn with the struggle I saved my life
from the enemy's grasp. The ocean bore me
to the land of the Finns, the flood on its current,
the surging waves. Of such dire struggles
10 not a word has been told me concerning thee,
no exploits of battle, for neither Breca
in the throes of the fight, nor thou yet more,
has ever done such deeds of courage
with a bloody sword—nor boasting am I—
though thou of thy brothers wert the bane and the
    slayer,
of thy dearest kin. Damned shalt thou be,
in hell make thy payment, though thy head be so
    clever.
I tell thee forsooth, thou son of Ecglaf,
that never could Grendel such numberless horrors,
20 that monster dire, have done to thy chief,
such shame to Heorot, if thy heart were at all,
thy courage so strong as thou hast claimed.
But he has found that the feud holds for him
little to fear from thy folk and thee;
a vaunt without worth, that of Victory-Scyldings.
He seizes his toll and spares no man
of the tribe of the Danes, but takes at his will,
slaughters and slays, and from Spear-Danes expects
no vengeance to follow. But Geats, he shall find,
30 have courage and strength, as full soon I to him
shall witness in battle. He who wills may then go
without fear to the mead-hall, when the morning
    light

of the day succeeding shall dawn upon men,
when the radiant sun shall shine from the south!'

This speech by Beowulf won him the trust of Hrothgar.
During the rejoicing that followed, Queen Wealhtheow
entered the hall and did the honors. To her Beowulf renewed his pledge to destroy the monster or die in the
attempt. Thereupon the Danes all withdrew from Heorot,
leaving it to the care of Beowulf and his companions.
(vv. 607-701)

Through the dark night gliding
came the shadow-goer. Asleep were the warriors
who were there to hold the horn-gabled hall—
but one was waking. Without the will of the Lord,
the men were sure that under the shadows
the demon enemy could never drag them;
but the vigilant leader the venture awaited,
10 sleepless and angry the issue of battle.
Then from the moors with their misty slopes
came Grendel forth with God's curse on him;
the ravager meant, of the men found there,
one to have as his prey in the high-built hall.
He made his way till, the wine-hall near,
the golden assembly of men he descried,
richly fashioned. Not the first time was it
he came to the home of Hrothgar the king;
but never before did he find such men,
20 so strong to grasp what fortune might give.
The joyless creature came creeping on
to the door of the hall. Though hasped with iron,
it withstood not long the strength of his hands;
he pushed wide open the portal then,
with anger stirred, and straightway entered.
Across the bright floor with a fury of heart
the monster shuffled, while there shone in his eyes
a horrid light most like to flame.
His furious glance fell on the warriors,

on the sleeping clansmen slumbering there,
the band of heroes, and his heart exulted.
The demon dreadful, ere day should come,
made sure of rending, wresting from all of them
life from the body, and likewise hoped
for a plentiful feast. His fate was other,
for he never tasted or touched a mortal
after that night. Now the mighty
kinsman of Hygelac the contest waited,
10 the sudden attack of the treacherous enemy;
nor did the monster a moment delay,
but seized at once a sleeping warrior
in his forward rush, rent him unwary,
tore his body, drank the blood from his veins,
devoured him straightway. Of the victim soon
remained not a limb, for the monster had bolted
every whit of the corpse. Came he then nearer,
laid hands on the hero, whose heart failed not,
on the warrior at rest; he reached forth for him,
20 clutching and clawing; but the chief was ready,
rising up on his arm against the enemy's thrust.
Soon discovered the keeper of wickedness
there was not to be found on the face of the earth,
though the world were searched, a stronger man
of greater power in the grip of his hands.
He feared for his life, but found no escape;
to flee and to hide was his heart's one wish,
with his demon brood; he endured what before
had never come to him in the course of his days.
30 Then the hero remembered, Hygelac's kinsman,
his boast of the evening; up he stood,
held the monster fast, though his fingers cracked;
away pulled the giant, the warrior followed.
The enemy longed, if ever he might,
to loosen the grip and get away,
to flee to the fens. He felt the power

of his enemy's grasp. A grievous journey,
this that the monster to Heorot made!
　There was din in the hall; to the Danes every one,
to the dwellers at court, keen men and warriors,
terror it brought. Both were angry,
the duel furious. The dwelling resounded.
Great wonder it was that the wine-hall stood,
fell not to earth as the foes there fought,
but the beauteous house with bands of iron
10 within and without was everywhere strengthened
by skilful craft. Crashed there many
a gold-decked settle, the story says,
to the floor of the mead-hall while the foes were
　　　struggling.
The Scylding leaders had believed not before
that any man ever in any fashion
could damage that hall, adorned with antlers,
by wiles destroy it, save the whelming of flame
with fire should raze it. Rose up the tumult
ceaseless and dreadful; on the Danish folk
20 a terrible fear fell while they listened,
from without through the walls the wailing heard,
the cry terror-stricken that came from God's foe,
from the hell-bound wight, wounded, defeated,
the dire lamentation. He was tight in the grasp
of the hero mightiest of mortal men,
strongest of grip. The guardian of warriors
would in no wise leave alive the destroyer,
accounting him wholly an encumbrance to folk.
Round about Beowulf brandished his comrades
30 their ancient weapons, wished to protect
the life of their prince, their lord so glorious,
if they in any wise a way might find.
They were not aware when they went to the battle,
those warriors eager who entered the fray,
hacking and hewing with hearts that were bold,

seeking with iron the soul of the monster,
that him no weapon, no war-bill on earth,
though the choicest of swords, might cleave or harm;
for he had upon him the power of a spell,
an enchantment had woven that warded from him
the edge of them all. Yet his end was to be,
when the time of death came, the day of departure,
a miserable one, for the monster afar
in the power of demons was doomed to go.
10 Now at length found he, who aforetime had
wrought
much trouble for man and many afflictions—
God's enemy he, hostile and wicked—
that his body's force was failing and feeble
in the clutch of the hero, Hygelac's kinsman.
Each to the other was ever hateful
while life remained. The monster dire
was sorely hurt; his sinews gaped;
a wound on his shoulder was seen, and asunder
the joints were burst. To Beowulf victory
20 in battle was given, while Grendel sore-stricken
must flee away thence to the fens and the marshes,
to his home unhappy. He then clearly
knew that his days were numbered and spent,
that his life was ended. To all of the Danes
after the contest had come their desire.
The man from afar, faithful, courageous,
had cleansed the hall of Hrothgar and saved it
from the enemy's wrath. In the work of that night,
in the valorous deeds he had done he rejoiced.
30 The prince of the Geats his promise and boasting
had performed to the East-Danes; their ills and
miseries
had ended at length, which inescapable
they before had suffered in sore distress
for no short time. The token was clear

when the proud in battle had placed the arm,
the shoulder of Grendel, and the hand he gripped
      with,
displayed them together under the gable.
    Then in the morning was many a warrior
about the hall, as I heard the tale;
from far and from near the folk-leaders came,
the wide ways over, the wonder to view,
the enemy's traces. Not at all did his death
seem a painful thing to the thanes who followed
10 the trail of the vanquished, tracking him down
where he went weary-hearted away from the hall,
smitten and dying, dragging his footsteps,
to plunge at last in the pool of the monsters.
Bubbles of blood broke on the surface,
the eddying swirls were swart with gore,
the crimson waters welled with his life-blood,
when he dove to his death. Doomed and joyless,
in the depths of the lake his life he gave up,
his heathen soul; then hell received him.
20   High of heart thence, home again riding,
the old men proud from the pool of death
came on their steeds, and crowding youths
borne on their horses. Then Beowulf's glory
was often recounted; they caught up the tale
that between the two seas, southward or northward,
the wide world over no other man
under heaven's dome was doughtier ever,
among shield-warriors more worthy to rule;
yet in praise were disloyal to their lord in no manner,
30 to Hrothgar the gracious, for a good king was he.
Sometimes the brave in battle their horses,
their tawny mounts, when they met smooth paths,
sent racing forward as rivals in speed.
Sometimes the thanes who had songs in remem-
      brance,

famed for their minstrelsy, the men in whose minds
lived the old sagas, who could set them forth
woven rightly in words interlocked,
such men with skill made about Beowulf
chants of adventure, his voyage and battle,
aptly reciting the story all knew,
but in varying words.

The court poets or minstrels went on to recount briefly
the adventures of Sigmund and the career of Heremod,
implying that Beowulf might now be accounted the equal
of the one great hero, and might take warning in his greatness from the sad end of the other. The company then
approached the hall, outside which formal speeches were
made by their leaders. (vv. 875-924)

Hrothgar began—to the hall he had come,
looked from the step where he stood to the roof,
10 gold-adorned, lofty, and Grendel's hand:
'At the first, to the Lord let us be giving
our thanks for this sight! I have suffered much
from the hatred of Grendel. Yet God the glorious
may accomplish at will wonder after wonder.
But lately I hoped not while life should last
for my release, or relief from my sorrow,
while battle-gory the best of dwellings
stood wet with blood—a woe far-reaching
to all of the council, since they could not hope
20 the fortress to hold against hostile creatures,
devilish monsters and demons of evil.
But now has a champion accomplished for us,
through the mercy of God, the mighty deed
which all of our wit, our wisdom and prowess,
contrived not before. Lo, this may she say,
whoever she be, the woman who bore him,
if yet she lives, that the Lord her God
showed her His favor when such a son

she brought into life. Now, Beowulf, thee,
noblest of heroes, I heartily ask
to be as my son; assume henceforth
that kinship forever. While I hold rule,
no want shalt thou have of worldly possessions,
since often for less to a lesser man
have I honors granted, and given wealth
to a feebler in deeds. Thou hast done such things
that thy glory shall live to the last of the world,
10 forever and aye. May the all-wielding Lord,
Who has guided thee hither, with good requite thee!'
    Beowulf spoke, the son of Ecgtheow:
'Great mercy it was that we won the fight,
the battle of strength, having boldly dared
the might of the foe. I had fondly hoped
to show thee the corpse of the creature here
as dight for the struggle but dead of his wounds.
I had thought to hold him so hard in my grip,
bind him so fast on the bed of death,
20 that he should there lie with his life as the forfeit,
in agony bound till his body should fail.
Though I would not loose him, the Lord did not
        grant
that I should stay him or stop his going,
my mortal foe; too mighty was he
in his power at the last. Yet he left his hand
in saving his life, his shoulder and arm,
nor was flight a help to the hapless creature
in any wise, for the evil-doer
is not destined to live the longer thereby,
30 pressed hard by his sins, for a sore wound has he,
holding him close in its hateful grip,
in its baleful clutch; abide he must there,
foul with his sinning, the final doom
when the Lord with justice shall judgment give.'

After these speeches, Unferth, who had derided Beowulf
earlier, was silent; but the other warriors, gazing at the
arm of Grendel, said that no sword could have served against
the monster. (vv. 980-990)

Then by eager hands was Heorot decked;
a throng there was of women and men
who dressed the wine-hall, adorned for the guests.
Golden-threaded the tapestries shone
the length of the walls, a wonder to see
for all of the men who might behold them.
Bright the house then and banded with iron,
though all within was injured and broken,
the joints of it rent; the roof alone
10 was wholly sound when the hostile demon,
stained with his crimes, despairing of life,
fled in confusion. To flee is not easy—
attempt it who will, and try as he may—
since every mortal by the mandate of fate,
all the children of men, all the creatures of earth,
must seek as appointed the place that is ready,
where his body shall lie on its bed in the grave,
asleep there forever.
                              Then into the hall
20 at the hour befitting went Healfdene's son,
the king himself to sit at the feast.
Never heard I of a nobler band
with a greater pomp round a giver of treasure.
There to the benches bowed the victors,
rejoiced in the feast, fairly receiving
many a mead-cup; the kinsmen together
sat strong-hearted in the towering hall,
Hrothgar and Hrothulf. Heorot was peopled
with friends on that day, nor deemed the Scyldings
30 that treachery ever or treason should rend them.
A golden standard the son of Healfdene
to Beowulf gave, a banner embroidered,

with helmet and corslet and costly sword.
In the view of the throng the victor's rewards
were borne aloft. Beowulf emptied
a cup while standing. He could not with right
feel shame of the gift in the sight of the warriors.
I think that but few have four such treasures,
adorned with gold, given to others
in sign of their friendship while sitting at ale.
Around the helmet a rim projected,
10 twisted with wire, to ward and preserve.
No blade that the files for battle made ready
could a warrior harm who bore to the contest
a guard so fashioned against his foes.
The protector of heroes eight horses, then,
with bridles plated, bade bring on the floor
of the hall itself, and the saddle on one
was wrought with art and rich with treasure;
the seat it had been of the son of Healfdene
when the high king sought the sword-play of men.
20 Never failed in the van the valor of Hrothgar,
renowned for his courage when the corpses fell.
And the staff of the Ingwines bestowed as a gift
both of the treasures on Beowulf then,
the horses and weapons: they were his to enjoy.
Thus nobly the prince of power and fame,
the warden of heroes rewarded the struggle
with treasures and steeds too splendid to scorn
by any man telling the truth as it is.

> After presents had been given to Beowulf's followers, a
> *scop* recited an heroic poem about a feud between the Danes
> and the Frisians, of whom Finn was the king. This poem
> is summarized in the text. Queen Wealhtheow thereupon
> gave Beowulf valuable gifts and begged him to act as pro-
> tector of her sons. (vv. 1050-1231)

She went to her seat. Splendid the banquet,
30 the drinking of wine, for their destiny grim

the men did not know, nor what to many
was fated that night to befall when Hrothgar
went forth to his dwelling, the famous to rest.
The hall was kept by a crowd of warriors,
who guarded it now again as of yore.
They pushed back the benches and placed on the floor
their beds and bolsters. Bowed to his slumber
one of the feasters who was fated to die.
They set at their heads their splendid shields,
10 protectors in battle; on the benches behind
the heroes rested their helmets tall,
their corslets of mail, their mighty spears.
Their custom it was for war to be ready
not only when forth on forays they went
but also at home at every season,
to furnish swift aid when befell the need,
the loyal clan to their liege lord dear.
　　Sank they to slumber. A certain one paid
for his sleep full heavily as happened before
20 while Grendel guarded the golden hall,
crimes committed, till came the end,
death for his sinning. It was seen that night,
made clear to the stalwart, that still there lived
an avenger and foe the feud to maintain,
the grievous strife. Grendel's mother,
a female monster, remembered her grief
in her watery den where she dwelt alone
in the cold, cold sea, after Cain long ago
his brother had slain, the son of his father.
30 Away into exile he went with his guilt,　.
marked with the murder from men had fled,
dwelt in the waste-lands. Thence woke the monsters,
the spirits of woe, of whom one was Grendel,
the hateful outcast who at Heorot met
a hero who watched, waiting the struggle.
The monster seized him, but soon he found

in the man a strength, a mighty power,
an abounding gift which God had bestowed,
for the Omnipotent Lord lent him His aid,
His solace and help. So he humbled the fiend,
overcame the demon, who to death went forth
abject, defeated, to the fen where he dwelt,
a foe of all men. But his mother now,
savage and ravenous, made ready to go
a sorrowful journey her son to avenge.
10   Came she to Heorot, where the hall was thronged
with sleeping Ring-Danes. Sudden and soon
the terror fell when the foe appeared,
the mother of Grendel, though greater the horror
he spread, as his might was a man's compared
with a woman's strength; like a warrior armed,
when his hammered blade with blood new stained
cleaves with its edge his enemy's helmet,
cuts through the boar-crest the bound sword keen.
Then they snatched in the hall their swords from the
       benches,
20 laid hands on their shields, but their helmets forgot,
gave no heed to their corslets, could not for terror
when the monster they saw. She was not staying,
but headed about in haste to be gone,
to save her life when she was discovered.
One of the heroes she hastily seized
fast in her talons, then turned to the fens.
Dearest to Hrothgar was he whom she slew
of all his retainers between the two seas,
a warrior mighty, a man of power.
30   Absent was Beowulf; after the banquet
another lodging had been allotted
to the famous Geat. A great cry rose
in Heorot then. The hand she had taken,
the blood-soaked trophe! A torture renewed
was this in the courts. The exchange was evil,

each party in turn paying a price
in the life of friends.   Then the leader wise,
the hoary king, in heart was troubled
when he knew that no longer was living the thane,
knew that his dearest of vassals was dead.
Swift from his bower was Beowulf fetched,
the hero victorious.   In the twilit dawn
the noble warrior, renowned among men,
went with his comrades where the wise king waited,
10 if ever the Wielder of All would change
to a happier tale the tidings of woe.
Along the floor strode the stalwart hero
with his handful of friends; the hall re-echoed.
In words he addressed the wise among rulers,
the lord of the Ingwines, asked of the night-time,
if aught had been done to dim his content.
    Hrothgar answered, the helmet of Scyldings:
'Ask not of rejoicing!   Anew comes sorrow
to the Danish folk.   Dead is Æschere,
20 the elder brother of Yrmenlaf,
my counsellor wise and constant helper;
at my shoulder he stood in the shock of battle,
in the crash of the conflict, the clash when we
        charged
like the boars on our helmets.   What is best in a
        warrior,
who seeks and achieves, such was Æschere!
He died in Heorot at the hand of a murderous
and wandering monster; whither she vanished,
content with her prey and proud of her killing,
I do not know.   Thy deed of the night
30 before this she avenged, when in violent wise
thou didst Grendel slay by the strength of thy hands,
because he too long had killed my folk,
wasted and ravaged.   He rests in death,
his life a forfeit; but forth came another,

a mighty slayer her son to avenge,
and far she has gone the feud in repaying,
as many a thane may think in his heart
who grieves for his ruler, the giver of rings—
woe hard to bear. The hand is gone
that was free to you all of all good things.
  'I have heard it said by inhabitants here,
who are people of mine and men of wisdom,
that they saw two monsters mighty and dreadful
10 haunting the borders and holding the moors,
creatures woeful. One had a semblance,
in so far as by them its form was descried,
in shape to a woman, while its wretched fellow
in the likeness of man, though larger than others,
the waste-lands haunted. Him while living
my people knew by the name of Grendel.
Not at all had they knowledge of any sire,
or whether before them were formed such demons
uncouth and strange. In a secret land
20 they keep to the wolf-slopes, the windy nesses,
the fearful fens, where the falling stream
under darkening forelands sinks down in shadow,
a flood into earth. Not far is it hence
in the measure of miles to the murky pool,
over which bend trees bright with hoar-frost,
a wood well-rooted the water shadowing.
There night by night may be noted a wonder,
a fire on the flood, and found can be no man
so wise among mortals who has measured the depth.
30 Though a hart be pressed hard, by the hounds over-
      run,
an antlered stag in search of cover
after racing from far, he will rather give up
his life on the bank than leap therein,
or plunge in the pool. The place is uncanny!
The waves of it stirred by the stormy winds,

when the weather is evil, rise up to the clouds,
heavy with darkness when the heavens are dark
and the sky sheds tears. On thee alone
is our sole reliance. Thou hast still to learn
that place of fear, to find if thou canst
the sinful creature. Seek if thou darest!
I will pay thee in treasure at a price unconsidered
to end the feud, as before I did,
in circles of gold, if again thou returnest.'
10   Beowulf spoke, the son of Ecgtheow:
'Grieve not, wise man! Mourning is feeble;
it avails much more to avenge one's friend.
For each of us must the end abide
of our course in the world, accomplish what may be
of glory ere death; to the doughty warrior
after life has gone is left but fame.
Arise, let us go, guard of thy people,
to track this monster, the mother of Grendel.
I give thee assurance, escape she shall not
20 in the womb of earth, or wood on the mountain,
or ground of ocean, go where she will!
Have patience to suffer thy sorrows so many
for the space of one day. I deem that thou wilt.'
    Then the old king up leaped, to the Lord gave
        thanks,
to the mighty God, for the man's good speech.
Straightway for Hrothgar a horse was bridled,
a curly-maned steed. In state he rode forth,
the king with his band of brave shield-bearers.
Through the forest they strode till they found on the
        plain
30 the trail of the monster, the track she had made
as forward she marched o'er the murky moor,
bearing along the best of the men
who had watched with Hrothgar the home of the
        folk.

Dead was he, taken, his doom accomplished.
Thus over the steeps of the stony hill-slopes
went the son of nobles by narrow paths
and lonely ways, a woeful region
of steep abysses, the abode of monsters.
Forward he went with a few of his men
whose skill he trusted to scan the place,
till he suddenly found dark fir trees leaning
over a grey and ancient cliff—
10 a joyless wood.   The water beneath
was gory and troubled.   Grievous it was
to the Danish warriors, a woe of the heart
to the Scylding thanes, sad of endurance
by all of the heroes when the head of Æschere
they found, as they gazed, at the foot of the cliff.
The waters were stirred and welled with blood;
a horn resounded with summons to battle;
the band of retainers on the bank sat down.
    They saw in the pool serpents swimming,
20 many sea-dragons of marvellous kind,
like the monsters which bask at the base of cliffs
and are seen in the mists of morning often,
braving all perils as they put out to sea.
Away these beasts of the wild, these serpents,
rushed in their anger, roused by the tumult,
the sound of the war-horn.   The warrior Geat
with his bow slew one in the waves where it swam,
for the keen arrow struck in the creature's heart;
more slowly it swam in the swirling pool
30 as death came near; and now in the waves
was assailed by the barbs of boar-spears quickly,
hard pressed by its foes when its force was spent,
and dragged to the shore up the shelving slope,
a monster wondrous.   The warriors viewed it—
a terror strange.

Beowulf then armed himself and addressed Hrothgar,
asking him to protect his followers and to send his treasures to Hygelac in case he did not survive the adventure.
(vv. 1442-1491)

After speaking these words, the Wether-Geat
        prince
would wait no answer, but went in haste;
in the surging pool plunged the warrior.
Though his might was great, it was many hours
ere he dove far down to the deep sea-floor.
Soon the greedy and savage creature,
who had held for half of a hundred years
the rule of the waters, became aware
that a mortal intruded on the monster's realm.
10 She clutched to seize him, but he clasped her firmly;
the hero's body was hurt in no wise
by the enemy's grip, for his armor was strong.
The mail withstood the strain of her fingers,
protected his life with its locked interweavings.
Then far in the depths, to her den the sea-wolf
bore the prince of rings. No power had he,
which angered him sorely, to swing his sword;
but many strange beasts, monsters of ocean,
pressed hard upon him, harassed him grievously.
20 With their tusks they threatened to tear his armor,
menaced the hero. Then the man perceived
he had entered what seemed the enemy's hall,
where no water could harm him, no hurt from the
        flood,
since a roof gave protection from the rush of the
        deep,
the fear of the sea. Then firelight saw he,
a gleaming blaze that brightened the dark.
It showed to the hero the sea-beast accursed,
the mighty water-wife. Amain he rushed
with his battle-sword, and stayed not his hand,

till the ringed blade sang on her scaly head
a fierce war-lay.   But the light of battles,
as the creature found, failed the warrior,
the bright sword he wielded was weak against her,
could do no hurt, though it had endured
many a combat, cut through the corslets
and helms of the doomed.   Now dimmed at last
was the pride in battle of the precious treasure.
   Yet faltered not, nor failed in valor
10 the kinsman of Hygelac, for his heart craved glory.
The angry champion cast away quickly
his well-chased sword strong and steel-edged,
to the earth flung it, having faith in his strength,
in the might of his hand-grip.   So a man must do
who desires to gain glory in battle:
be careless of life but cherish his fame.
The prince of the Geats was glad in the struggle;
manful in contest he caught by the shoulder
the mother of Grendel, gripped her so fiercely
20 in his furious onrush that she fell to the ground.
She recovered quickly and caught him in turn,
repaid the attack with a terrible onset.
Though the strongest of warriors, he with weariness
      staggered
and crashed to the earth.   The creature uncanny
pressed down upon him and drew her broad knife
with its shining edge her son to avenge,
her only born.   But his armor woven,
a corslet linked, his life protected,
kept from entering sword-edge and sword-point.
30 Save for his armor, the son of Ecgtheow,
the prince of the Geats, would have gone his far
      journey
that day under ground.   His doughty corslet
helped him and saved him; the holy Lord

the victory gave, for God the wise,
the Heavenly Counsellor decreed it thus.
    He won to his feet, and the war-gear among
saw a victory-bringing blade gigantic,
a sword strong of edge, ancient, splendid,
a glory of warriors, of weapons the choicest.
So mighty it was that no man but he
could ever have wielded that work of giants
or borne into battle the beautiful sword.
10 The Scyldings' defender, fierce and enraged,
seized the chased hilt, swung the sword on high,
for his life was at stake; then struck with fury.
So strong was the blow that the bones of her neck
broke with the might of it; the blade pierced through
her fated body. On the floor she died.
    The sword dripped gore; the swordsman rejoiced.
The gleam of the firelight filled all the cavern,
like the candle of heaven shining clear in the sky.
About the hall gazing, Hygelac's kinsman
20 turned to the wall with his weapon upraised,
grim and resolute gripped the strong sword.
The blade had not failed in his glory the warrior,
and now was his purpose to pay back to Grendel
the harm he had wrought to the West Dane folk,
the attacks he had made and the murders done
more often by far than only that once
when he had Hrothgar's hearth-companions
slain in their slumber and, sleeping fast,
devoured fifteen of the folk of the Danes,
30 and a band of like number had borne to his den,
a hideous prey. Him the champion
sternly requited, when he saw at rest
the lifeless body of Grendel lying,
doomed in the struggle he suffered at Heorot,
dead in the cavern. His corpse sprang wide

as the sword-blade fell, for the stroke of the hero
was strong and hard; and the head he severed.
   Soon the warriors who waited above
and scanned with Hrothgar the shadowy pool
saw that the waters were welling and troubled
and reddened with blood. About the hero
the grey old men together were speaking.
They said that the noble would never return,
would never come back from the battle victorious
10 the mighty prince; and many were sure
that the wolf of the sea had slain him there.
Came the noon of day. The ness was forsaken
by the Scylding heroes; and homeward departed
the gold-friend of men. But the Geats stayed on,
though sick of heart, and stared at the mere.
They desired, but hoped not, to see again
their comrade and lord.
        Then because of the blood
the battle-sword wasted, and a wonder came,
for the blade dissolved in shreds of iron,
20 melted wholly, as melts the ice
when the Father unwinds the fetters of frost,
the water-bonds loosens, Who wields all power
of times and seasons. In truth is He Lord!
Though he saw much wealth, the Wether-Geat prince
took from the cavern treasures but two:
the head of the monster and the hilt of the sword,
richly adorned. The damascened blade
had perished before in the fire of blood,
in the demon's venom, who had died in the cave.
30 Then he who in conflict had compassed the downfall
  of his enemies swam, plunging up through the
      waters.
Cleansed was the pool, purified wholly,
since the demon uncanny his days had ended,

relinquishing the fleeting life of this world.
Came to the surface, swimming stout-hearted,
the guard of mariners glad in the sea-spoil,
the mighty burden he bore to land.
Giving thanks to God, his thanes went towards
    him;
the mighty clan in their chief rejoiced,
were glad when they saw him safe after battle.
    Then from the hero were his helmet and corslet
speedily loosened. The lake grew quiet,
10 though still the water was stained with bright blood.
In mood exultant they marched from the shore,
the known path followed, went forth on their way.
Bold were the warriors who bore from the sea-cliff
the mighty head; heavy the burden;
no two, though sturdy, had strength sufficient
to carry it forth, but four were needed
to bring with labor, bound on a spear-shift,
to the golden hall the head of Grendel.
Forthwith to the hall, warlike and valiant,
20 the fourteen Geats together came.
Among them their prince, proud with his comrades,
was treading the plain on the path to the mead-hall.
Then entered at length the lord of the thanes,
the valorous man mighty in glory,
the hero high-praised, and Hrothgar greeted.
By its hair was borne in the head of Grendel
across the wide floor where the warriors feasted,
a terror indeed to the Danes and their queen,
a spectacle strange; they stared with dismay.

Beowulf then recounted to Hrothgar his adventure, and
gave him the sword-hilt which he had brought back.
Hrothgar responded by a speech praising Beowulf and
moralizing at length. At the end of it, Beowulf took his
seat, and feasting continued. (vv. 1651-1788)

Night's helmet darkened
over king and companions. The company rose;
the grey-haired king would go to his bed,
the Scylding lord, while a longing unmeasured
for sleep overcame the conqueror Geat.
The stranger prince was soon guided forth,
worn with adventure, by one of the thanes
who for courtesy's sake was assigned to attend
such needs as the chief and his clan should have,
10 the length of their stay, the sea-farers all.
The noble lord slumbered. Spacious and gold-
    adorned
the high hall rose, while rested the guest
till the gleaming raven in gladness of heart
gave news of the sun. Then soon on the shadows
daylight was waxing. The warriors hastened,
for the clansmen were glad to go to their people;
the bold-hearted stranger would seek his ship,
on the journey afar was fain to depart.

Unferth then presented Beowulf with his sword Hrunting,
thus making amends for his earlier rudeness. Beowulf
pledged to Hrothgar his continued help, and that of Hygelac.
Hrothgar replied with renewed compliments to Beowulf
and protestations that peace would continue between Geats
and Danes. (vv. 1807-1865)

Then the son of Healfdene, helmet of warriors,
20 made gift of treasures twelve to the hero,
bade him seek in peace his people beloved,
but straightway return when time should avail.
Kissed him in parting the king high-born,
the prince of Scyldings his most precious of thanes,
and grasped his shoulders with the shedding of tears,
the grey-haired elder. No expectation
had they of meeting once more in council,
he more than the other, whom age had made wise.
So dear was the man that he might not restrain

what rose in his breast; his blood was quickened
with longing deep-seated and love of the hero
who was bound in his heart by the bonds of affec-
tion.
Away turned Beowulf the warrior from him,
trod the greensward with gold resplendent,
with his treasure exultant. At anchor riding,
the sea-goer waited, the ship its master.
But still in going the gifts of Hrothgar
they often acclaimed; a king was he
10 blameless in all wise until age the destroyer
had snatched away his strength and his joy.
    Then came to the sea the company proud
of youthful warriors, wearing their corslets,
their woven armor. The warder perceived
the return of the band from the tip of the headland,
again as before, and greeted the strangers
with words of welcome when he went to meet them,
said that as friends, to the folk of the Wethers,
brave and bright-armored, they embarked on their
journey.
20 There beached on the sand was the ship ring-prowed,
a roomy vessel with riches laden,
with horses and armor. High above it
the mast overtowered the treasures of Hrothgar.
To the guard of the boat was given a sword
with a golden hilt, which gained him thereafter
in the mead-hall much honor for the heirloom he
owned,
for the treasure's sake. Then the ship to the sea
was launched, and went forth from the land of the
Danes.
    From the mast was spread a sail like a mantle,
30 made fast with cordage; there was creaking of
timbers;
not at all did the wind or the waves on the voyage

oppose the sailors. The ship went forth
with foam at its prow, floated seaward,
a craft well-caulked on the currents of ocean,
until they came to the cliffs of the Geats,
to the forelands they knew. Forward the vessel
by the wind was driven, and dashed to the shore.
The harbor warden, who had waited long
on watch by the sea for the warriors dear,
straightway perceived them from the strand where
    he stood.
10 The craft wide-bosomed he bound to the sand,
made it fast by cables, lest the force of the waves
should sweep the fair ship seaward and crush it.
The æthelings' treasure, the trappings and gold,
he bade them bring forth; nor far was it thence
they must go to seek the giver of riches,
Hygelac Hrethling, at home where he dwelt
with his comrades about him, close to the sea-wall.

In connection with the might of Hygelac and the splendor of his hall, Queen Hygd is contrasted with Thryth, the
haughty and cruel consort of Offa. (vv. 1925-1962)

To seek him the hero o'er the sands came marching
with his band of comrades, o'er the plain by the sea,
20 the wide-spreading shore. Shone the world's candle,
the sun risen high. They hastened forward
till they reached the courts where the king, they
    knew,
the warriors' protector awaited their coming,
young and yet valiant, the victor of Ongentheow,
the giver of treasure. They told to Hygelac
their tale of adventure, the voyage of Beowulf,
their chieftain in war, their comrade in battle,
who in safety had come as conqueror homeward,
surviving the struggle with strength unweakened.

Then quickly was made, as the mighty king bade,
a place in the hall for the heroes returning.

Beowulf then related his adventures, and shared with
Hygelac and Hygd the treasure he had brought from the
land of the Danes. He then established himself in Geat-
land, where, after the deaths of Hygelac and his son
Heardred, he ruled as king for fifty years. At the end of
that time, a fire-dragon began to lay waste the country,
having been stirred to anger by a fugitive slave who had
robbed its hoard. (vv. 1977-2323)

Straightway the terror was told to Beowulf,
made known in truth that the noblest of dwellings,
his home had crumbled in the clutch of the fire,
the throne of the Geats. Great and dire woe
the good king suffered, sorrow of heart.
In his wisdom he deemed he had deeply angered
the Ruler Eternal, Whose right is of old,
10 the Lord Everlasting. There leapt dark thoughts
in his surging breast which was steady before.
The fortress of peoples had the fire-dragon
destroyed with its flames, the stronghold wasted,
the land by the sea. The lord of the Wethers,
the war-king devised vengeance therefor.
He bade them make a marvellous shield
all of iron, the aid and protector
of nobles and warriors, for he knew right well
that a shield of linden could shelter him not,
20 wood against flame. He would wait the end
of his mortal days; but the dragon, too,
should finish its life with the lord of the people,
though long it had held its hoard of treasure.
Too proud was the king, the prince long famed,
the far-flying monster to fight with his band,
with an army in force. He feared not the contest,
nor dreaded at all the dragon's power,
its strength and its might; for struggles many

he had braved and endured, daring adventure
in the crash of battle, since he cleansed by his deed
the hall of Hrothgar and, hailed as a victor,
by his grip of death crushed Grendel's kin,
the hateful race.

Other exploits of his life are reviewed, including Hygelac's
death and a feud with the Swedes. (vv. 2355-2509)

For the last time Beowulf with brave words spoke:
'Many deeds of war I dared in my youth;
and once more still in the wisdom of age
as the guard of my people I will go to the conflict,
10 will add to my glory, if the evil creature
shall seek me out from its earth-hidden hall.'
Then greeted he the helmeted warriors,
each loyal man in a last farewell,
his comrades dear: 'I would carry no sword
against the dragon, nor deign with a weapon
to meet the monster if I might in some wise
proudly grapple, as with Grendel I did;
but I deem that its breath is deadly and hot,
a venomous flame. I shall venture, therefore,
20 with corslet and shield. Not the space of a foot
will I give by the cliff to the guard of the cavern,
but there shall await what Wyrd may decree,
the Lord of mankind. With courage of heart,
but making no boast, I shall meet the dragon.
Abide near the cave, ye bold men in corslets,
armed with your war-gear, and wait there the out-
        come,
which one of us twain shall win in the contest,
come forth as the victor. The venture is mine,
for no other man has might sufficient
30 or measure of power the monster to fight—
the deed of a warrior. I shall win the gold

by boldness and strength or in battle shall perish;
and dreadful shall be the death of your lord.'
   With helmet and shield, the hero bold
arose and went forth, firm in his courage,
to the mouth of the cave. No coward's adventure!
He trusted the strength of his stalwart arm.
Endured had he much in the day of battle,
the crash of arms, the clashing of standards.
His courage was steadfast. Then he saw in the cliff
10 an archway of stone, and out there issued
a stream from the cavern, the surge of it hot
with death-dealing fires. In the depth of the rock
could no man remain for a moment's space
alive and unburnt by the breath of the dragon.
Stirred with fury, the stout-hearted Geat
let words from his bosom break in his anger,
shouted defiance. Resounding and clear,
his voice was heard in the hollowed rock,
and roused the warder, for its wrath was kindled
20 that a man came near. No more was there time
to ask for a truce. Out from the cavern
the breath of the fiend came forth in a flood,
a venomous reek. The rock resounded.
Against the monster the man made ready
his shield as a guard, the Geats' dear lord.
   Then was the rage of the ring-dragon stirred
to enter the conflict, while the king of battles
drew out his sword, the ancient heirloom,
his bold-flashing weapon. Both felt terror,
30 each of the other, as their enmity stirred.
Behind his tall shield with stout heart waited
the lord of his clansmen, while quickly the dragon
coiled for the onset; in his corslet he waited.
Then breathing out fire, to its fate the monster
came snakily gliding. The glorious prince

not long was protected in life and in body
by the shield he carried. He could not tell,
and his mind sought to fathom, why fate had not
        granted
for the first of all times triumph in battle.
He lifted his hand, the lord of the Geats,
and struck the dragon dreadful in motley
with his ancient blade. Though bright the edge of it,
it bit but feebly on the bone, and failed,
when its master had need, by the monster hard
        pressed.
10 Then savage of mood at the stroke of the weapon,
the guard of the barrow belched out its venom
in deadly flame; the fires spread wide.
    No joy of victory had the generous prince
of the folk of the Geats; failed him in battle
had his unsheathed sword, the iron he trusted,
his faithful weapon. For the famous king
hard was the voyage, the venture new,
hard the departure from the plains of the world
for a dwelling elsewhere, as each man must go
20 when his fleeting days are finished here,
though his will be to stay. They waited little,
the combatants fierce, but the contest renewed.
The treasure guardian again took heart
and breathed forth flame; with fire surrounded
the hard-pressed lord who had long borne rule.
No longer stood comrades in a company round him,
warriors noble, known for their valor.
They had fled in terror to the forest far off
to save their lives. But sorrow of heart
30 filled the mind of one, for may not forget
what to kinship is due the clansman loyal.
The man was called Wiglaf, Weoxstan's son,
a shield-warrior keen and kinsman of Ælfhere,

of the Scylfing stock. He saw that his lord,
despite his helmet, by the heat was oppressed.

Wiglaf recalled the benefits he had received from Beowulf.
(vv. 2606-2624)

                    The first time it was
that the champion young with his chieftain and
        lord
had come into battle; but his courage of heart
was steadfast in danger, and the sword of his sires
did not weaken in combat, as the war-dragon found
when they met together. Much that was truthful,
many words that were just, Wiglaf uttered
10 as he spoke to his comrades in sadness of heart.
'I remember the time when mead we were drinking
and he gave us these bracelets in the banquet hall,
these helmets, these swords hardened and tempered;
we promised our lord we would pay him at need
for the trappings of war if a time should come
like this now upon us. Therefore he took us
himself from the army, holding us worthy
of adventure and glory, gave us these treasures,
because he accounted us chosen warriors,
20 courageous and loyal, though our lord intended
alone to accomplish this combat of strength
as guard of his folk, since glorious deeds
he was fain to perform, was the first of all men
in reckless daring. Now the day is come
when our lord requires the loyal strength
of valorous warriors. Let us venture and go,
give help to our chief, since here in the terror
of flame he has need. God knows that to me
it seems far better that my body perish,
30 with the giver of gold engulfed by the fire.
It would ill become us to enter the court
still bearing our shields, save as preservers

of the life of our prince, the lord of the Wethers,
having vanquished his foe. For verily he
has better deserved than to battle alone,
to fall in the combat, affliction to suffer
bereft of comrades. Corslets and helmets,
our swords and our mail, must be shared by us all.'
 Through the deadly reek he rushed in his helmet
to the aid of his lord, while he eagerly spoke:
'Beowulf beloved, thy boast accomplish .
10 which was uttered in youth when thy years were
 few,
that never while living thou wouldst let thy glory
crumble and fall. In defence of thy life
show thy full power, prince strong-hearted;
be steadfast in courage. I come to thy aid!'
When he had spoken, came a second time
the enemy dire, the dragon enraged,
attacking with waves of terrible fire
the men it hated. In the heat of the flames
his shield with its boss was burned, while his corslet
20 was useless to aid the youthful warrior,
but the shield of his kinsman gave shelter to him
when his own was devoured in the vomit of flame.
 Then the king once more, the mighty in battle,
remembered his glory, with main strength struck,
wielded with fury his war-blade Nægling,
and drove it home in the head of the dragon.
But shivered and failed the sword of Beowulf,
the grey and ancient. His gift it was not
that blades of iron might ever in battle
30 help him to conquer. His hand was too strong,
the strain too great when he struck, I am told,
for any weapon he wielded in combat,
though wondrously tempered; nor well was it for
 him.
 Then a third time advanced the violent foe,

the furious dragon in a fiery charge;
rushed on the chieftain when its chance had come
with a fierce attack, and fastened its jaws
in the neck of Beowulf, whose blood with his life
poured out from the wound in waves of gore.
In the king's distress his comrade in arms
showed forth his courage by a feat of might,
with the boldness and strength that were bred in
 his line.
He took no heed of the head of the dragon,
10 but the bold man's hand was burned when he struck
a little below in his lord's defence
and drove his sword so deep in the monster,
his fine-wrought blade, that the fire thereafter
began to lessen. Then the king of the Geats,
with his senses returned, seized the battle-knife
that hung on his corslet, a keen-edged blade,
and split the dragon with his stroke asunder.
   They had slain the foe, slain it with valor,
shared in the enemy's end and destruction,
20 the kinsmen noble! At need should be
all thanes like Wiglaf. But this for the prince
was the last of victories, the latest of deeds,
of his works in the world. For the wound that
 before
the earth-dragon gave him began now at length
to burn and to swell, and soon he found
that the venom within him with violent rage
rose up in his breast. The bravest of heroes,
the wise-hearted warrior, by the wall sank down
and leaned against it. He looked on the work
30 of giants about him, the great stone arches
and the columns supporting the cave immemorial.
Then the loyal thane laved with water
his chieftain and friend, the famous prince
bloody and wounded, worn with the battle,

with his hand he laved him, and his helmet un-
fastened.
Now Beowulf spoke despite his hurt,
the wound that was mortal, for well he knew
that his days were ended, that done was he
with the joy of earth, that all the tale
of his days was spent—and death most near:
'Now I to my heir, had any been granted me,
to the son of my body, had son been given,
to wear it hereafter my armor of war
10 would here bequeath.   I have held this people
for fifty winters; no folk had a king
of the neighbors about us, none had a leader
who dared undertake an attack upon me
with swords and warriors.   I waited unmoved
the judgments of fate, with justice ruled,
never sought to win by the wiles of war,
nor swore false oaths.   Now stricken with wounds,
with death nigh at hand I am happy in this,
that the Lord of men need lay at my charge
20 no slaying of kinsmen when I come to depart
and leave my body.   Now boldly go,
Wiglaf beloved, and look at the hoard
in the cavern grey, since the guardian lies
asleep from its wounds, despoiled of its treasure.
Make haste that I may behold the wealth,
view well the gold and the gems in their radiance,
and so beholding for the sake of the treasure
more peacefully go, giving then over
my life and my lordship, which long I have held.'
30   The son of Weoxstan the speech of his lord
who was wounded in battle obeyed then quickly;
wearing his corslet of woven mail,
of intertwined rings, he entered the cave.
There the young thane perceived, and seeing exulted,
as he passed by the seat, a great pile of jewels,

on the earth the glitter of gold wide-scattered,
and the walls of the cavern a wonder to see,
for cups adorned the den of the dragon,
vessels once shining but now shorn of their beauty,
from the days of old. No dearth was of helmets
ancient and rusted, arm-bands aplenty
cunningly twisted. For treasures of gold,
when buried in earth, may easily last
far longer than he who hid them therein.
10 And a banner he saw shining all golden,
hanging high o'er the hoard, of handiwork marvellous,
skilfully woven. He scanned by its radiance,
so wondrous the light of it, the walls with the
treasure
and the floor of the cave; but he found of the
dragon
no sign at all, for the sword had destroyed it.
Thus a single man, they say, in the cavern
plundered the treasure of plates and cups,
till his arms were laden with the old work of giants;
and the banner, too, brightest of standards,
20 he brought forth with him. The blade of the hero,
the iron sword, had slain already
the monstrous guard which for many a year
had kept the hoard by the heat of flame,
which filled with terror and the fires of death
the darkness of night while the dragon lived.
   The brave envoy hastened, eager to show
the wealth he had brought and wondering much
if he still should find where before he had left
him
the prince of the Wethers with wounds that were
mortal,
30 his lord still living. Laden with treasure,
he came to the famous king and found him

spent and bloody, expiring, it seemed,
with life at an end. But at length when **water**
he had cast upon him, the king began
in words that broke from his breast in sorrow
to speak, as the gold he saw before him:
'For all these riches to the Ruler Almighty,
to the King of Glory I give my thanks,
to the Lord Eternal, that I leave such wealth,
may have ere I die what here I see
10 to bestow on my people. The price I have paid
is my ripened years; they are reaped for the treasure.
Hold then in keeping, since the hoard is so bought,
the care of the tribesmen. I can no longer.
Let the warriors famous, when the fire consumes me,
build on the foreland a barrow splendid,
which shall keep me in memory among my people,
as it rises high on the headland Hronesness;
and sea-farers ever, seeing, shall call it
Beowulf's barrow, when the ships high-built
20 through the mists of ocean come sailing from far.'
    Then took the brave prince from his throat a
        necklace,
a golden collar, and gave the young warrior
his gold-decked helm from his head and his ring,
his corslet gave him, bade keep them well.
'Last remaining thou art left of our kinsmen,
of the Wægmund tribe, for Wyrd has swept
away my clansmen, the warriors valorous,
all to destruction; and I must follow.'
For the last time thus the thoughts of his heart
30 the old king uttered, ere he came to the pyre,
to the searing flame. His soul departed
the triumph to find of the true and the steadfast.

    After Beowulf's death, the cowardly warriors emerged
from their refuge in the forest and were rebuked by Wiglaf.

Wiglaf then sent a messenger to announce the news to the
Geats. In doing this, the messenger foretold the troubles
that were likely to follow, calling to mind past wars with
Franks and Swedes. The Geats then went to the scene
of the fight and viewed the bodies. At Wiglaf's bidding,
they brought the rest of the treasure from the cave, shoved
the corpse of the dragon over the edge of the cliff into the
sea, and bore the king's body to the headland. (vv. 2821-
3136)

Then the folk of the Geats a funeral pyre
built on the headland, a bale-fire splendid
hung over with shields, with shining corslets,
with helmets of war, as he had desired.
They laid upon it the prince illustrious
with lamentation for their lord so dear.
Then the warriors kindled on the cliff-side the flame
of the mighty pyre. Murky the wood-smoke
uprose all dark, while roared the fire;
10 and weeping was heard, but the winds were quiet,
till the heat in its breast the body consumed.
Their hearts were sad, and with sorrow stricken
they lamented the death of their dearly-loved lord.
Then an aged woman in her woe for Beowulf,
with her locks bound up, a lay of mourning
sang, and repeated that sorely she feared
days of evil, enmity, slaughter,
the terror of war, and the taking of captives.
The heavens consumed the smoke of the pyre.
20   The folk of the Geats a barrow fashioned,
a mound on the cliff massive and lofty,
to be seen afar by sailors who journeyed,
built it in honor of the brave in battle,
in ten days made it in memory of him,
to guard his ashes. Whatever the wise
could find that was noble his name to recall
they bore to the mound: bracelets and jewels,
all the treasure that enemies earlier,

men who were hostile, in the hoard had seized;
resigned the warriors' wealth to the earth,
the gold to the mound, where yet it remains
as useless to men as erstwhile it was.
Then around the barrow there rode together
twelve who in battle were bravest and best,
gave voice to their care, the king lamented,
chanted their sorrow in a song of grief.
10 They praised the might of the man and his deeds,
sang of the hero as seemly it is
that comrades acclaim their king and lord,
in heart hold him dear when hence from the body
the hero has left his hearth-companions.
Thus lamented the men of the Geats
the death of their lord, for they deemed him to be
of the kings of the world the kindest and noblest,
the gentlest of men, most good to his people,
acclaimed by all most eager for fame.

CYNEWULF

From only two poets of the period before the Norman Conquest have we any verse remaining to which the author's name can be attached. One of these men is Cædmon, from whom Bede in his Latin history of the early days of the British Church quotes a few lines. The other is Cynewulf, who signed four poems with acrostics, which spell out his name in runic letters. These are *Juliana, Elene, Christ,* and *The Fates of the Apostles.* The author cannot be definitely identified with any Cynewulf of whom we have knowledge from other sources; but he was certainly an ecclesiastic who lived in the north of England, and he probably wrote towards the end of the eighth century. Whether he composed other poems like *The Phoenix, Guthlac,* and

Andreas we do not know. They have similar characteristics. It is more difficult to show in translation the virtues of Cynewulf and his school than of the *Beowulf* poet. Cynewulf was gifted with amazingly keen sense perceptions, and depended largely upon sensory images for his effects. These inevitably become dulled and blurred in a translation. Yet the rhapsodic hymns and emotionalized descriptive scenes of *Christ* have great beauty, while such a poem as *Elene* cannot be ignored by any lover of narrative verse in the heroic manner.

From CHRIST

AN ADVENT HYMN

O radiant and glorious, Thou God exalted,
Thou High and Holy, heavenly Trinity!
Broad creation brings its praises;
and rightfully should we, though wretched mortals,
our voices lift to laud and honor,
to give Thee praise, since God the faithful
has shown Himself, the Savior, to us.
Aloft in heaven the holy Seraphim,
the true and brave, in throngs unwearying,
10 among the angels ever with their praises
raise songs to Thee and sound aloud,
both near and far, fairly with their voices
their hymns of joy. They have of duties
the noblest to the King, for Christ has granted
that they may ever with their eyes behold Him,
may there adore, celestially adorned,
the Lord Who rules through regions without end.
And with their wings they guard our God eternal,
the majesty and glory of the mighty Lord;
20 and ever round His throne they throng, for each
desires
with fluttering wing to fly the nearest
our King and Savior in the courts of peace.

The Well-beloved they laud, and in the light He
    spreads
they sing these words and sound His praises,
Creator glorious of all created things:
'Holy art Thou, holy, of the hosts of the arch-
    angels
very Lord and Prince! The Victor art Thou, holy,
Lord of Lords forever! Everlasting shall endure
Thy glory in the world, and widely honored
till time is gone, for Thou art God of hosts,
and earth and heaven are ever filled,
10 O Guard of warriors, with the glory of Thy pres-
    ence,
O Protector all-powerful! Eternal be
in the highest heights Thy glory, and in earth Thy
    praise
be bright forever! O blest and loved
Who comes to men, to give comfort to the wretched
in the name of Him Who in the heights shall have
praises without ending, everlasting honor!'

From ELENE

CONSTANTINE'S VISION AND BATTLE
WITH THE HUNS

Of the circling years, counted by number,
two hundred and thirty and three had passed,
and so many winters that measure the world,
20 since God the Ruler, the Glory of kings,
the Light of the faithful, in the form of man
was born on earth. The sixth it was
of Constantine's rule in the realm imperial,
since as leader of war in the land of the Romans
he was raised to command. To his men he was
    gracious,

his people's protector, and of praise he was eager.
The realm of the prince, which he ruled under
    heaven,
grew mighty withal. He made it great,
for a true king was he, and a help in battle
to the warriors all. For his worth God blessed him
with glory and power; and he gave to many
his comfort and aid through the earth far and wide;
did vengeance on foes when violence stirred him
to lift his weapons.

10   Then war was proclaimed,
the terror of battle. There were thronging hosts,
the folk of the Huns, and the Hrethgoth people,
while forth there came the Franks and the Hugs.
Brave were the warriors and bold for fighting;
their lances gleamed, and their linked mail glittered.
With shouts and the clash of clattering shields
the heroes raised on high their standard,
assembled in force; and forth together
came marching the host. In the midst of the forest
20 the wolf gave voice and of violence chanted,
while the dewy-winged eagle on the enemies' track
sang of slaughter to be. The soldiers to battle
moved fast, to attack the fortified places,
as mighty a concourse as the King of the Huns
could in any way summon from all his neighbors
of warriors to battle. So went they forth,
the finest of armies, with foot and with horse;
marched to the Danube, and made their camp
in that alien land, those lancers brave,
30 by the surge of the water with sound and with
    tumult.
They would ruin the realm of the Romans, and
    sack it
with their plundering hosts.

Then the Huns' approach
became known in the city.   Caesar commanded
to summon the soldiers in squadron formation
against the foe, and to form at once
the army for battle, to bring forth for conflict
the warriors in haste under heaven's arch.
Valiant and eager for victory were they,
the dwellers in Rome, and ready they made them
with their weapons for war, though weaker their
          forces
10 in number and power for the press of the combat
than those that came riding with the King of the
          Huns.
But their bucklers clashed, and clattered their shields.
The King with his troop, with his conquering host,
led them to battle.   Aloft the dark raven,
greedy for carrion, cried from the heavens.
To the marching host the heralds gave orders,
the trumpeters ran, and the tread of the horses
on the earth was loud.   Eager for battle
the army came; but the King was afraid,
20 troubled with care, when the throng he saw
of Huns and of Hreths, as his host he collected
at the river's bank on the bounds of his kingdom.
The King of the Romans was racked with care,
lest for lack of men he should lose his realm.
Too few were his warriors, too frail his support
against the might overpowering he must meet in
          battle.
   Near the river waited the warriors and leader
for the space of a night, after sighting first
the host assembled.   Then to Caesar a dream
30 was revealed in his slumber, as he slept with his
          men;
longing for victory, a vision he saw.
A beauteous being, brilliant and shining,

in form like a man, but far more splendid
than ever before under the arch of heaven
he had seen with his eyes, it seemed there appeared.
His head he raised, the helmeted warrior,
and the angel spoke, the envoy of glory,
the messenger radiant, called the man by name
in haste, while the darkness grew dim and was light.
  'The King of the angels, Constantine, greets you,
the Lord of Hosts, Who allots our destinies.
10 He offers a covenant, so fear not at all,
though the foreign host make a fearful threat
of battle hard. To the heavens look
on the Warden of glory; there weal you shall find,
a sign of victory.' Then soon he obeyed
the behest of the holy one; his heart he opened,
and he gazed on high, as had given command
the beauteous angel. There brightly adorned
the Tree of Glory, with rich gold gleaming,
he saw in the heavens, splendid with jewels.
20 And words were written on the radiant Cross,
shining and brilliant: 'In this sign you will conquer
the host of your foes in the fearful battle,
will hinder and let them.' Then the light departed
and vanished away, and with it the angel
to the host of the blessed. But blither the ruler,
the more free of care the King in his heart
because of the sight he had seen so fair.
  Then the lord of nobles a likeness commanded
of that he had seen there in the heavens;
30 the famous king, Constantine bade them
to make in haste, the mighty ruler,
the giver of rings, a Rood of Christ
as a symbol and token of the sight in the vision.
In the twilight gray he gave his commands
to awaken the warriors for the battle of weapons,
to raise the standards, and the Rood all holy

to bear before them as the beacon of God,
to carry it forward when the foe they attacked.
   Loud the trumpets sang as they surged on the
      enemy;
the raven grew eager, and the eagle damp-winged
gazed at the conflict of cruel warriors;
the wolf gave tongue, the woodland companion.
The battle arose. There was rushing of warriors
and clashing of shields, combat furious
and the slaying of men when they met the arrow-
      flight.
10 In showers the arrows, over shields the spears
they sent on the doomed and desperate foe;
on the enemy bold the battle-adders
they speeded forth by the strength of their hands.
They advanced strong-hearted, they hastened for-
      ward,
tore shields asunder and their spears thrust in,
pressed forward boldly. Then the banner was
      raised,
the standard before them, and they sang of victory.
The golden helmets gleamed like the lances
on the field of, battle. Fell there the barbarous;
20 the heathen perished. The Hun folk at once
fled on beholding the Holy Tree
which the King of the Romans had reared in battle.
Widely were scattered the warriors bold.
Some in the conflict were killed with weapons;
some saved their lives, but saved them hardly,
by their sudden flight; and some half dead
fled to a fastness, and found there refuge
in the rocky cliffs, reaching the Danube
and a strong place near it; while some in the stream
30 were drowned as they swam, and their doom there
      met.
   Then the host of the brave was happy and joyous;

pursued the aliens until evening came
at the end of day, while the darts still flew,
the adders of battle. The enemy perished,
the force of the foe, for few went thence
of the host of the Huns to their homes again.
Then was it clear that Constantine
the King Almighty had made the victor,
had endowed him with honor in the day of battle,
with rule under heaven through His Rood Tree there.

THE WANDERER *

APART from heroic poems of various sources, and such inno-
vations as we associate with Cynewulf, the best things surviving from the wreckage of Old English literature are a
few poems in the elegiac mood. Of these *The Wanderer*
is the most striking and poignant. It was probably written
in the eighth century. Like almost all the Old English verse
that is left, it has come down to us in a single manuscript,
which has been preserved in Exeter Cathedral since about
the time of the Norman Conquest.

10 Many a lonely man at last comes to honor,
Merits God's mercy, though much he endured
On wintry seas, with woe in his heart,
Dragging his oar through drenching-cold brine,
Homeless and houseless and hunted by Wyrd.

These are the words of a way-faring wanderer,
This is his song of the sorrow of life,
Slaughter of foemen, felling of kinsmen:

* From Old English Poetry by J. Duncan Spaeth. By permission
of Princeton University Press, publishers.

Oft in the dark alone, before dawning,
All to myself my sorrow I tell.
No friend have I here to whom I may open
My heart's deep secret, my hidden spring of woe.
Well do I know 'tis the way of the high-born,
Fast in his heart to fetter his feelings,
Lock his unhappiness in the hold of his mind.
Spirit that sorrows withstandeth not destiny,
Heart that complaineth plucketh no help.
10 A haughty hero will hide his suffering,
Manfully master misery's pang.
Thus stricken with sorrow, stript of my heritage,
Far from kinsmen and country and friends,
Grimly I grappled my grief to my bosom,
Since long time ago, my giver of bounty
Was laid in the earth, and left me to roam
Watery wastes, with winter in my heart.
Forsaken I sought a shielder and protector;
Far and near I found none to greet the wanderer,
20 No master to make him welcome in his wine-hall;
None to cheer the cheerless, or the friendless to
befriend.

He who has lost all his loved companions
Knoweth how bitter a bedfellow is sorrow.
Loneliness his lot, not lordly gold,
Heart-chilling frost, not harvest of plenty.
Oft he remembers the mirth of the mead-hall,
Yearns for the days of his youth, when his dear
lord
Filled him with abundance. Faded are those joys!
He shall know them no more; no more shall he
listen
30 To the voice of his lord, his leader and counsellor.
Sometimes sleep and sorrow together
Gently enfold the joyless wanderer:

Bright are his dreams, he embraces his lord again,
Kisses his liege, and lays on his knee
Head and hands as in happy days,
When he thanked for a boon his bountiful giver.
Wakes with a start the wanderer homeless;
Nought he beholds but the heaving surges,
Seagulls dipping and spreading their wings,
Scurries of snow and the scudding hail.
Then his heart is all the heavier,
10 Sore after sweet dreams sorrow reviveth.
Fain would he hold the forms of his kinsmen,
Longingly leans to them, lovingly greets them;
Slowly their faces swim into distance;
No familiar greeting comes from the fleeting
Companies of kinsmen. Care ever shadows
The way of the traveller, whose track is on the
      waters,
Whose path is on the billows of the boundless deep.

Behold I know not how I may keep
My heart from sinking, heavy with sorrow,
20 When all life's destiny deeply I ponder,—
Men that are suddenly snatched in their prime,
High-souled heroes; so the whole of this earth
Day by day droopeth and sinketh to decay. . .
How dread is the doom of the last desolation,
When all the wealth of the world shall be waste,
He that is wise may learn, if he looks
Abroad o'er this land, where lonely and ruinous,
Wind-swept walls, waste are standing;
Tottering towers, crusted with frost,
30 Crumbling wine-halls, bare to the sky.
Dead is their revelry, dust are the revellers!
Some they have fallen on far fields of battle,
Some have gone down in ships on the sea;
Some were the prey of the prowling gray-wolf,

Some by their loved ones were laid in the earth.
The Lord of the living hath levelled their mansions,
Silenced the sound of the singing and laughter.
Empty and bare are all their habitations,
Wondrous works of the giants of old.

He that considers this scene of desolation,
And this dark life deeply doth ponder,—
Battle and blood-shed, burning and slaughter,
10 It bringeth to mind, and mournfully he asks:
Where is the warrior, where is the war-horse?
Where is the giver of bounty, where are the boon-
    companions,
The "dream and the gleam" that gladdened the hall?
Alas the bright ale-cup, alas the brave warrior!
Alas the pride of princes! Their prime is no more;
Sunk under night's shadow, as though it had never
    been!
Where lusty warriors thronged, this lone wall
    towers,
Weird with dragon-shapes, wondrously carven;
Storm of ash-spears hath stricken the heroes,
20 Blood-thirsty weapons, Wyrd the supreme.
Wintry blasts now buffet these battlements;
Dreary snow-storms drift up the earth,
The terror of winter when wild and wan
Down from the north with the darkness drives
The ruinous scourge of the ruthless hail.

All this life is labor and sorrow,
Doom of destiny darkens o'er earth.
Wealth is fleeting, friends are fleeting,
Man is fleeting, maid is fleeting,
30 All this earth's foundations utterly shall pass.

THE VISION OF PIERS PLOWMAN

OF THE poets who had a part in the remarkable revival of writing in English, which came about during the second half of the fourteenth century, one of the most interesting is the unknown author of *The Vision of Piers Plowman*. This work used to be confidently ascribed to a William Langland, about whom a biography was built up which is now seen to have been based on quite insufficient evidence. Three different versions of the poem exist. Version A consists of a prologue and twelve sections, or passus, and contains 2567 lines. The following translation is from this text. Version B is much longer, 4242 lines in all, and includes nine sections not in the A-text. Version C is a still more expanded form, consisting of 7357 lines. It is the present belief of scholars that the poem was first written in 1362 or soon afterward, that the B-text was composed in 1376 or 1377, and that the final version appeared in the last decade of the century. Opinions differ as to whether or not the man who first made the poem was also responsible for the longer forms of it.

Such unsettled problems need not blind us, however, to the importance of the work. Unquestionably the first author was one of greatest satirists who have ever written in English, and he produced one of the best allegorical visions of all time. He must have known London well; but he chose as his medium the old alliterative verse that had sprung into vogue in the west and north of England with the contemporary growth of national consciousness, and he used language that smacked of the country—used it, probably, with the conscious intention of making his poem seem rustic. Unlike Chaucer, whom he resembles in his powers of observation, the author was aflame with moral indignation against the evils of his time. He was too generous and too large-hearted to be a crabbed commentator, but he lacked no vigor in his denunciation of wickedness and folly. As a vision, his poem has the merit of moving the characters across the scene in a wholly dreamlike fashion; as an allegory, it rivals the work of Bunyan in clearness of visualization and sharpness of outline; as a satire, it compares favorably in vividness of detail and picturesqueness of phrase with anything in the language. No writer has ever expounded more ably the virtues of honesty and common sense and simple faith.

In a summer season when soft was the sun,
I got me the garments and garb of a shepherd,
Like those of a hermit unholy of works,
And wandered wide through the world wonders to
　　　hear.
But on a May morning on the Malvern Hills
A marvel befell me, a fairy thing, it seemed.
I was weary from wandering and went to take rest
By the side of a brook where the bank was wide;
And there as I lay and looked at the waters,
10 I dropped off to sleep, the sound was so pleasant.
　　Then began I to dream a dream that was mar-
　　　vellous,
That I was in a wilderness, but where I could not
　　tell.
As I looked to the east where aloft rose the sun,
I saw a splendid tower set on a hill,
With a deep dale below it, and a dungeon therein,
With a deep and dark ditch dreadful to see.
　　A fair field full of folk found I between them,
Of all manner of men, both the mean and the rich,
Working and wandering as the world compels.
20 Some were at the plough and played full seldom,
Labored full hard as they harrowed and sowed,
Worked for what these wasters in gluttony destroy.
　　And some were very proud and apparelled ac-
　　　cordingly,
Cleverly disguised by the cut of their clothing,
While many were praying and doing their penance,
For the love of Our Lord living full hard,
Like anchorites and hermits who hold them in their
　　　cells
And care not to wander the country about

To get a fat livelihood and feed up their bodies.
And some bought and sold, the better to thrive,
As it seems to our thinking that such men should.
And some made mirth as minstrels know how,
And got gold by their glee—guiltlessly, I trow.
But jesters and clowns, the children of Judas,
Mimicked and mimed, and made themselves fools,
Though they had wit enough to work if they wished.
Paul preaches of them, though I stay not to prove it:
10 *Qui loquitur turpiloquium* he is Lucifer's servant.
Mendicants and beggars went about their business
Till their bags and their bellies were brimful
    crammed;
Whined for their food and fought at the ale-house,
Going to bed in gluttony, God knows the truth is,
And rising up with ribaldry, these knaves of Robert.
Sleepiness and sloth pursue them forever.
Pilgrims and palmers plighted together
To seek St. James of Spain and the saints in Rome;
Went upon their way with many a wise tale,
20 And had leave to lie all their lives thereafter.
Hermits, a heap of them, with hooks on their staves,
Were walking to Walsingham—each had his wench
    with him.
Husky tall lubbers who were loath to labor
Clothed themselves in copes, and called themselves
    brothers;
And some became hermits simply for idleness.
I found there the friars, all the four orders,
Preaching to the people for the profit of their bellies,
Twisting the Gospel as it seemed good to them,
Construing it badly to bring a new cope,
30 For many of these masters may dress as it pleases
    them,
Since money and their merchandise meet together
    often.

Now that charity has turned chapman, and chiefly
  shrives lords,
Many wonders have befallen within a few years.
Unless Holy Church begin to hold herself better,
The greatest mischief on earth will mount up fast.
  There preached a pardoner as though he were a
    priest,
And pulled out a bull with a bishop's seals on it,
Said that he himself could assoil them all
From falsehood and fasting, and from the vows
  they had broken.
The ignorant liked him and believed what he said,
10 Came up and kneeled and kissed his bull.
He banged them with his bull and bleared their
  eyes,
So his bull brought to him brooches and rings.
Thus you give your gold for gluttony's sustenance,
Turn it over to fellows who follow after lechery.
Were the bishop truly blessed and worthy of both
  his ears,
They would not be so bold in bamboozling the
  people.
Yet do not blame the bishop that the beggar preaches,
For the parish priest and he go halves on the silver
That poor folk would have if it were not for them.
20   Parsons and parish priests complain to their
    bishops
That their parishes are poor since the time of the
  pestilence,
And ask leave and licence to live up in London
And sing masses for simony, since silver is sweet.
  Then appeared a hundred in hoods of silk;
Sergeants they seemed, who serve at the bar
And plead the law for pence, or pounds more likely,
But never for the love of God will unloose their
  lips.

You might better meet the mist on the Malvern
    Hills
Than get a mumble from their mouths till money is
    shown.
I saw there bishops bold and bachelors of divinity,
Who had turned accounting clerks in the king's
    service.
There were deacons and archdeacons, whose duty it
    was
To preach to the people and the poor to feed,
Who went loping off to London by leave of their
    bishops
To be clerks of the King's Bench for the country's
    harm.
Barons and burgesses and bondmen, too,
10 I saw in that assembly, as you shall hear hereafter.
There were bakers and butchers and brewsters
      aplenty,
Female woolen weavers and weavers of linen,
Tailors and fullers and tanners among them,
Masons and miners and men of other crafts,
Ditchers and delvers who do their work ill
And pass the long day with "Dieu vous save, Dame
    Emma!"
Cooks and their knaves cry "Hot pies! Hot!
Good geese and pigs! Go dine! Go!"
Tavern-keepers with them told the same tale
20 About good wine of Gascony and wine of Alsace,
Of Rochelle and the Rhine, the roast to digest.
All this I saw while sleeping, and seven times more.

Passus I

What the mountain means and the dark dale be-
    neath it,
And the fair field full of folk, fairly I will show you.

A very lovely lady garbed all in linen
Came down from the cliff and called to me cour-
 teously,
Saying "Son, do you sleep?   Do you see these
 people,
How busy they are about the foolish maze?
The great part of the people who pass their lives
 on earth
Have their reward in this world and wish for noth-
 ing better;
Of any other heaven they have no care at all."
 I was afraid when I saw her, though fair was her
 face,
And said "I thank you, madam.   What does all this
 mean?"
10 "This hill and this tower," quoth she, "truth dwells
 therein;
And would that you wrought as His word teaches.
For he is Father of our faith, who formed you
 wholly
Both with skin and with features, and gave you five
 wits
To worship Him therewith the while you dwell here.
He made the earth for you to match all your needs
With woolen and linen, and a living to give you;
Within measure, moreover, to make you at ease.
He decreed in his courtesy three things in common,
And what their names are it is needful that I tell
 you,
20 Rehearsing them in order by rule and by reason.
The one thing is clothing to keep you from the cold,
The second meat at meals to keep you from misery,
And the third drink when thirsty, but drink not
 out of reason.   -
 "For Lot in his lifetime, because of liking for
 drink,

Did with his daughters what the devil loved;
Took delight in drink as the devil wished,
And so fell into lechery and lay with them both.
He said that the wine he drank made him do the
    wicked deed.
Take care of pleasant drink, and you will come off
    better;
Be moderate in all things, no matter how you yearn.
What the body longs for is not always best for
    spirit,
Nor pleasing to the body what is pleasant to the soul.
Do not believe your body, for a liar misleads it,
10 Which is the wicked world that works to betray you.
The fiend and your flesh follow on together,
And your soul will destroy unless you search your
    heart.
For your better guidance I give you this counsel."
    "I thank you, madam," quoth I. "Your words
    please me well.
But what of the money that men hold so fast?
Tell me to whom the treasure belongs."
"Go to the Gospel," quoth she. "What did God
    Himself say
When the people in the temple placed a penny before
    Him,
And asked if they should honor Caesar as their
    king?
20 He asked them in turn the teaching of the letters,
And whose was the image that was printed thereon.
'It is Caesar,' they said, 'as all of us can see.'
'Then *Reddite*,' quoth God, 'what to Caesar belongs,
Et que sunt dei deo, or else you do a wrong.'
For rightful reasoning should rule you in all things,
And native wit be warden and keeper of your
    wealth,

The guardian of it, to give it you at need.
Thrift and common sense thrive well together."
   Then I questioned humbly by Him Who made
      her:
"The dungeon in the dale that dreadful is to see,
What does that mean, madam? I beg you to tell
      me."
   "That is Care's castle," quoth she, "and he who
      goes therein
May curse that he was born in body or in soul.
Therein dwells a wight who is called Wrong,
The father of falsehood. He founded it himself.
10 Adam and Eve he urged to do wickedness;
Gave counsel to Cain to kill his brother;
Judas he deceived with the Jews' silver
And on an elder tree hanged him thereafter.
He keeps men from love, and lies to all of them
Who trust in their treasure, where is no truth at all."
   Then I wondered in mind what woman it was
Who such wise words of Holy Writ showed me.
I begged her by the name of God before she went
      away
To give me her name, since she guided me so well.
20   "Holy Church am I," she quoth. "You ought
      to know me.
I received you at first and the faith taught you.
You brought me sponsors who promised your obedi-
      ence,
That you would love me loyally while your life
      endured."
   Then I knelt on my knees and cried for her grace,
Praying her piteously to pray for our sins
And also to teach me to trust in Christ,
That I might work His will Who wrought me a
      man.

"Give me no treasure, but tell me this only,
How I may save my soul, since a saint you are held."
"When all treasures are tested, truth is the best.
I base it on *Deus Caritas,* deeming it right.
It is something as precious as dear God Himself.
Whoso is true with his tongue and tells nothing but
    truth,
Does his work thereby, and does no man ill,
He is reckoned on earth and in heaven to be
    righteous,
And like to our Lord, by St. Luke's words.
10 Clerks who know truth should teach it widely,
For Christians and pagans both lay claim to it.
   "All kings and knights should carefully rule,
And by right should journey about through the
    realm,
Taking trespassers and tying them fast
Until Truth has probed the trespass to the bottom.
For David in his days dubbed him knights,
Made them swear on their swords to serve Truth
    always.
That is the true profession that pertains to knights,
And not to fast one Friday in five score years,
20 But to hold with him and with her who desire the
    truth,
And for love or for gift never to leave it.
He who fails in that point is apostate to his order.
Christ, the King of Kings, gave knighthood to ten,
Cherubim and Seraphim in all the four orders,
And gave them mastery and might in His majesty,
Making them archangels over all His host,
And taught them through the Trinity the truth to
    know,
To be obedient to His word, but bade them nothing
    else.

"Lucifer learned truth with his legions in heaven,
Being loveliest to see after our Lord,
Until he disobeyed through boasting and pride.
Then fell he with his fellows, and they fiends be-
came;
Thrust from heaven into hell, they were hobbled
fast,
Some in air and some in earth and some in depths
of hell.
But Lucifer the lowest lies of them all;
For the pride that he showed, his pain has no end.
And all who work evil they shall wend, be sure,
10 After their death day and dwell with the rascal.
But those who keep the word that Holy Writ
teaches
And end their lives, as I have said, in meritorious
works,
May be sure that their souls shall be saved in
heaven,
Where Truth is with the Trinity and shall set them
all on thrones.
For I say certainly by the sight of the texts,
When all treasure is tested, truth is the best.
Let ignorant men learn it, since the lettered know
it now,
That truth is the treasure most trustworthy on
earth."
"I have no native knowledge," quoth I. "You
must teach me better,
20 By what power it begins, and where in my body."
"You are doting and a fool," quoth she; "dull
are your wits.
It is native knowledge that makes known to your
heart
To love your lord liefer than yourself,

And no deadly sin to do, though you die for it.
This, I trow, is truth! Whoso can teach you better
Let him tell you about it and afterward teach others!
Thus His word teaches—and according to it live—
That love is the dearest thing that our Lord asks,
And the plant of peace, too.   Preach it with your
 harp
When you are merry at your feasts and when men
 bid you sing.
For by natural knowledge you may know what to
 sing.
That comes from the Father Who formed us all.
10 He looked on us with love and let His Son die
Meekly for our sins, and to amend us all.
Yet He wished them no woe who brought the pain
 for Him,
But meekly with His mouth He besought mercy for
 them,
Pity for the people who tortured Him to death.
"Here may you see an example in Himself.
Though strong, He was meek, and mercy showed to
 them
Who hanged Him high and His heart pierced
 through.
And so I charge the rich to have ruth on the poor.
Though mighty you be, be meek in your works.
20 *Eadem mensura qua mensi fueritis, remecietur vobis.*
For the same measure you mete, amiss or otherwise,
You shall be weighed therewith when you wend
 hence.
Though you be true of tongue and true in your
 winnings,
And as chaste as a child that wails in church,
Unless you live truly and also love the poor,
And give of such goods as God may you send,
You have no more merit in masses and in hours

Than Malkin in her maidenhead which no man de-
    sires.
For the gentle James put it in his book
That faith without works is feebler than naught,
And dead as a door-nail unless the deed follow.
Chastity without charity, know you right well,
Is as useless as a lamp that has no light in it.
Many chaplains are chaste, but charity fails them;
No men are harder when higher they rise,
Unkind to their kin and to all Christian men.
10 They chew up their charity and chide the more
    afterward.
Such chastity without charity may be claimed by
    hell!
"Curates who keep themselves clean in their bodies
Are so cumbered with cares that they cannot creep
    out,
For avarice holds them bound hard and fast.
That is no truth of the Trinity but the treachery of
    hell,
An example to the ignorant to be niggardly, too.
These are the words that are written in the gospel,
Date et dabitur vobis, for I deal out to all
Your favor and your fortune in finding a livelihood;
20 Wherefore make your acknowledgment out of what
    I have sent.
The key of love is this, to release my grace
For the comfort of the troubled who are cumbered
    with sin.
Love is the chief thing that our Lord asks
And the straight way, too, that leads into heaven.
So I say as before, having seen these texts,
When all treasures are tested, truth is the best.
Now that I have told what truth is, that no treasure
    is better,
I may no longer stay. May the Lord keep you!"

THE AUTHOR OF *THE PEARL* AND *SIR GAWAIN*

APART from Chaucer, the most accomplished English poet of the fourteenth century was his contemporary, the unknown author of *The Pearl,* who with good reason is thought to have written also *Sir Gawain and the Green Knight,* together with two or three less important works. Who he was has not been discovered, but he must have been writing in the last quarter of the century. Like Chaucer, he knew both books and the ways of the world. There is evidence of his acquaintance not only with Latin literature and the French poetry which was still the birthright of Englishmen, but with the new Italian masters, Dante and Boccaccio; and he was equally familiar with the aristocratic manners, conversation, and sports of his time. The ideals of chivalry and its fine-spun courtesies are mirrored in his verse, as well as the eager aspirations of men who sought at once earthly honor and heavenly comfort. Curiously enough, since he was so learned a person and so accomplished an artist, he chose to write in the dialect of remote Lancashire at just the time when the speech of London was coming to be generally current.

In metrical form *The Pearl* is the most elaborate elegy in English, as can be seen from the following translation of the opening stanzas; but it is no mere exercise in versification. Only a poet with the power of expressing profound feeling in images of beauty could have made it what it is. The appeal to all the senses is sharp, but the appeal is used to stimulate more complicated emotions. Seldom has the beauty of poetic language been so well combined with beauty of formal design. *Sir Gawain and the Green Knight* is equally admirable in another way, being our best English example of the pure mediæval romance. The reader who comes to it for the first time will be struck by the strangeness of the tale: the interweaving of fantastic adventure with sophisticated courtly manners. He will find, if he looks more carefully, that the story is told with exquisite art. Each incident is given its due emphasis, and suspense is maintained to the end with the greatest skill. The loyalty test, which is the main plot, leads so naturally to the sec-

ondary plot that the transition is scarcely noticed. Even
the elaborate hunting scenes of the third part are justified
by the purpose they serve by way of foils to the experiences
of Gawain with Bercilak's lady. Another point to observe
is that the characters, though thinly drawn as is proper in
a romance, always behave like real human beings throughout
their amazing adventures. The poet, furthermore, understood the art of using atmosphere to heighten the effect of
his story. Not until the age of Burns and Wordsworth can
another verse narrative be found in which there is so careful
an adaptation of setting to the moods of the characters involved. That such a poem suffers by prose translation must
not be forgotten, but certain of its values cannot well be
destroyed by the unfortunate necessities of such a rendering.

From THE PEARL

Pearl, formed to be a prince's pride
When chastely set in purest gold,
Came never from the Orient wide
One worthy to be so extolled,
So round, so radiant—every side—
So delicate and smooth to hold!
When gems a judgment must abide,
To set mine first I dared be bold.
Alas! upon a green it rolled
10 Through grass to ground; I marked it not.
And now my grief cannot be told
For my pearl without a stain or spot.

Since in that spot it sprang from me,
Oft have I waited, wished to feel
The joy that erst could set me free
Of baleful chance and bring me weal;
Yet still that comfort cannot be,
Nor solace come my wounds to heal.
But once in thought I seemed to see
20 A vision that began to steal
Upon my heart like music's peal,

Though sad that clay my gem should blot.
O earth, thy stain hath set a seal
On my dear pearl without one spot!

That spot of spices needs must spread
Where wealth like that to earth is run;
Blossoms pale and blue and red
Shine there full bright beneath the sun;
Flower and fruit may there be fed
By the jewel wrapped in earth-folds dun.
10 For each herb grows from seed struck dead;
No wheat were else for harvest won.
From good all good is aye begun;
So that fair seed can fail us not.
Of spices rich shall want not one
From that precious pearl without a spot.

To that spot, then, as it befell,
I entered, to that sheltered green,
In August on a festival,
When corn is cut with sickles keen.
20 The hillock where my pearl once fell
Was pied with flowers sheer and sheen:
Gilliflower, ginger, and gromwell,
And peonies scattered all between.
Fair sight it was that there was seen
And sweet the perfume there, I wot,
Where rests in honor, as I ween,
My precious pearl without a spot.

Before that spot I wrung my hands;
Upon me swept care's swift increase;
30 My heart redoubled its demands
Though reason counselled me to peace.
I wailed my pearl's imprisoning bands,
Complained, and prayed for her release.

Although I knew Christ's mercy stands,
My wretched will I sought to please.
But there I found a strange surcease,
Such fragrance to my brain there shot;
I swooned upon the turf—and these
My visions—pearl without one spot!

From that spot my spirit sprang in space,
My body rested there behind;
My ghost went forth by God's good grace
10 To seek adventures He designed.
I knew not where in earth it was,
But all the place with cliffs was lined;
Towards a wood I turned my face
Where splendid rocks were clear defined.
The light of them could be divined
By no man—a gleaming glory they.
For ne'er were fabrics, to my mind,
Of half their radiance in array.

Arrayed were all the hill-slopes high
20 With cliffs of crystal clear of hue;
A forest bright about them nigh,
With tree boles of the Indies' blue.
Like burnished silver, flung awry,
Leaves quivered in the breeze that blew,
When shafts of sunlight swift to fly
Their shimmering darts intensely threw.
The gravel thick they seemed to strew
With orient pearls like dawn of day;
The very sunbeams paler grew
30 Before their radiance of array.

The sweet array of the hill-sides there
Made my heart's sorrow swift retreat;
The fresh and fruity perfumes were

Refreshment to me like strong meat.
Birds fluttered through the woodland air,
Flame-hued the dusky shadows beat.
The citole and the cithern ne'er
Their mirth could mock, and ne'er defeat;
For when they sang, those birds could cheat
The heart from grief to dance and play,
So gracious were they and so feat
To hear and see in their array.

10 Thus sweetly was arrayed the wood
Where fortune chanced that I should go.
The glory of it no man could
With tongue declare, and none can know
How joyously I strayed, or stood
Even the threatening cliffs below.
The farther, the fairer! Ah, how good
To see the flowers, row on row!
Green hedges and rich rivers show
With golden banks where I might stray.
20 To a stream I won and watched its flow.
Lord, glorious was its array!

The dear array of that great deep
Was a bank as green as beryl bright;
I saw the rushing waters sweep
With murmuring music, running aright.
In the river's bed, where the shadows sleep,
Gleamed stones like the glow through glass of
    light;
Like the streaming stars, when all men sleep,
That glitter aloft in the wintry night.
30 Each pebble that in the pool was pight
Emerald or sapphire I saw display;
The whole deep glowed to my wondering sight,
So precious and proud was its array.

That glory rare of down and dale,
Of wood and water and proud plain,
Brought me to bliss and eased my bale,
O'ercame my grief, destroyed my pain.
Joyous I sped adown the vale
Of that bright stream with surging brain;
And still the greater, without fail,
My joyance grew and did not wane.
For fortune fares as she is fain
10 To grant of weal or woe a store;
And when she favors, one may gain
Delight unceasing, more and more.

More joy came to me in that wise
Than I could tell, though space I had,
For mortal heart may not suffice
To the tenth part of that gladness glad.
Methought in truth that Paradise
Was on those slopes so richly clad;
Methought the river a device
20 To mark the pleasances there made
Beyond it; yet my heart grew sad
To find no crossing there before,
For the water was deep—I durst not wade.
I longed to pass, aye more and more.

Yet more and more I longed to dare
The stream, the while those slopes I scanned;
For though the vale I trod was fair,
Yet lovelier far was yonder land.
Round I began to search and stare
30 To find some ford where I might stand,
Yet of more dangers was I ware,
The farther I strode along the strand.
Was I then from that glory banned
That waited me on the farther shore?

Then came a wondrous thing to hand
That moved my mind aye more and more.

A greater marvel came to light!
I saw beyond that river clear
A cliff of crystal shining bright,
And at its foot I saw appear
A child who gleamed in purest white;
A maiden was she debonair,
And all in glistening raiment dight.
10 I knew her well—I had no fear—
She seemed of glittering gold; all sheer
And shining on the farther shore.
The longer I looked upon her there,
I knew her the better, more and more.

The more I gazed on her fair face,
Her lovely form, a glory came;
Transporting joy began to race
Throughout my heart; and her to name
I longed. Yet for a moment's space
20 The syllables I could not frame
To call her: in so strange a place
She came to me, yet seemed the same.
Her brow that ivory put to shame
She lifted towards me as of yore.
My heart, amazed, could but exclaim—
And ever, as I looked, the more.

SIR GAWAIN AND THE GREEN KNIGHT

When the siege and assault of Troy had come
to an end, and the city destroyed and burnt to
brands and ashes, the man responsible for the
treason there was tried for his treachery, the completest on earth. It was the noble Æneas with his

mighty kindred, who afterwards conquered provinces in the Western Isles and became lords of almost all the wealth therein. When noble Romulus came to Rome forthwith, he built that city with great pride, first of all, and named it from his own name, as it is now called; Ticius came to Tuscany and began settlements; Langobard in Lombardy set up homes; and far across the French Sea Felix Brutus joyfully established Britain on many a wide shore,
10 where war and trouble and marvel have appeared by turns, and both happiness and turmoil have often interchanged very quickly ever since.

When Britain had been established by this noble ruler, valiant men were bred there, who loved strife and in the course of time frequently stirred up trouble. More marvels have befallen here in this land than in any other that I know, ever since that day. But of all the kings of Britain who have dwelt here, Arthur was in all ways the noblest, as I
20 have heard. Therefore I intend to recount an adventure that some men hold to be a marvel: something exceeding strange among the wonderful tales about Arthur. If you will listen to this lay for a little while, I will tell it straightforwardly, as I have heard it narrated and as it is set forth and written, brave and strong, wrought into a narrative that has long been known in the land.

The king lay at Camelot during Christmas with many gracious lords, his best knights, all the noble
30 brethren of the Round Table, namely, enjoying splendid revel and unhampered mirth. There at times full many heroes journeyed, and gentle knights jousted full gallantly, then went to the court to dance and sing carols. For there the feast continued without interruption for full fifteen days, with all the banqueting and mirth that men could

devise, merry-making loud and glorious to hear, a
pleasant din by day and dancing by night. All was
at the peak of happiness for the lords and ladies,
whatever they most enjoyed. With all the prosperity in the world they dwelt there together, the
most famous knights under Christ and the loveliest
ladies who ever lived, and he who held the court
the most gracious of kings. For all these fair folk
in the hall were in the prime of their age, the most
10 fortunate people under heaven, with a king whose
spirits were the highest of all. It would be hard
in our time to name so brave a company on any
castle hill.

While the New Year was brisk because new
come, the assembly on the daïs was served double
portions when, after mass in the chapel had ended,
the king with his knights came into the hall. Loud
shouts arose from clerks and the others, who cried
"Noel! Noel!" again and again. Forthwith the
20 nobles ran about to offer their gifts, demanding New
Year's presents while they gave their own, and
talking eagerly about the gifts. Ladies laughed
aloud though they had lost in the exchange, and he
who won was not displeased, you may well believe.

All this mirth they made until time for meat, when
they washed suitably and went to their seats, the
best man placed ever above, as was most seemly.
In the midst of them the very lovely Guenevere was
seated on the splendid daïs, surrounded by adorn-
30 ments. There were thin silk hangings all about her,
while above rose a canopy of excellent cloth of
Toulouse, with tapestries of Tharsia cloth which
were embroidered and set with the finest gems that
could be bought for any price at that day. She was
most comely, and her grey eyes shone. No man

could say with truth that he ever saw anyone more fair.

But Arthur would not eat till all were served, he was so gay in his youth, and in a way so boyish. Life sat lightly upon him. He loved neither to lie long nor long to sit, so stirred within him his youthful blood and his restless brain. And another custom he had, too, which he had adopted in his magnificence: on such a high feast he would never
10 eat until there had been related to him a wonderful tale of something adventurous, of some great marvel that he could trust, of princes, of arms, of other great events; or until some trusty knight had besought him to joust and lay in peril dear life against life, each one the other, as fortune favored. This was the king's behavior at every feast that came, when he was in court among his noble household in the hall. Therefore with proud mien he stood boldly in his place on that New Year's Day, a very
20 valiant man. Much mirth he made withal.

Thus stood the brave king in his place before the high table, talking with courteous lightness. Good Gawain was placed beside Guenevere, and Agravain de la Dure Main sat on the other side, both of them sons of the king's sister and very trusty knights. Bishop Baldwin began the table above, and Iwain, Urien's son, ate with him. These were set on the daïs and splendidly served, and there were many brave knights besides at the side tables.
30 Then came the first course with the blaring of trumpets, which were hung with many bright banners. The sound of drums waked the echoes, with the tremulous notes of noble pipes, so that many a heart rose high at the sound. Full fair and dainty foods appeared therewith, abundance of fresh meats on so many plates that it was hard to find a place

on the cloth to set the silver dishes which held the
divers viands. Each man took ungrudged whatever
he pleased. Each pair had twelve dishes as well as
good beer and bright wine.

Now I will tell you no more of their service, for
every man can well understand that there was no
stinting. Another burst of sound followed quickly,
giving leave to each knight to begin his repast.
Scarcely had the music ceased, however, and the first
10 course been properly served, when in at the hall
door came a terrible lord, one of the greatest and
tallest on earth. From his neck to his waist he was
so squarely built and so thick, and his loins and his
limbs were so long and so large, that he was half a
giant of earth, I believe, yet I declare him to have
been a man nevertheless, and the best formed for
one of his size who ever went riding forth. Although his body was thick in back and breast, his
belly and waist were becomingly slender, and all
20 parts of his body were clean-cut and shapely. Men
wondered at his color no less than at his form and
size. He bore himself like a valiant man and was
bright green all over.

The man and his garments were altogether green.
A straight narrow tunic clung to his body, with a
fair mantle over it lined with plain fur of a single
color, a brilliant and pleasant white, as was his hood
also, which was thrown back from his head and
laid on his shoulders. Neat well-fitting hose of the
30 same green encased his calves, and his bright golden
spurs were set on barred straps of rich silk, while
there were facings under his thighs to protect him
as he rode. All his clothing, indeed, was green,
even to the stripes of his belt and the bright gems
richly set against silken embroideries on his fair
garments and his saddle. It would be tedious to

tell half the designs that were worked in these embroideries—birds and insects of bright green mingled with gold. The pendants of the steed's breast-trappings, the magnificent crupper, the studs at the ends of the bit, and all the metal work were enamelled in the same fashion; the stirrups were of the one hue, as likewise were the bows and noble skirts of the saddle, which glimmered and gleamed with green jewels. The horse he rode was gay with the same
10 color, you may be sure, a green steed large and strong, with an embroidered bridle, difficult and restive to manage but perfectly under the knight's control.

Very gaily attired in green was the man, and the hair of his head matched that of his horse. A comely waving thatch of it covered his shoulders, and over his breast fell a great beard like a bush, which with the hair of his head hung down all about above his elbows in such a way that half of
20 his arms were covered, just as a king's neck is covered by his cape. The mane of the great horse was much like the man's, well curled and combed, with very many knots and with gold thread plaited in the handsome green—ever a strand of the hair and another of the gold. The tail and the forelock were arranged in the same way, and both were tied with a band of bright green, while the dock of the tail was ornamented with very costly gems as well as bound tight with a thong that had an intricate
30 knot at the top, on which tinkled many shining bells of refined gold. Such a steed and such a rider were never seen in that hall ere that time. He looked, said all who saw him, as brilliant as lightning. It seemed that no man could endure his blows.

Yet he had neither helmet nor hauberk, nor gorget, nor any plate armor, nor spear to smite with,

nor shield for protection; but in one hand he carried a bunch of holly, which is greenest when the woods are bare, and in the other he bore a huge and monstrous axe, a cruel weapon, whoever might describe it. The head had the length of an ell, the spiked end was made of green steel and gold, and the bit was burnished bright, with a broad edge as keen as a sharp razor. It was fastened to a helve, the end of a strong staff, which was wound with
10 iron to the tip and chased with pleasant designs in green. A thong was wrapped about it, to which were attached both at the head and along the shaft, here and there, fine tassels set on richly embroidered buttons of bright green.

This knight came forward and entered the hall, making his way to the high daïs as if fearful of no danger. He greeted no one, but kept his eyes aloft. The first word he said was: "Where is the ruler of this company? Gladly would I see him and
20 hold speech with him." He cast his eyes over the knights, looking them up and down, then halted as if trying to see who was the most famous man in the hall.

There was prolonged scrutiny of the man, for everyone marvelled at the hue of the knight and his horse, as green as grass and greener, it seemed, glowing brighter than green enamel on gold. All who were standing about studied him and stepped nearer, wondering what in the world he was going
30 to do. Many wonders had the folk seen, but never before one such as this, on account of which they considered it illusion and magic. Many of the noble knights were thus afraid to answer, being altogether astonished at his voice, and sat stonestill in the dead silence that fell throughout the splendid hall. Their voices stopped at once, as if all had fallen

asleep—I think not wholly from fear, but partly from courtesy, in order to permit him whom all of them reverenced to address the man.

Then Arthur, as he beheld the strange thing happening before the high daïs, promptly saluted the knight, for he was never afraid. He said: "Welcome, indeed, sir knight, to this place. I am called Arthur and am the head of this house. Graciously dismount, I pray you, and what it is you wish we
10 shall learn hereafter."

"Nay," quoth the knight, "it is not my mission to remain any long while in this dwelling; but because your praise, my lord, is raised so high, and because your castle and your men are held the best in the world, and your knights the bravest who ride forth in steel armor, the strongest and most honorable of mankind, and valiant to sport with in all noble games, and because the chivalry here is famous, as I have heard, I have come hither at this time. You
20 may be certain by this holly bough which I bear that I come in peace and seek no quarrel, for had I set forth on this business in fighting wise, I have a hauberk at home and a helmet, too, a shield and a sharp spear shining bright, as well as other weapons to my hand, I assure you. But because I desired no protection, my equipment is less warlike. Only, if you are so brave as all men say, you will grant me by your grace the sport that I rightfully ask."

Arthur answered and said: "Courteous sir knight,
30 if you ask nothing more than battle, you shall not fail of a contest here."

"Nay, I ask for no fight, I tell you truly. There are only beardless children about this table here. If I were armed and set on a high steed, there is no man here to match me, their strength is so feeble. Therefore I am merely asking a Christmas game in

this court, for it is Yule and New Year's, and many bold knights are here. If anyone in this castle holds himself so brave, and is so valiant in mettle and so reckless as to dare the exchange of one stroke for another, I will give him this splendid battle-axe, which is heavy enough, to handle as pleases him; and I will suffer the first stroke unarmed as I sit here. If any knight be so bold as to try what I propose, let him come to me quickly and take the
10 weapon. I give him a quit-claim of it forever; he may keep it as his own. I will accept unflinchingly from him the blow as I stand. In recompense, you will adjudge me the legal right to give him a stroke in my turn, but grant him the respite of twelve months and a day. Hasten now, and let us see whether anyone here dare speak."

If he had astonished them at first, all the courtiers in the hall were now even more quiet, both the high and the low. The knight on the horse turned
20 and rolled his red eyes about fiercely, wrinkling his bristling green eyebrows and sweeping his beard from side to side, while he waited for someone to rise.

When none would address him, he gave a loud cough, cleared his throat resoundingly, and proceeded to speak. "Lo," quoth the knight, "is this the house of Arthur, the fame of which runs through so many kingdoms? Where now are your pride and your conquests, your fierceness, your wrath,
30 and your boastful words? The gaiety and the glory of the Round Table are destroyed by one man's word, for all of you are cowering with fear before a blow has been offered!"

Therewith he laughed so loud that Lord Arthur grieved, and the blood rushed for shame into his bright face. He grew as angry as the wind, as did all who were there. The king, whose nature was daring, approached the bold man, and said: "By heaven, knight, what you ask is foolish, and it is right for you to get what your folly demands. I know of no man who is afraid of your bragging words. Give me now your battle-axe, in God's name, and I will grant the boon you ask."

Swiftly he stepped towards him and grasped at his hand, while the other knight dismounted in proud 10 fashion. Now Arthur had the axe and, gripping the helve, brandished it grimly, thinking to strike with it. The bold man stood upright before him, taller by a head and more than any other in the hall. With serious face and unmoved countenance, he stroked his beard and pulled down his tunic, no more troubled or dismayed by the power of Arthur's strokes than he would have been if someone were bringing him wine to drink.

Gawain, from his place by the queen, bowed to 20 the king, saying: "Honored lord, I beg earnestly that this affair may be mine. If you would bid me come from this bench and stand by you there— if I might without discourtesy and displeasure to my liege lady leave the table—I would advise you thus in the presence of your noble court. It seems to me unseemly, if the truth be known, when such a demand is made openly in your hall, that you take it on yourself, capable though you be, when so many brave men are sitting about you on the benches. 30 None is more warlike of spirit than they, I believe, none stronger on the field of battle. I am the feeblest of them, I know, and the weakest of understanding. To acknowledge the truth, the loss of my life would matter least. Only inasmuch as you are my uncle do I merit praise; no worth but your blood have I in my body. Since this affair is so foolish that it concerns you in no way, and since I have first asked to undertake it, turn it over to me. If I speak not what is right, blame not this honorable court."

The nobles took counsel together, and forthwith advised with one voice that the crowned king be released, and that the game be given to Gawain. Then the king commanded the knight to rise from his place; and he got up at once and approached 10 the king courteously, kneeling down before him and taking the weapon. The king graciously released it and with uplifted hand invoked God's blessing on Gawain, bidding him cheerfully to be strong in heart and hand.

"Take care, cousin," quoth the king, "how you manage the cut you give him. If you dispose of him well, I readily believe that you will be able to endure any blow he can offer afterwards!"

With the battle-axe in hand Gawain approached 20 the man, who awaited him boldly, in no wise dismayed.

Then the knight in green spoke to Sir Gawain. "Let us rehearse our agreement before we go further. First, knight, I beg that you will tell me your name truly."

"On my honor," quoth the good knight, "I am called Gawain. I will give you this blow, irrespective of what may befall hereafter; and a twelve-month hence I will take another from you with what-30 ever weapon you please, but from no other man alive."

The other answered: "Sir Gawain, on my life I am wondrously glad that you are to give the stroke. By God," went on the green knight, "it pleases me that I am to receive at your hand what I have sought here. You have fully and properly rehearsed in very correct form all the covenant that I asked of the king, save that you shall assure me, sir, on your honor, that you will seek me out yourself wherever on earth you believe I may be found, and receive payment in kind for what you give me to-day before this noble company."

"Where shall I find you?" quoth Gawain. "Where is your dwelling? By Him Who made me, I know not where you live, and I know not you, sir knight
10 —neither your court nor your name. Instruct me rightly, and tell me by what name you are called, and I will use all my power to win thither; and that I swear to you in truth by my honor."

"That is enough at New Year's," quoth the man in green to gracious Gawain. "Nothing more is necessary. If, indeed, after I have received the buffet and you have given me your skilful stroke, I tell you at once my house, my home, and my name, then you may seek me out and fulfil your agreement;
20 and if I do not speak, then you shall speed the better, for you may remain in your land and inquire no further. But stay! Take your grim weapon, and let us see how you give a blow."

"Gladly, sir," quoth Gawain. He stroked his axe.

The green knight promptly took his stand with his head a little bowed to uncover the bare flesh. He drew his splendid long locks up over his head and exposed his neck for the business in hand. Gawain, setting his left foot forward, gripped his axe and
30 raised it aloft, then let it fall swiftly on the neck. The edge clove the bones of the man, going through the bright flesh and cutting it asunder, and the shining steel blade pierced the ground. The fair head fell from the neck to the earth, so that many thrust at it with their feet as it rolled away. Blood spurted from the body and showed bright against the green.

Nevertheless the man neither faltered nor fell; but
started forth vigorously on sturdy legs, groped about
in a terrible way where people were standing,
clutched his fair head, and lifted it up. Then he
turned to his steed, caught the bridle, put his foot
into the stirrup, and swung aloft, holding the head
in his hand by the hair. Though he was headless,
he sat as firmly in the saddle as if no mishap had
befallen him. The ugly bleeding body turned the
10 horse about. Many a man had fear of him by the
time his speech was ended.

For he held up the head in his hand, turning the
face towards the most noble lady on the daïs; and
it lifted up its eyelids and gazed with eyes wide open,
and spoke as you may hear. "See that you be ready
to go as you have promised, Sir Gawain; and search
loyally until you find me, as you have promised in
the hearing of these knights. Go to the Green
Chapel, I charge you, to receive a blow like the one
20 you have given—as you merit—which will be
promptly delivered on New Year's morn. Many men
know me as the Knight of the Green Chapel. Therefore you will not fail to find me if you make the
quest. So come, or you will deserve to be called
recreant."

With a fierce roar he tightened the reins and,
holding the head in his hands, passed out of the hall
door so quickly that sparks flew from the hooves of
his steed. To what race he belonged none there
30 knew, any more than they could tell whence he had
come. What of that? The king and Gawain smiled
and laughed aloud at the green knight. Yet it was
accounted wholly a marvel among those men.

Although gracious King Arthur wondered in his
heart, he let no such impression be seen, but said
aloud to the beautiful queen with courteous words:

"Dear lady, do not be troubled at all to-day. Such affairs are well suited to Christmas, with playing of interludes, and laughter and song and the courtly dancing of carols by knights and ladies. Nevertheless, I may well sit down to my meat, for I cannot deny that I have seen a marvel." He glanced at Gawain, and said courteously: "Now, sir, hang up your axe, which has hewed enough."

And it was placed above the daïs, hanging against
10 the tapestry at the back, where all men might see and marvel at it, accounting it truly a wonder. Then the two lords, the king and the good knight, sat down at the table, and brave men served them double portions of whatever was best. With all manner of feasting and minstrelsy they passed the day happily till it came to an end. Now take heed, Sir Gawain, and do not try because of the danger to avoid this adventure you have taken in hand.

II

This handsel of adventures had Arthur at the
20 New Year, because he was eager to hear of bold undertakings. Although there was lack of vaunting words when they sat down, they were now well provided with serious business, their hands over-full of it. Gawain was glad when he began the game in the hall; but do not be surprised though the end be grievous. For though men are merry when they have taken strong drink, a year runs very quickly and never brings back what has passed. The end is very seldom like the beginning.
30 So this Yule went by, and the year thereafter, and one season followed another in due course. After Christmas came crabbed Lent which tries the flesh with fish and simpler food. But then the weather

contends with winter. The cold shrinks away, clouds rise, bright falls the rain on the fair meadows in warm showers, flowers appear. Both earth and forest are clothed in green. Birds prepare to build and sing bravely from delight in the soft summer which is coming on the hill-slopes; and blossoms swell to their bloom in the richly luxuriant hedge-rows, while splendid song is heard in the proud wood. Afterward comes summer with its soft breezes, when 10 Zephyr blows gently over seedlings and herbs. Very lovely is the plant that grows up while the dampening dew drips from the leaves, awaiting the happy gleam of the bright sun. But then follows autumn apace, hardens the plant, and warns it to come to full ripeness ere winter. Autumn stirs the dust to rise with drought, flying high above the face of earth. Fierce winds of heaven wrestle with the sun, the leaves drop from the trees and light on the ground, and the grass fades that erstwhile was 20 green. Then all that has grown up ripens and decays.

Thus runs the year away into many yesterdays, and winter returns again, as in truth is the way of the world. The Michaelmas moon came with its pledge of winter. Then Gawain thought full soon of his troublesome journey.

Yet until Allhallows' Day he remained with Arthur, who made an entertainment for the knight's sake on that feast, a great and splendid revel of the 30 Round Table. Full courteous knights and lovely ladies were grieving on account of the prince; but none the less they were ready of speech and mirth-ful. Many who were sorrowful on the gentle knight's behalf made their jests there.

After the feasting he spoke soberly to his uncle about his journey, and without pretence said thus:

"Liege lord of my life, I beg permission to leave you. You know the nature of this matter: I need by no means tell you the trouble of it. But I am bound without fail to start forth to-morrow for the blow, to seek the green man as God may guide me."

Then the noblest in the castle assembled, Iwain, and Eric, and full many others: Sir Dodinal de Sauvage, the Duke of Clarence, Lancelot, Lionel, and good Lucan, Sir Boor and Sir Bedivere, both
10 strong men, Sir Mador de la Port, and many another honorable knight. All this courtly company approached the king with sorrowful hearts to give counsel to the knight. There was much lamentation in the hall that one so honored as Gawain should go on that errand, to endure a grievous blow and make no return with his sword.

The knight made good cheer throughout, and said: "Why should I hesitate? What may a man do but go to meet his fate, however harsh and terrible?"
20 All that day he remained there, and in the morning made ready. He asked for his arms early, and they were all brought. First a carpet of red Toulouse was spread on the floor, and much gilded gear glittered upon it. The brave man stepped thereon and fingered the steel. He was dressed in a doublet of fine Tharsia cloth, with a well-cut cape, short and full and fastened together at the neck, which was trimmed inside with brilliant white fur. Then they put sabatouns on the knight's feet, and enclosed his
30 legs in splendid greaves of steel with polished knee-pieces attached thereto, which were tied about his knees with gold knots. Goodly cuisses, which skilfully protected his sturdy thighs, were fastened on with thongs. The knight was then enfolded in a linked corslet of bright steel rings, with a backing of noble cloth. There were well-burnished arm-pieces,

and elbow-guards strong and bright, and gloves of plate, and all the fine gear that could serve him: a gorgeous coat-armor, gold spurs splendidly fastened, and a very trusty sword belted on with a girdle of silk. When he was clasped in his arms, his harness was rich indeed. The least latchet and loop gleamed with gold.

Dressed as he was, he heard mass, which was offered and celebrated at the high altar. Then he 10 came to the king and to his companions of the court, and graciously took leave of the lords and ladies; and they kissed him and escorted him forth, commending him to Christ.

By that time Gringolet was ready, girded with a saddle that gleamed very bright with many gold fringes and in preparation for the adventure was newly studded with nails. The bridle was striped transversely and bound with bright gold; the ornamentation of the breastpiece and of the superb sad-20 dle-skirts, the crupper, and the horsecloth matched the saddle-bows; and all were red, studded with rich gold nails which glittered and glinted like the gleaming sun.

Then the knight took his helmet and quickly kissed it. It was stoutly stapled and padded within, set high on his head, and fastened behind. Over the beaver was a light covering, which was embroidered and adorned with the finest gems on a broad silken hem, with birds on the seams, parrots preening at 30 intervals, turtle-doves and true-love knots set so thickly that it seemed many a damsel must have been seven winters at work upon it. The circlet that surrounded the crown of the helmet was even more precious, a device of bright and shining diamonds.

Then they brought to him his shield, which was of bright gules, with a pentangle depicted upon it

in pure gold. Taking it by the baldric, the knight put
it about his neck, and it became him most excellently.
Why the pentangle belonged to this noble prince I
must tell you, even though it delay me. It is a symbol that Solomon once devised to betoken truth, as
can be seen from the description; for it is a figure
having five points, and each line overlaps and locks
in another, and everywhere it is endless. The English always term it, as I hear, the endless knot.
10 Therefore it suited this knight and his bright arms,
for ever faithful in five ways, and five times in
each way, was Gawain known to be; and like refined
gold he was free from all unchivalrous qualities as
well as graced with virtues at court. On this account
he bore the new pentangle in his shield and coat-
armor, as a man accounted most true and as a knight
most gentle of conduct.

First, he was found faultless in his five wits; and
again, the man never failed with his five fingers; and
20 all his trust in the world was in the five wounds
which Christ received on the cross, as the creed tells
us. And wheresoever he was fighting, he steadfastly
kept in mind, no matter what occurred, that all his
pride must be in the five joys which the gracious
Queen of Heaven got of her Child. For this reason the knight had her image beautifully depicted
in the upper half of his shield, so that when he
looked thereto his courage never failed. The fifth
five that the man showed, as I find, were generosity
30 and love of his fellow men more than all things
else, purity and courtesy that never wavered, and
pity, which surpasses all points. These noble five
were more firmly attached to this knight than to
any other. With all of them he was, in truth, five
times girt about; and each one was joined to another
so that they had no end; and they were fixed upon

five points which never failed, neither gathering together on one side nor sundering, being without an end at any angle, wherever one started or finished. Therefore the figure was fashioned royally on his bright shield with red gold on red gules. This is what learned men call the true pentangle.

Now was fair Gawain ready. He took his spear straightway, and bade them all farewell—forevermore, as he thought. Then he struck the steed with
10 his spurs and hastened forth so fast that sparks flew from the stones as he rode away. All who saw the comely knight sighed in their hearts and said, indeed, each to the other, grieving for him: "By Christ, it is wrong that you, my lord, who are noble of life, should be so lost! To find his equal on earth, in faith, is not easy. To have wrought more carefully would have been more sensible. It would have been better to make yonder noble knight a duke, for he would have been a brilliant leader
20 in war; and that would have befitted him better than to be destroyed for naught, beheaded by a monster for the vanity of pride. Who ever heard of any king's so sacrificing his knights for the sport of Christmas games!" Many tears fell from their eyes when the noble lord went from the court that day. He stopped not, but sturdily went forward. Many a bewildering path he rode, as the story tells us.

Now rode Sir Gawain, as God willed, through the realm of Logres, though it brought him no pleasure.
30 Often companionless and alone he stayed at night in places where his fare was by no means to his liking. He had no comrade but his steed through forests and across downs, no being but God to speak with by the way, until he came near to North Wales. All the islands of Anglesey he kept on his left hand, and passed over the fords by the headlands of Holy

Head, coming to shore in the Forest of Wirral. But few dwelt there who loved either God or man with good heart. And ever he inquired, as he journeyed, from the men he met, if they had heard of a green knight in any place thereabout, or of the Green Chapel. All denied that ever in their lives they had seen a man of such a green hue. The knight took strange roads on many a dreary hillside. His mood changed often ere he found that chapel.

10 Many cliffs he scrambled over in strange regions, and rode as an alien far removed from his friends. At each riverside or ford where he passed, he found an enemy before him, as a rule: a foe so evil and so fierce that he had to fight. The knight encountered so many marvels among the hills that it would be tedious to tell the tenth part of them. Sometimes he warred with dragons, and with wolves, too; sometimes with forest creatures that dwelt in the rocks; with wild bulls, with bears, and with boars 20 at other times; and with giants who pursued him from the high fells. Had he not been doughty and steadfast, and served the Lord, he would surely have been slain full often. For troublesome as the fighting was, the winter weather was worse, when the clear cold rain fell from the clouds and froze ere it touched the sere earth. Almost dead with the sleet, he slept in his armor more nights than enough, where the cold stream ran clattering from the mountain-top and hung in hard icicles above his head. 30 Thus in peril and distress and hardship the knight journeyed alone through the country till Christmas Eve. At that tide he made his petition to Mary that she would direct his course and guide him to some habitation.

In the morning he rode pleasantly along a mountain slope into a very deep and wild forest, which

was flanked by high hills on each side. There were clumps of hoary oaks, a hundred together, and tangles of hazel and hawthorn everywhere clothed with rough ragged moss. On the bare twigs many unhappy birds, distressed by the cold, piped sorrowfully. The knight on Gringolet went on beneath the trees through many a bog and swamp, all by himself, troubled about his religious duties, lest he should not be able to attend a service to the Lord, Who on
10 that same night was born of a virgin to end our sorrow.

Therefore he said, sighing: "I beseech Thee, Lord, and Mary Thy dearest and gentlest mother, for some lodging where I may hear mass solemnly, and Thy matins to-morrow. I ask this meekly, and to that end I pray forthwith my Pater Noster and Ave and Creed." While he prayed, he rode on, confessing his misdeeds, and crossed himself repeatedly, saying: "The Cross of Christ aid me!"
20 He had crossed himself but thrice when he became aware on a hill above a glade of a moated dwelling, framed in by the boughs of many great trees which grew along the moat: the most lovely castle that ever knight owned, set on a meadow, with a park all about surrounded by a spiked palisade that enclosed the trees for more than two miles. The knight viewed the stronghold as it shimmered and shone through the bright oaks, then reverently took off his helmet and solemnly thanked Jesus and
30 St. Julian, who in their gentleness had shown courtesy to him and hearkened to his cry. "Now," quoth the man, "I beseech you yet for good lodging!" Then he spurred Gringolet with his gilt heels, and by good fortune found the main road that brought him speedily to the bridge end. The bridge was drawn up securely, the gates were shut fast; the

walls were strongly fashioned. No blast of the winds had it need to fear.

The knight waited on his steed by the bank of the deep double moat that surrounded the place. The walls plunged marvellously deep into the water and rose aloft to a very great height, all of solid hewn stone up to the cornice with its horn-works under the battlement. Above were fair watch-towers, provided at intervals with many fine loop-holes that 10 fastened securely. The knight had never looked upon better outworks; and within he beheld a very lofty hall, as well as many turreted towers and beautiful high pinnacles with skilfully carved and ornamented summits. He saw many chalk-white chimneys that gleamed on the tower roofs. So many pointed pinnacles were scattered everywhere, clustered so thickly about the embrasures of the battlements, that the castle seemed cut out of paper.

The nobleman on his steed thought it very fair, 20 if only he might enter the refuge and find lodging there while the holy day lasted that was at hand. He called, and soon a very civil porter, coming out on the wall to know his errand, hailed the errant knight.

"Good sir," quoth Gawain, "will you take a message from me to the high lord of this house, to beg lodgement?"

"Yea, by Peter," quoth the porter, "but indeed I am sure, sir knight, that you are welcome to dwell 30 here while you please."

Quickly the man returned with other folk to give the knight courteous reception. They let down the great drawbridge and, coming out, knelt down on the cold earth to welcome him as seemed honorable to them. As they had set the broad gates wide open for him, he bade them at once to rise, and rode over the bridge. Several equerries assisted him to dismount, and then brave men led his steed to stable. Knights and squires came down to convey him joyfully into the hall. When he lifted up his helmet, there were many to serve him and receive it at his hands; and they took from him both his sword and his shield. He greeted each of the proud nobles graciously, as they pressed forward to do him honor. Still dressed in his splendid armor, they took him 10 into the hall, where a delightful fire burned proudly on the floor.

The lord of the people came forth from his chamber to greet the visitor with honor. He said: "You are welcome to rule as you like all that is here. Everything is yours, to have and to hold at your will."

"Many thanks," quoth Gawain. "May Christ reward you!"

The knights embraced with seeming gladness. 20 Gawain looked at the man who had greeted him so courteously, and thought the owner of the castle a brave knight, a huge one, too, and in the prime of life. Stalwart was he, and his beard was reddish brown; stern was he, and he stood firm on his sturdy legs. His countenance was as terrifying as fire, though in speech he was courteous. It seemed to Gawain that he was well fitted to hold rule over good lieges.

The lord turned to a chamber, bidding them 30 assign people quickly to serve the guest with deference. At the command, men enough were ready, who brought him to a bright chamber, where the bedding was splendid: the sheets of pure silk hemmed with bright gold, the coverlets very elaborate, with beautiful panels of brilliant white fur and embroidered besides, the curtains sliding on cords with red gold rings. On the walls were hangings of Toulouse cloth and Tharsia silk, and similar tapestries under foot on the floor. There the knight was relieved of his corslet and the rest of his bright armor. Men quickly brought him rich robes to wear at his choice. As soon as he took one and donned it, it became him well with its spreading folds. Almost like the springtime he appeared to every man in his varied colors, with all his limbs 10 beneath glowing and delightful. It seemed to them that Christ never made a more comely knight. No matter where he might go through the world, he would be a prince without a peer on any field of battle.

A chair with coverings and quilted cushions, both cunningly made, was pleasantly arranged for Sir Gawain before the hearth, where burned a fire of charcoal. And then there was thrown over him a beautiful mantle of bright silk, richly embroidered 20 and furred within with the best skins trimmed with ermine, as was also the hood. So he sat in the splendid chair and warmed himself until his frame of mind grew more cheerful.

Soon a table was set up on trestles very fairly, covered with a clean cloth of pure white, with an over-cloth, a salt-cellar, and silver spoons. The knight washed at his good pleasure and began to eat. Men served him in seemly fashion with various excellent broths, admirably seasoned, double portions 30 as was right; and many kinds of fish, some baked in bread, some broiled on the coals, some boiled, some in stews flavored with spices, and all with such well-made sauces that the hero was pleased. Often with courtesy and graciousness he called it a feast indeed, though the knights, as was good manners, encouraged him to eat by saying: "Accept this penitential fare. Later it shall be bettered." The knight grew mirthful as the wine went to his head.

Then by discreet and tactful questions they made inquiry of the prince, until he courteously acknowledged that he came from the court held by noble and gracious Arthur, the splendid royal king of the Round Table, and that he was Gawain himself sitting there, come, as chance befell, to that Christmas celebration.

10 When the lord heard that he had the knight as guest, he laughed aloud at the news, so pleased was he; and all men in the company were happy that they were soon to be in the presence of one to whom belonged all excellence and valor and courtly manners, a man ever praised and honored beyond all others on earth. Each knight said to his comrade: "Now shall we see courtesy well exemplified, and hear noble speech without reproach. We may learn without asking what conversation ought to be, since 20 we have caught the fine father of good breeding. God has surely been gracious to us in granting us such a guest as Gawain at this time when men sit and sing of Christ's birth. This man shall instruct us in noble manners, and those who hear him shall learn the art of lovers' dalliance."

By the time dinner was at an end and the noble visitor had risen, it was nearly night. Chaplains went to the chapel and rang very loudly, as was proper, for the devout evensong of the high festival. 30 The lord went thither, and his lady gracefully entered her closed pew. Gawain hastened in happy mood and followed them. The lord took him by a fold of his mantle and led him to a seat, calling him familiarly by name and saying that he was most welcome of all men in the world. Gawain thanked him hastily, and they embraced and sat soberly one by the other throughout the service.

Then the lady wished to look upon the knight, and came forth from her closet with many lovely maidens. She was the fairest of them all in the texture of her neck and face, in her color, her figure, and her gentle ways—more beautiful than Guenevere, as it seemed to the knight. He went through the chancel to salute the gracious lady courteously. At
10 her left hand she was attended by another lady who was older than she, an ancient dame highly honored by the company of knights. Unlike to look on were those ladies, for if one was young and fresh, withered was the other. Rich red mantled the cheeks of the one, while the rough and wrinkled cheeks of the other hung in loose folds. The head-dress of the one, ornamented with many gleaming pearls, left bare her breast and white throat, which shone brighter than snow new fallen on the hills;
20 the other's neck was covered with a gorget, her black chin bound up with a white veil, her forehead hidden by silk, and she was muffled up everywhere, turreted and tricked out with ornaments, so that nothing was visible of the lady but her black eye-brows, the two eyes, the nose, the bare lips, and those were unpleasant to see and strangely bleared. One may call her, before God, a worshipful lady! Her body was short and thick, with broad and rounded hips. Sweeter to look upon was the lady
30 she led!

When Gawain saw the fair lady, who surveyed him graciously, he went up to the two with per-mission of the lord, saluted the elder with a low bow, but lightly embraced the more lovely, and kissed her in seemly fashion, while he spoke as a knight should do. They received him in a friendly way,

and he quickly asked that if it pleased them they would accept him as their servant. They took him between them and led him, as they talked, to the hearth in the chamber, where they called for spices and good wine, which men hastened to bring them in profusion. The lord often sprang from his seat, urging them many times over to be merry. Gaily he pulled off his hood and hung it on a spear, offering the honorable possession of it to the one
10 who made the most mirth during Christmas. "And I shall try, by my faith, if my friends will help, to contend with the best, before I lose my hood." Thus the lord made merry, to gladden Sir Gawain that night with sport in the hall, until the time came when he called for a light. Sir Gawain took leave and went to his bed.

On the morning which recalls to every man the time when the Lord was born to die for us, happiness comes to each dwelling in the world for His
20 sake. So did it there on that day with many delights. Cunningly made dishes were served on the daïs by stout retainers. The ancient dame sat in the highest place, with the lord courteously leaning towards her. Gawain and the fair lady sat together in places of equal honor, as the service duly began. And afterward throughout the hall, in a way to please them, each man was promptly served according to his degree. There was meat, there was mirth, there was so much joy that to recount it all
30 would be hard for me if peradventure I tried to describe it in detail. Yet I know that Gawain and the beautiful lady had so much pleasure of each other's company in their private dalliance, the pure and virtuous courtesy of their talk, that their play truly surpassed the enjoyment of the other nobles. Each man minded his sport, and those two minded

theirs, while trumpets and drums and pipes sounded about them.

Much joy there was on that day and the next; and the third was equally filled with delight, for the merriment of St. John's Day was pleasant to hear. That was the last of the entertainment, they thought, and the guests were to depart at the gray dawn thereafter. So they held high revel and drank wine, dancing unceasingly in joyous carols. At 10 last, when it was late, they took their leave, each strong man to wend his way on the morrow. As Gawain bade farewell, the good lord held him back and led him to the chimney-place in his own chamber. There in privacy he thanked him warmly for the honor he had done to him and his house at that high festival, by adorning the castle with his gracious presence.

"Indeed, sir, while I live, I shall fare the better because Gawain has been my guest at God's own 20 feast."

"Many thanks, sir," quoth Gawain, "All the honor is your own, in good faith. The High King reward you! I am your man, as I rightly should be, to work your will in high things and low."

The lord insistently tried to keep the knight longer, but Gawain answered that he could by no means stay. Then the lord asked him very courteously what serious business had driven him to journey all alone from the king's court so daringly at that time 30 of the year, before the holidays were past.

"Truly, sir," quoth the knight, "you say but the truth. A high and pressing errand took me from court, for I am summoned to a place that I know not how to seek for, or whither in the world to go to find it. For all the land in Logres I would not fail to come to it on New Year's morning, so our Lord

help me! Therefore, sir, I make this request of
you here, that you tell me truly if ever you have
heard any tale of the Green Chapel and where it
stands, or of the Green Knight who holds it. A
solemn agreement was made between us that I should
meet the man there if I lived. It now wants but
little of the New Year; and, by God's Son, I
would see the man more gladly, if God would permit, than have any other blessing whatsoever. I
10 have now barely three days, and I would as gladly
fall dead as fail of my mission."

Then, laughing, the lord said: "It is better for
you to stay on, for I can direct you to the place
where the Green Chapel stands by the end of the
time you have set. Grieve no more. You shall
remain at your ease in your bed here while the days
pass, and set forth on the first of the year, yet reach
your goal by mid-morning, to do what pleases you
there. Dwell here until New Year's Day, then
20 rise and go. You shall be set on your way. It
is but two miles hence."

Then Gawain was very glad, and laughed merrily.
"I thank you heartily above all else. Since my adventure is achieved, I shall stay at your will and
do whatever you judge best."

At this the lord placed him by his side, had the
ladies fetched for their greater delight, and in this
privacy they took their pleasure together. The lord
in his high spirits made merry speeches like a man
30 who had lost his wits and knew not what he did.

He cried out to the knight: "You have agreed to
do whatever I bid. Will you hold to the promise
here and now?"

"Yea, forsooth, sir," said the loyal man, "while
I remain in your castle, I will be obedient to your
command."

"You have travelled from afar," quoth the lord, "and because you have revelled with me since, you are not well recovered either in food or sleep, as I know of a truth. You shall stay in your upper room and lie at your ease to-morrow morning until time for mass, and go to meat when you will with my wife, who will sit with you and give the pleasure of her company till I return to court. Remain you here, and I shall rise early and go
10 hunting."

Gawain agreed to all this, bowing courteously.

"Yet further," quoth the lord, "we shall make a covenant. Whatsoever I get in the forest shall be yours, and whatever fortune you win give it to me in exchange. Swear on your honor, dear lord, to make this exchange, whether worse come or better."

"By God," quoth the noble Gawain, "I agree thereto, and I am glad it pleases you to make this sport."
20 Said the lord of the castle: "The bargain is made. Who brings us drink to seal it?"

They laughed and drank, trifling and exchanging badinage, these lords and ladies, while it pleased them. And afterward with Gallic courtesy and many fine words they rose and stood for a little, speaking quietly, then kissed one another graciously and separated. With many deft attendants and gleaming torches each man was brought to his bed at last in comfort. Yet ere they went to bed, they
30 often rehearsed their covenant. The old lord of the people knew well how to keep a game in hand.

III

Full early before dawn the folk arose; and those guests who were leaving called their servants, who

hastened to saddle the horses, prepare their gear, and pack their bags. The nobles, all arrayed for riding, made ready, mounted lightly, and took their bridles, each man on the way he pleased. The noble lord of the land with his retinue of knights was not the last one ready to depart. When he had heard mass, he ate a morsel of food hastily, and with a bugle-call hastened swiftly to the hunting-field. As soon as daylight dawned upon earth, he and his
10 knights were on their tall steeds.

Then the well-trained dog-grooms coupled their hounds, opened the kennel door, and called them out, blowing loudly three single notes on their bugles. The hounds bayed at the sound and made a brave noise. A hundred huntsmen of the best whipped in and turned back the ones that strayed away. The keepers went to their stations, and the huntsmen unleashed the hounds. There rose in the forest the great tumult of bugle blasts.
20 At the first cry of the hounds, the wild deer trembled, rushed through the valley in their terror, and away to the hills; but they were promptly stopped by the cordon of sharp-eyed beaters. The beaters let the harts with the tall heads pass by, and the brave bucks, too, with the broad palms on their antlers; for the noble lord had forbidden anyone to touch the male deer in the close season. The hinds were held within the circle by cries of "hay!" and "ware!", the does driven back with a great
30 noise to the deep valley. There one could see, as they passed, the rushing flight of arrows; at each turn in the wood sped an arrow, which mightily pierced a shining hide with its broad head. Lo! they cried out, they bled, they died on the hillslopes. All the while, the racing hounds tore after them swiftly, and the hunters with loud horns hastened

on with such a ringing cry as if the cliffs had burst
asunder. Whatever game escaped the men who
were shooting was pulled down and slain at the
receiving stations, after the beasts had been driven
from the heights and down to the waters. The men
at the lower stations were skilled, and the greyhounds so powerful that they seized them at once
and pulled them down straightway, as fast as men
could look. The lord, enraptured, rushed in again
10 and again, and dismounted, passing the day joyously in this manner till came the dark night.

While the lord was making sport on the edge of
the forest, good Gawain lay in his magnificent bed,
idling until daylight gleamed on the walls, under
bright covers and curtained about. As he was
quietly dozing, he heard a slight noise cautiously
made at his door, and heard it quickly open. He
lifted his head out of the clothes, raised a corner
of the curtain a little, and looked warily to see what
20 it might be.

It was the lady, most beautiful to behold, who
closed the door after her very quietly and moved
towards the bed. The knight in embarrassment
lay down, and craftily pretended to be asleep. She
stole in silence to his bed, lifted the curtain, and
crept inside, where she sat down gently on the
edge of the bed and stayed there, waiting for him
to awake. He lay quiet for a long while and pon-
dered on the possible results of the affair. It seemed
30 to him very strange, yet he said to himself: "It would
be more courteous of me to find out as soon as may
be what she wishes." Rousing himself and stirring, he turned towards her and opened his eyes,
then pretended to be astonished and made the sign
of the cross, as if to protect himself. With the
white and red blended in her face, she began to

speak most graciously, and on her delicate lips was a smile.

"Good-morrow, Sir Gawain," said the fair lady. "You are a careless sleeper to allow anyone to steal in like this. Now that you are caught, I shall imprison you in bed, you may be sure, unless we come to terms." Laughingly the lady uttered the jest.

"Good-morrow, fair one," quoth the merry Gawain, "I am in your power, and that pleases me well, for I yield at once and beg for mercy, which is best, I am sure, since I can do nothing else." Thus he turned the jest with a happy laugh. "But if you would give me leave, lovely lady, by releasing your prisoner and asking him to rise, I would remove myself from this bed and array myself more suitably. I should have the more comfort in talking with you."

"Nay, forsooth," said the sweet lady, "you shall not rise from your bed, I assure you. I shall keep you here and talk with my knight whom I have captured. For I know very well you are that Gawain whom all the world honors, wherever you journey. Your honor and courtesy are praised by lords and ladies—by every living creature. And now you are here, to be sure, and we are alone. My lord and his train have gone afield; other men are in their beds, as are my ladies; the door is closed and securely fastened. Since I have the favorite of everyone here in the house, I shall use my time well in conversation while it lasts. You are welcome to my body to do with it what you will. I ought to serve you, and so I shall do."

"On my honor," quoth Gawain, "though I am not the man you picture me, I seem to profit by it. I know well that I am unworthy of such honor as you mention; but I should be glad, by God, if you permitted, to have the joy of pleasing you in word or deed. That would rejoice me."

"In good faith, Sir Gawain," quoth the lovely lady, "if I found fault with the excellence and prowess that please all others, or held them lightly, I should fail in courtesy. There are plenty of ladies who would rather have you in their power, gracious knight, as I have you here, to enjoy the dalliance of your charming speeches and to get comfort and
10 relief from their sorrows, than all the treasure and gold they possess. But I praise the Lord of Heaven that through His grace I have what all desire."

Very gracious was the fair lady, but the knight replied discreetly to everything she chanced to say. "Madam," quoth the courteous man, "Mary reward you! Your generosity, in very truth, is noble. People most commonly take their line of conduct from others, and they foolishly exaggerate the courtesy they pay me. In reality, I am to be valued
20 only on account of the honor you pay me, because you cannot go wrong."

"By Mary," quoth the lady, "it seems otherwise to me. If I were equal to all the women alive, and had the entire wealth of the world in my possession, and if I were to bargain for the choice of a lord, no knight on earth should be selected before you, sir, both on account of your manners that I have observed, your beauty, your courtesy, and your happy demeanor—what I knew by report earlier
30 and now find to be true."

"You might certainly choose much better, dear lady," quoth the knight, "but I am proud of the praise you give me, and as your true servant I hold you my sovereign, and make myself your knight. May Christ reward you!"

Thus they talked of many things until morning

passed, and ever the lady made it appear that she loved him greatly, while the knight was on the defence, but acted very courteously. "Though I were the most beautiful of ladies," the lady thought to herself, "he would show me no love." It was because of the terrible event he was soon to meet, the unavoidable blow that would strike him down. The lady then spoke of departure, and he did not restrain her. She said good-bye with a laugh-
10 ing glance, but amazed him by the gibe she gave as she lingered: "May He Who gives us speech reward you for this entertainment! But that you are Gawain I am inclined to disbelieve."

"Why?" asked the knight, and repeated the question, fearful lest he had been at fault in the manner of his speeches.

The lady blessed him, and said as follows: "Anyone so courteous as Gawain is held to be—and that is pure courtesy itself—could not well have been
20 so long with a lady without begging her for a kiss, out of politeness and by some trifling hint, at least, at the end of some speech or other."

Then said Gawain: "Let it be as you will, to be sure. I shall kiss you at your command, as a knight should, and go further to avoid your displeasure. So plead no more."

She approached at that and caught him in her arms, bending down and kissing him. Thereupon they commended each other to Christ, and she left
30 the room without further speech.

He prepared hurriedly to rise, called to his chamberlain, selected his garments, and when he was ready went forth to mass. Then he passed on to the meal which awaited him, and made merry all day till the rising of the moon. A knight was never more fairly placed between two ladies of such worth as the older and the younger. Much pleasure they had together.

And ever the lord of the land continued at his sport, hunting the barren hinds in forest and heath. A marvellous number of does and other deer he killed while daylight lasted. Then at length the folk assembled proudly and made a quarry of the slain deer. The nobles came thither with their attendants, selected the fattest of the beasts, and ceremoniously 10 cut them open, as custom demands. Certain ones made the assay, and found two fingers of fat on the poorest of them.

Then they made a slit above the breastbone, seized the first stomach, cut it open with a sharp knife, and tied it up. Next they slashed the four legs and stripped off the hide, then broke open the belly and took out the bowels, cunningly removing also the flesh of the knot in the flanks. Gripping the throat, they carefully separated the gullet from the wind- 20 pipe and took out the lungs. Then they cut out the shoulders with sharp knives, slitting round them along a narrow passage in order to keep the sides uninjured. Next they broke up the breast, separating it, and, beginning at the throat, ripped it quickly to the fork of the legs, taking out the advancers. After that they cut the membranes along the ribs, and stripped off the hide along the back- bone straight down to the haunches, so that it all hung together and could be lifted as a whole and 30 cut off. This they took for the numbles, as I believe they are called. At the forks of the thighs they cut the loose folds of skin from behind, and quickly cut the forks in two, to separate them from the backbone. Then they cut off the head and neck, and separated the sides from the backbone, throw- ing the ravens' fee of gristle into the branches of a tree. Next they pierced each thick side through by the ribs, and hung them up by the hocks of the legs, each man to have his portion as is the custom. On one of the deerskins they fed their hounds with liver, lights, and tripe, mixed with bread soaked in blood.

Bravely they blew the signal call of capture, while the hounds bayed. Then they took their venison and turned towards home, sounding loud many a
10 note on their horns. By the time daylight had gone, the whole company had returned to the fair castle, where the knight had remained without stirring. Joyously the lord came in where the bright fire was kindled, and greeted Gawain with delight.

Then the lord commanded all the household to assemble in the hall, and bade call both the ladies down with their maidens. In sight of all the folk he told his men to fetch his venison, and called out to Gawain in high glee, showing him the tally of
20 nimble beasts and pointing out the bright fat on the ribs.

"How like you this sport? Have I won your praise? Have I deserved your hearty thanks by my skill?"

"Indeed, yes," quoth the other man, "here is the finest hunting I have seen these seven years in the winter season."

"And I give you all, Gawain," said the lord, "for by our covenant you may claim it as your own."
30 "That is true," quoth the knight. "I say the same to you. What I have honorably won in this house is certainly yours with equally good will." He clasped the lord's fair neck in his arms and kissed him as courteously as he knew how. "There you have my winnings. I achieved nothing more;

but if there had been more, I would give it to you completely."

"Many thanks," quoth the good man. "It is good, yet perhaps it would be even better if you would tell me where you won this treasure by your wit."

"That was not the agreement," said he. "Ask me nothing more, for you have received what is due you, as you must truly believe."

10 They laughed and made merry together with praiseworthy courtesy. Soon they went to supper, where there were dainties in plenty. Afterward they sat in the chamber by the hearth, while attendants brought choice wine to them often; and again they agreed jestingly to carry out in the morning the same agreement as before: namely, to exchange their winnings when they met at night, whatever chance befell them or whatever new thing they got. They made the covenant before all the court, while drink 20 to seal the bargain was brought forth with jests. Then they took leave of one another courteously at last, and each man hastened to his bed.

When the cock had crowed and cackled but thrice, the lord leaped from his bed, as did all his attendants. Ere daylight came, as soon as mass and food had been properly despatched, the company repaired to the forest for the chase. The huntsmen's horns were loud as they crossed the plain, and among the thorns they uncoupled the racing hounds.

30 In a copse beside a marsh the hounds soon cried the finding of scent, and the huntsmen with loud shouts encouraged those which first gave tongue. The hounds that heard the noise hastened thither, and fell quickly in pursuit, forty at once. Then rose such a babel and tumult of the hounds in the

pack that the rocks re-echoed. The hunters heartened them with horn and with voice.
In a compact body the hounds rushed forward between a forest pool and a forbidding crag. On a rocky hillock beside a cliff, not far from a marshy thicket, where rough rocks had fallen in confusion, they found the game at length; and the men came after them, surrounding both crag and hillock, because they knew well that within the circle was
10 the beast which the bloodhounds had announced. They beat on the bushes, and bade him rise up, and he rushed out with disaster to the men in his path—one of the most marvellous of swine. Long separated from the herd was the old, old creature, and savage, the greatest of all boars. When he had grunted fiercely, he brought trouble to many, for in his first plunge he knocked three men to the earth, and sped forth at high speed without pausing. The hunters called aloud "Hi!" and hallooed
20 "Hay! Hay!", put their horns to their lips, and vigorously blew the assembly call. Many were the merry voices of men and of hounds, as they rushed noisily after the boar with threats to kill him. Often he stood at bay and maimed the pack, injuring the hounds, while they howled and yelled. Men pressed forward to shoot at him, loosed their arrows, and often hit him. But the points failed on his tough shields, and the barbs would not pierce his brawn, though the smooth shafts broke in pieces. The ar-
30 row-head rebounded, wherever it hit. Yet when the blows hurt him, striking so hard, he rushed on the men in his madness for battle and wounded them in his rushes, so that many were afraid and withdrew a little. But the lord on a swift horse dashed after him, blowing his bugle like the brave man he was on the hunting-field. He gave the assembly call, and

rode through the thickets, pursuing the wild boar until the sun was high.

Thus through the day they went on, while our gracious knight Gawain lay pleasantly at home in his bed under rich-hued covers. The lady did not forget to come to salute him. Very early she came to cheer his spirits. As she approached the curtain and peeped at the knight, Sir Gawain welcomed her courteously at once. She replied very eagerly, sit-
10 ing down quietly by his side and laughing much.

With a gracious look she said: "Sir, if you are Gawain, it seems wonderful to me that a man so well-disposed at all times to what is good does not understand the manners of society, and that, when instructed by anyone, you put them out of your mind. You have forgotten at once what I taught you yesterday in the best way I could."

"What is that?" quoth the knight. "Truly I do not understand. If what you say be true, I am to
20 blame."

"I instructed you about kissing," said the beautiful lady. "It is proper for any courteous knight to claim a kiss quickly wherever he finds favor."

"My dear lady," quoth the doughty man, "say not so! I dare not do that, lest I be denied. If I were refused, I should surely be wrong in having made the request."

"My faith!" said the merry woman. "You cannot be refused! You are strong enough to get your
30 will by force if you please, should anyone be so ill-bred as to deny you."

"That is all very well, by God," quoth Gawain, "but threats are unlucky in the land where I dwell, and so is any gift not bestowed with good will. I am yours to command, to kiss when you will. You may take kisses when you please, and stop only when it seems to you best."

The lady bowed down and graciously kissed his cheek. Much talk they had of the sorrow and happiness of love.

"If you will not be angry," the noble lady said, "I should like to ask you, sir knight—young and valiant as you are, courteous and chivalrous as you are widely known to be, the best of all knights—
10 why I have never, though I have sat here by you two several times, heard any word from you, less or more, that pertained to love. Yet the chief thing praised in the lore of arms is the faithful sport of love. This labor of true knights is the very title given to their works, and the text of it: how men have ventured their lives for their true love, have endured grievous times of trouble on account of it, and afterward have avenged themselves by their valor and rid themselves of their sorrow, bringing
20 joy into the bower by their virtues. You are known as the most noble knight of your time; your fame and honor are spread abroad everywhere; and you ought, being so gracious and so skilled in courtly vows, to be willing to show and teach a young creature such as I am something about the art of true love. Can it be that you are ignorant, in spite of the fame you bear? Or do you consider me too dull to listen to your courtly conversation? For shame! I have come hither by myself, and here
30 I sit in the hope of learning some craft from you. Teach me, I beg you, out of your wisdom, while my lord is away from home."

"In good faith," quoth Gawain, "may God reward you! My happiness is great, and my pleasure extreme, that so noble a lady should come hither and trouble herself about such a poor man as I am. It gives me delight that you can amuse yourself with your knight, showing him favor of any kind. But as for taking on myself the task of expounding true love, and preaching about the text and tales of arms, to you who have twice the craft in that art, I know well, than a hundred men such as I am or ever shall be while I live on earth, it would be manifold folly, noble lady, by my troth. As far as I can, I would do what you will, because I am greatly your 10 debtor, and I will be your servant always, so save me the Lord!"

Thus the noble lady made trial of him, and often tempted him to make him woo her, whatever was her intent. But he defended himself so fairly that no fault appeared, nor any wrong on either side, and they were happy together. They laughed and sported for a long time. At last she kissed him, took her leave courteously, and went her way.

Then the knight bestirred himself, and rose for 20 mass, after which their dinner was prepared and splendidly served. The knight amused himself with the ladies all the day; but the lord galloped over the countryside, pursuing his monstrous boar.

The beast rushed along the slopes; and when he stood at bay, snapped asunder the backs of the hounds, till bowmen subdued him and made him plunge on for his life, so many were the arrows shot at him when the hunters collected. Yet at times he made the boldest of them flinch. At last 30 he was so weary that he could run no more, but made as fast as he could for a hollow where a stream ran at the base of a rock. He got the bank at his back and began to paw the earth and whet his white tusks, while the foam frothed horribly at the corners of his mouth. All the brave men disliked to attack from a distance, but they dared not approach because of his savagery. He had injured so many before that all were loath to be torn by his tusks. Fierce he was and mad.

Then came the lord himself, urging on his horse, and saw the creature at bay, with the group of men about him. He dismounted with grace, left his courser, drew out a bright sword, rushed forward, and came fast through the stream where the enemy had taken his stand. The wild boar saw the
10 man with weapon in hand, and with hair rising he snorted so violently that many were afraid on the nobleman's account, lest evil befall him. The pig rushed, and man and boar were fighting in the middle of the stream. The boar had the worst of it, for the man eyed him well when they met, set his blade straight at the creature's breast, and drove it up to the hilt, piercing the heart. Snarling he yielded; and down the stream a hundred hounds were at him quickly, biting him with fury. The
20 men brought him to the bank, and the dogs gave tongue to proclaim his death.

The horns blew high triumphal blasts, and the knights who had breath left hallooed aloud. The hounds bayed at the creature, as the chief huntsmen of the toilsome chase gave them the signal to do. Then a man wise in woodcraft began to cut up the boar with ceremony. First he hewed off the head and set it aloft, then tore him roughly along the backbone and took out the guts, which he singed
30 on hot coals. With these, mixed with bread, he rewarded his hounds. Next he cut out the brawn in wide slabs, and removed the edible entrails, as was proper. Then they fastened the halves together and slung them on a strong pole. Now with their boar they hastened home. Before the man who

had slain him in the stream by the mighty strength of his hand was borne the head of the beast. It seemed long to him until he saw Sir Gawain in the hall. He called, and Gawain came towards him to receive his payment. The lord laughed loud and merrily when he saw him, and greeted him joyously. The good ladies were fetched and the household gathered. The lord showed them the slabs of boar's flesh, and told the tale of the wild boar's
10 great size and length, and of his ferocity in the wood where he stood at bay. The other knight commended his deed very courteously and gave him praise for the skill and courage he had shown. Such brawn and such sides, the bold man said, he never before saw taken from any swine. Then they handled the huge head, while the courteous knight admired it and was loud in praise of the lord.

"Now, Gawain," quoth the good man, "this game is yours according to our fixed agreement, as you
20 know well."

"That is so," quoth the knight, "and just as certainly all I have got I shall pass on to you, by my troth." He clasped the nobleman about the neck and graciously kissed him, and a second time did the same. "Now we are fairly quit, this evening," said the knight, "in respect to all the covenants we have solemnly made since I came hither."

The lord said: "By St. Giles, you are the best I know! You will be rich presently, carrying on a
10 trade like this!"

Then they set up tables on trestles and put cloths on them. Bright lights appeared along the walls, where men fastened waxen torches, and the knights were served in the hall. Much noise of merrymaking and joy sprang up about the fire; and both at supper and afterward there were many noble songs such as Christmas processionals and new carols, with all the customary mirth that one can imagine. And ever our courteous knight was beside the lady. She made such an effort to please the stalwart man with her secret looks of favor that he was altogether astonished, and angry inwardly; but on account of his good breeding he could not refuse to be agreeable, but treated her courteously, no matter how twisted the affair became.

10 When they had sported in the hall as long as they pleased, he asked them to his chamber, where they sat by the fire. There they drank, and made game, and the lord proposed the same terms for New Year's Even. The knight craved leave to depart in the morning, for it was near the time when he ought to be gone.

The lord restrained him, bidding him linger, and said: "As I am a true man, I pledge my word, my lord, that you shall reach the Green Chapel, to do 20 your business, long before prime on New Year's Day. So keep to your chamber and take your ease, while I hunt in the forest. I will hold to the terms of our covenant and exchange my gains with you when I return. I have tested you twice, and I find you faithful. Remember, to-morrow morning, that 'The third time pays for all.' Let us make merry and think only of joy while we may, for at any time we may have sorrow."

Gawain promptly agreed to remain, and drink 30 was joyously brought ere they were lighted to their beds. Sir Gawain lay sleeping very softly and quietly through the night; the lord was early dressed, being anxious about his affairs. After mass he and his men took a morsel of food, and in the pleasant morning he called for his mount. All the nobles who were to ride in his train were ready on their

steeds at the gates of the hall. Very lovely was
the earth, for hoar-frost lay on the ground and
the sun rose red from a cloud-bank, while above in
the heavens bright clouds were drifting.

The hunters unleashed the hounds at the edge of
a wood, and the rocks of the forest rang with the
sound of their horns. Some of the hounds fell on
the scent of the fox in cover, but trailed this way
and that to make sure. When a harrier gave tongue,
10 the huntsmen called to him, and his fellows rushed
towards him from all sides, panting and running
forward on the right course in a pack. The fox
scuttled before them; but they soon found him,
and when they were in sight went fast away, crying
out on him in their clear, fierce voices. He dodged
and twisted through many a rough wood, doubled
back, and often stopped to listen under the cover
of hedges.

At last he leaped a thorn hedge by a little ditch,
20 stole out very quietly by the edge of a thicket, and
thought by the trick to get away from the hounds
and out of the wood. But then, before he knew it,
he ran upon a hunting station, where three fierce
dogs, all grey, rushed out at him together. He
swerved again quickly, and started fast in a new
direction, going away, much distressed, into the
wood. Then it was joyous sport to listen to the
hounds, when all the pack together were after him.
They set up such a clamor at the sight of him that
30 it seemed all the lofty cliffs had fallen in a heap.
Here he was hallooed, when the knights came up
with him, and was greeted with loud jeers; there
he was threatened and often called a thief; and always the greyhounds were at his tail, not letting
him slacken speed. Often he was chased as he

made for the open, and often he turned suddenly into cover again, so wily was Reynard.

He led them on like this, indeed, splashed with mud, the lord and his company, over the mountains until midday, while the gracious knight at home slept healthfully through the cold morning within his fair curtains. But the lady could not sleep for love, lest the purpose in her heart should fail. She rose early and came to him in a beautiful mantle splen-
10 didly furred with well-trimmed skins, which reached to the earth. There were no colored ornaments on her head, but only the gems that were skilfully twisted into her fret in clusters of twenty. Her lovely face and firm throat were bare, as was her breast both in front and behind. She came into the chamber and closed the door after her, swung open a window, and called to the knight with pleasant and cheerful words, rallying him thus: "Ah, man, how can you sleep when the morning is so
20 clear?"

The noble knight was sunk in gloomy sleep, but he heard her. He was muttering in the heavy oppression of a dream, for he was troubled and distressed with many thoughts of his destiny: how he was to accomplish his fate the next day at the Green Chapel, when he should meet the man there and accept a blow without resistance. But when the fair lady came, he recovered his wits, came suddenly out his dreams, and quickly answered. The
30 lovely lady approached, laughing sweetly, bent over his handsome head, and kissed him gracefully. He welcomed her with courtesy and with excellent cheer, for she appeared to him so glorious and so gaily dressed, so faultless in form and so fine in color, that joy welled up and warmed his heart. With gentle and courteous smiles they fell into merry

speech, and everything they said was altogether joyous and happy. Much delight they took in the pleasant words that were spoken. If Mary had not been mindful of her knight, there had been great peril for the two. For that noble princess pressed him so continually and was so urgent, that he had either to accept her love or refuse it discourteously. He was concerned about his honor, lest he should be a craven, and yet more about the disaster of 10 committing sin and becoming a traitor to the lord of the castle.

"God guard that may not happen!" quoth the knight. With pleasant laughter he countered all the fond speeches that came from her lips.

Said the lady to the knight: "You deserve blame if you love not the person you lie beside beyond all lovers in the world, unless you have a dearer mistress who pleases you better, and have your faith so plighted to that lady, and set so firmly, that you 20 care not to break the troth—which I nowise believe. I beg that you will now tell me the truth, and by all the loves in the world conceal it not deceitfully."

The knight said, smiling gently: "By St. John, I have no love, in faith, nor will I have one at present."

"That is the worst saying of all," quoth the lady. "But I am answered truly, grievous as it is to me. Graciously kiss me now, and I will go away. All 30 I can do on earth is to mourn, as a woman who greatly loves." Sighing, she bent down and kissed him sweetly, then rose and said as she stood by his side: "Do me this pleasure, my dear, now that I am going away. Give me some gift, your glove perhaps, that I may remember you by it and lessen my grief."

"Now surely," quoth the man, "I would I had here the dearest of my possessions to give you for your love, for you rightly deserve many times over a recompense such as I could not offer. But as to giving you for a love-token what is of such little worth as a glove of Gawain's, it is not honorable for you to have the keepsake at this time; and I am here on a mission in strange lands and have no men with saddle-bags filled with things of worth.
10 That disinclines me to love, my lady, for the present. Each man must do as he is circumstanced. Take it not ill, and do not grieve."

"Nay, gracious and highly honored sir," quoth the lovely lady, "though I have nothing of yours, yet you shall have something of mine."

She offered him a splendid ring made of red gold, set with a brilliant stone that flashed gleams like the bright sun. It was worth, be assured, a very great sum. But the knight refused it, and
20 at once.

"I will accept no gifts now, lovely lady; I have none to offer, and I will take none."

She pressed it on him very earnestly, but he refused her offers, and swore by his honor that he would not have it.

Sorrowful that he would not accept it, she said: "If you refuse my ring because it seems too precious, and you would not be so much beholden to me, I will give you my girdle, which will profit you
30 less."

Quickly she took off a belt that clasped her, bound about her kirtle under the bright mantle. It was fashioned of green silk and ornamented with gold, embroidered only at the edge and adorned with pendants. This she offered to the knight, and besought him merrily to take it, though it was unworthy. And he said that he would in no wise touch either gold or keepsake until God should send him grace to achieve the adventure he had undertaken.

"Therefore, I pray you, be not displeased, and do not insist, for I shall never consent to it. I am greatly beholden to you for your favor, and I shall be your true servant through heat and cold."

"Are you then refusing this piece of silk," asked 10 the lady, "because it is too simple a thing? So it seems, to be sure. It is small, and its value is even less. But anyone who knew the qualities woven into it would perhaps appraise it at a higher value, for a man neatly girded with this green belt could not be slain by any knight under heaven, or by any means whatsoever."

Then the knight reflected, and it came into his mind that this would be a treasure on the adventure to which he was destined, when he came to 20 the Green Chapel to receive the return blow. It would be a noble device if by means of it he could escape death. So he grew indulgent of her pleading and let her speak on; and she pressed the belt upon him and strongly urged him until he consented. She gave it to him with good will, beseeching him, for her sake, never to reveal it but to keep it loyally concealed from her lord. The knight promised that on no account should anyone ever know aught of it except the two of them. He thanked her very 30 warmly and earnestly both with heart and mind. Thereupon she kissed the valiant knight three times, and took her leave, for no more entertainment was to be got from the man.

When she had gone, Sir Gawain made his preparations for the day: rose and arrayed himself splendidly, and put away his love-token, the girdle the lady had given him, hiding it carefully where he could find it afterward. Then he went straightway to the chapel, quietly sought out a priest, and begged to be instructed and taught how his soul might be saved when he went hence. The priest had from him a clean confession and showed him his sins, both the greater and the less, then prayed for mercy and for his absolution, thereupon absolving him securely and making him as pure of sin as if doomsday were about to come on the morrow. Then the knight made more merry among the noble ladies until nightfall, with seemly carols and every sort of festivity, than he had done on any day earlier. Every man had pleasure of him there, and said: "Surely he was never so joyous since he came hither."

Leave him now in his shelter, where love befell him! The lord, meanwhile, was pursuing his sport in the field. He killed the fox that had led him so long a chase. As he leaped a thorn hedge to get sight of the rascal, following the cry of the hounds that were hot on the scent, Reynard darted through a rough grove with the pack racing at his heels. The lord caught sight of the creature, stopped warily, and whipping out his bright sword, slashed at the beast. The animal swerved and would have made his escape if a hound had not rushed at him before he could get away. Right before the horse's feet all the dogs fell on him and worried the crafty beast with savage din. The lord dismounted briskly and seized the fox, snatching him quickly out of the mouths of the hounds. He held him high over his head and gave the halloo, while the pack of furious dogs bayed at him. Huntsmen with horns came rushing towards them, blowing the assembly call till they saw the knight. When the noble company had come together, all those who had bugles blew at once, and all the others shouted. It was the merriest baying that man ever heard, the tumult which rose there for Reynard's soul. The hounds had their reward, for they were fondled and their heads were stroked. Then the men took Reynard and stripped off his coat. Thereupon they started homeward, for it was close to nightfall, sounding their mighty horns vigorously.

At length the lord dismounted at his beloved home, 10 and found a fire on the hearth with good Sir Gawain beside it. The knight was happy withal, having enjoyed himself in the friendly company of the ladies. He wore a blue mantle that swept the earth, while his softly furred surcoat became him well; and the hood of the same stuff, which hung on his shoulders, was likewise adorned with fur.

He met the good lord in the centre of the hall, and greeted him merrily, saying with courtesy: "First I will fulfil the agreement that we made as 20 to our good fortune—without sparing drink!" Then he embraced the lord and kissed him three times as coolly and soberly as he could manage.

"By Christ," quoth the other knight, "you have good luck in what you win by this trading, if, that is, you made a good bargain."

"No matter about the price," quoth the other at once. "What I have won I have paid you openly."

"Mary!" quoth the other man. "My winnings are less than yours, for I have hunted all day and have 30 got naught except this foul fox hide. The Devil take it! That is very poor payment for three such treasures as you have pressed heartily upon me here —three such good kisses!"

"Say no more!" quoth Sir Gawain. "I thank you, by the Rood."

As they stood together, the lord told him how the

fox was killed. With mirth and minstrelsy, with good food at their pleasure, they made as merry as men could, with laughter of the ladies and jesting speech, both Gawain and the good lord, so happy were they. As if the company had lost their senses or been drunk, both the lord and his household joked and made merry until the time came when they must separate, for at last they had to go to their beds.

10 Then the noble knight, taking leave of the lord first of all, thanked him courteously. "May the High King reward you for the wonderful sojourn I have had here and for the honor you have done me! If you will please to accept it, I offer myself as your servant. I must needs depart to-morrow, as you know, if you will give me some man according to your promise to show me the road to the Green Chapel, since God wills that I meet my fate there on New Year's Day."

20 "In good faith," quoth the lord, "everything I have ever promised you I will perform with good will."

Thereupon he assigned him a servant to put him on his way and conduct him over the downs, so that he might get through the forest without trouble, and journey by the most direct path. Gawain thanked the lord for the honor he did him, then took his leave of the proud ladies. Sorrowfully he kissed them and made his parting speeches, begging them 30 to accept his hearty thanks. To this they replied in kind, commending him to Christ with grievous sighs. Then he bade farewell ceremoniously to the members of the household, thanking each man in turn for his services and his kindness and the great trouble they had been put to in attendance upon him. And every man was as sorry to part with him as if he had dwelt with him always and been honored by him.

Afterward with attendants and lights he was conducted happily to his chamber and his bed to rest. That he slept soundly I dare not say, for he had much on his mind to reflect upon with reference to the morrow, if he would. Let him lie there. He is close to what he has sought. If you will be patient for a little, I will tell you what happened.

IV

10 Now came the New Year with the passing of night, and day dispersed the darkness, as the Lord willed. But wild weather had risen in the world outside; bitterly the clouds flung their chill on the earth, with enough of the north wind to be a torment to the thinly clad. The snow came shivering down, biting what it touched and nipping the creatures of the wild, while the shrill wind rushed from the heights and filled the valleys with great drifts.

Lying in his bed, the knight listened. Though he 20 shut his eyes, he slept little, but heard the voice of each cock that crew. Ere daybreak he sprang up, for a lighted lamp burned in his chamber. He called for his chamberlain, who answered him promptly, and bade the man fetch him his corslet and saddle his horse. The other quickly brought his weeds and arrayed Sir Gawain carefully. First he put on his clothing to ward off the cold, then his other harness, which had been faithfully kept: the body armor and steel plates polished clean, and 30 the rings of his splendid corslet rolled to free them from rust. All was as fresh as when new; and the knight was fain to give thanks for the care with which each piece had been treated. From here to

Greece no knight was so resplendent when he
bade them bring his steed.
Meanwhile he put on the fairest trappings: his
coat-armor with its cognizance of bright embroid-
ery worked upon velvet, set and adorned with precious gems, the seams of the coat stitched and the
inside lined with beautiful fur. Nor, for his own
good, did Gawain forget the girdle, the lady's gift.
When he had belted his sword on his sturdy hips,
10 he wound the love-token twice about himself, wrap-
ping the girdle of green silk quickly around his
waist. It became the fair knight well, for it showed
richly against the fine red cloth. But the man did
not put on the belt for display, for pride of the
pendants, though they were polished, and though
glittering gold shone on the ends of them, but to
save himself when he came to the test and had to
meet death without being able to defend himself
by sword or dagger. Thus prepared, the brave man
20 walked forth from his chamber, thanking all his
noble attendants heartily and often.
Gringolet, who had been stabled with care and
skill, was ready and eager to be off. The knight
went to the proud horse, huge and tall, and examined his coat, then said soberly, swearing it on
his honor: "The household in this castle take thought
for courtesy. May joy be with the man who keeps
them, and love betide the dear lady while she lives!
As they have entertained a guest for charity's sake
30 and paid him honor, may the Lord Who rules High
Heaven reward them—and also all of you. If I
could continue to have life in the world for any time,
I should do whatever I could to recompense you."
Then he put his foot into the stirrup and mounted.
His attendant passed him his shield, which he
slung on his shoulder; and Gringolet, at a touch of

the gilt spurs, no longer stood prancing but leaped forward on the pavement. Bearing his spear and lance, the knight on his steed commended the castle to Christ and asked good fortune for it. The drawbridge was let down, and both sides of the wide gates were unbarred and flung open. When he had made the sign of the cross, the knight rode out over the planks of the bridge, thanking the porter, who knelt and bade him good-bye, commending him to
10 Christ for safety.

Thus the prince went on his way accompanied only by the man who was to guide him to the dismal place where he must receive the grievous blow. They passed along the hillslopes beneath the bare boughs of the trees; they mounted by cliffs in the penetrating cold. The clouds hung high, but the weather beneath them was threatening. On the moors there were damp mists, and on the mountains fell drizzling rain. Each hill was capped with a huge
20 cloak of fog. The brooks boiled and foamed against their banks, dashing and breaking as they plunged downward. Very perplexing was the way the men followed through the forest until sunrise, which found them on a high hill with an expanse of white snow before them. The attendant bade his master halt.

"I have brought you hither, sir knight, and now you are not far from the famous place for which you have inquired and sought with so much zeal.
30 Since I know you and you are a lord whom I love well, I will tell you truly that you would do better to follow my advice. The place you are hastening to is thought extremely perilous. The worst man in the world dwells in that wild spot. He is strong and grim and loves to give a blow, he is taller than any other man in the world—more huge of body

than any four in Arthur's house, Hector, or any other. He so manages at the Green Chapel that no man, however proud, can ride by the place without being slain by a blow from his hand, for he is ruthless and has no mercy. Be he churl or chaplain who passes by, monk or priest, or any other man, he likes as well to kill him as to live himself. As truly as you are sitting in your saddle, I tell you, you shall be killed when you come there if he can accomplish 10 it, though you had twenty lives to spend. Trust what I say. He has lived here long and done much harm by his fighting. Against his terrible blows you cannot defend yourself. Therefore, good Sir Gawain, let the man alone, and for God's sake go away by some other road and seek some other land. May Christ speed you! I will hasten home again, and I promise you further—and I will swear it by God and all his good saints, so help me God and the holy relics and plenty of other oaths!— 20 that I will keep your counsel loyally and never set going any tale about how you fled from any man, as far as I know."

"Many thanks," quoth Gawain, and he spoke reprovingly. "May good befall you, my man, for wishing me well, and I believe you would loyally keep my counsel. But if you kept it ever so secret, and I fled away for fear while passing here as you suggest, I should be a coward knight and not to be excused. Whatever may befall, I will go to the 30 Chapel and hold with the man the conversation that I please, be it for weal or woe as fate may decree. Although he be a grim fellow to deal with, and stand there with a club, the Lord may full well save his servants."

"Mary!" quoth the other man. "Since you say at such length that you will take your own hurt on

yourself, and if you wish to lose your life, I will not hinder or hold you back. Put your helmet on your head and take your spear in your hand, and ride down this same path by the side of yonder cliff until you come to the bottom of the wild valley. Then look a little across the glade on the left side, and you shall see the Chapel itself in the valley and the sturdy man who keeps it. Now farewell, noble Gawain, with God's blessing! I would not go with
10 you for all the gold on earth, nor bear you fellowship through this wood a foot further."

With that, the man turned his horse in the forest, hit him with his heels as hard as ever he could, and galloped away, leaving the knight there by himself.

"By God Himself," quoth Gawain, "I will neither cry out nor lament. I bow myself to God's will and commit myself to Him."

Then he spurred Gringolet and followed down
20 the path, making his way by a bank on the edge of the wood and riding forward along the rough slope straight into the dale. There he paused to look about, for the place seemed deserted; and he saw no sign of habitation, but only steep and high banks on both sides and rough crags knobbed with jutting rocks. The clouds seemed to him to graze the crags. Reining in his horse, he halted and looked this way and that, in search of the Chapel. He saw nothing of the kind on any side, which seemed to
30 him strange; but soon he descried, a little way down a glade, something like a mound, a broad hillock on the bank of a stream, near a waterfall that tumbled down there. The brook bubbled as if it were boiling.

The knight urged on his steed and came to the mound, where he dismounted and tied the rein of his horse to a rough branch. Then he went to the

mound and walked about it, debating within himself
what it might be. It had a hole in one end and
holes on each side, and was overgrown everywhere
with patches of grass. Inside, it was hollow—nothing but an old cave or a crevice in a crag, he could
not determine which.

"Lord!" quoth the gentle knight. "Whether or
not this be the Green Chapel, the Devil might well
say his matins here at midnight! Surely this is a
10 desolate place, an ugly oratory overgrown with
weeds. It well befits the man in green to make his
devotions here after the devil's use. Now I feel sure
by all my five senses that it is the Fiend who has
trapped me into this covenant in order to destroy
me. This is a chapel of misfortune, ill luck take it!
It is the cursedest church that ever I came to."

With his tall helmet on his head and with lance
in hand, he went up to the rough rocks of the place.
Then he heard from a crag on the slope of a high
20 hill beyond the brook a marvellously loud noise. Lo!
it clattered as if it would split the cliff apart, like
someone sharpening a scythe on a grindstone. Lo!
it whirred and made a grinding noise, like water at
a mill. Lo! it rang and rushed at the same time—
something terrible to hear.

"By God," quoth Gawain, "that contrivance, I
think, is being made ready for our meeting, sir
knight, according to our agreement. Let God bring
weal or woe, it helps me in no wise to be afraid.
30 Though I lose my life, no noise shall frighten me."

Then the knight called out very loud: "Who has
a mind to hold tryst with me in this place? Good
Gawain is walking here. If any man wishes aught
of him, let him hasten hither to do his business,
either now or never."

"Stay," quoth someone on the bank above his

head, "and you shall quickly receive all that I once promised."

Yet he went on with the rushing noise for a short time, and changed to the sound of whetting before he would come down. At length he made his way along a crag and came out of one of the holes, brandishing as he emerged a terrible weapon—a newly sharpened Danish axe—wherewith to give the blow. It had a heavy bit, four feet wide, curved back in 10 line with the helve and sharpened with a whetstone. It was no smaller than the one used before, if measured by the gleaming thong; and the man in green was arrayed in the same way, both face and legs, hair and beard, except that he advanced on foot, setting the handle of the axe on the stones and marching beside it. When he came to the stream, he would not wade across, but vaulted over by the help of his axe, and came forward rapidly over the snow-covered ground in a fury. Gawain met the 20 knight, but did not bow to him.

The green man said: "Now, sweet sir, one may trust you to keep an agreement. God must guard you, Gawain! You are truly welcome to my place, and you have timed your journey as a loyal man should. You know the covenant between us. A twelvemonth ago you took what came to you, and at this New Year I was to be promptly repaid. We are here in this valley altogether by ourselves. There are no men at hand to separate us, no matter what 30 we do. Take off your helmet and receive your payment, nor make more resistance than I offered when you struck off my head at one blow."

"Nay," quoth Gawain, "by God Who gave me life, I shall in no way bear ill will for any hurt that comes. If you confine yourself to one blow, I shall stand still and make no resistance to your doing what you please."

He bent forward, bowing, and showed the flesh of his neck all bare, pretending not to be afraid. He would not flinch for terror. Then the man in green made ready quickly, lifting up his grim weapon to smite Gawain. With all the strength in his body he raised it aloft, making a mighty feint of destroying him. Had it fallen as powerfully as he pre-
10 tended to make it, the ever valiant knight would have been slain by the blow. But Gawain glanced sidelong at the axe as it came rushing down through the air to destroy him, and flinched a little from the sharp steel with his shoulders. The other man, with a sudden jerk, pulled back the bright blade, and reproved the prince with many scornful words.

Quoth he: "You are not Gawain, who is held so good a knight and never quailed at any force on hill or in valley, for now you flinch with terror before
20 you feel any hurt. I have never heard such cowardice reported of that knight. I did not flinch or draw back, man, when you took aim, nor did I raise any difficulty in King Arthur's house. My head dropped to my feet, and yet I never flinched. Yet you, before you have received any harm, are terrified in heart. Wherefore I am to be reckoned the better man."

Quoth Gawain: "I flinched once, but I will do so no more. Only I cannot restore my head if it falls
30 to the ground. But make haste, man, in faith, and come to the point with me. Give me my destiny, and do it out of hand, for I shall wait your stroke and not move again till your axe has hit me. You have my pledge."

"Have at you, then!" quoth the other, and raised the axe aloft, looking as furious as if he were mad.

He feinted at his man mightily, but did not cleave him, withholding his hand just before the stroke fell. Gawain waited it steadfastly and did not flinch at all, but stood like a stone, or like a stump which is fastened in rocky ground by a hundred roots.

Then the man in green said playfully: "Since your heart is so steadfast, it behooves me to strike. Hold fast to the noble knighthood that Arthur gave you, and keep your neck at this blow if you can
10 manage it."

Fiercely angry, Gawain replied: "Smite on, you cruel man! You threaten too long. I believe that your own heart is terrified."

"Truly," quoth the other man, "you speak so fiercely that I will no longer delay your business."

Then he took his stance to give the blow, with a frown on lip and forehead. No wonder that Gawain, hoping for no rescue, was troubled. The green man raised his weapon lightly and let the cutting
20 edge of the blade drop squarely on the bare neck. Though the stroke was fierce, it did no more hurt than to give him a scratch, for the blade merely cut through the skin and the outer layer of flesh. And when he saw the bright blood spurting over his shoulders and gleaming on the snow, he sprang forward more than a spear-length in a sudden leap, clutched his helmet quickly and placed it on his head, slipped his shield into place on his shoulder, pulled out his bright sword, and fiercely spoke. Never in the world
30 since he had been born of his mother had he been half so happy a man.

"Cease, man, to strike! Threaten me no more! I have taken one blow here without resistance, and if you give me another, I shall promptly return it, requiting you without hesitation—fiercely, too, you may be sure. One stroke only I owe you, as the covenant made in Arthur's hall provided. Stop, then, good sir!" The knight moved away and rested on his axe, setting the helve on the ground and leaning on the blade. He looked at the prince, who was ready for battle, saw how boldly he stood there armed, doughty, fearless, and completely without dread. In his heart he was pleased. Then in a loud, ringing tone he said playfully to 10 the knight: "Bold man, be not so fierce. No one here has ill-used you or treated you discourteously, except as the covenant of the king's court provided. I promised you a stroke, and you have it. Consider yourself well requited. I release you from the remainder of all other rights. If I had not been skilful, I might perhaps have given you a worse blow and done you harm. In the first place I threatened you merely and did not cleave you with a sore wound (which I might have given you rightfully) because 20 of the agreement we made on our first night together, and because you kept faith with me loyally and justly, passing on to me all your gains as a good man should. The second threat I offered you, man, because of the morning when you kissed my beautiful wife—the kisses came back to me! For both of them I gave you mere feints without doing you harm. An honest man gives back honestly, and need fear no danger. The third time you failed, and for that you should accept the tap I gave you.

30 "The woven girdle you wear is mine. My own wife gave it to you, as I know well. I know well, too, your kisses, and all your behavior, and my wife's wooing of you. I arranged it myself. I sent her to test you, and methinks you are truly one of the most flawless men who ever stepped on foot. As a pearl is of more value than a white pea, so is Gawain,

in truth, when compared with other fair knights. Here you failed a little, sir, and were wanting in loyalty! but that was on account of no intrigue, or love-making either, but because you loved your life. I blame you the less."

The other brave man stood in meditation for a great while, so grieved and mortified that his heart cried out in anguish within him. All the blood of his breast streamed into his face, and he winced for 10 shame while the knight spoke.

The first words he uttered were these: "Cursed be cowardice and covetousness both! Lack of chivalry and the vice that destroys knightly virtue are in them." Then he took hold of the knot of the belt, loosened the fastening, and thrust it violently at the man. "Lo! there is the faith-breaker! Evil befall it! For fear of your blow, cowardice taught me to make a pact with covetousness, forsaking my proper nature—the generosity and loyalty which be-20 fit knights. Now am I guilty and disloyal, I who have ever been afraid of nothing save treachery and lack of truth. Sorrow and care come to both!. I acknowledge to you, sir knight, here between us two, that my behavior has been altogether faulty. If you will restore me to your good will, I will be more wary hereafter."

Then the other lord laughed and said courteously: "I consider the wrong I received completely amended. You have made a clean confession, ac-30 knowledging your mistakes, and have done your penance at the point of my sword. I regard you as cleansed of your offence, as well purified as if you had never done wrong since you were first born. I give you the gold-bordered belt, sir, for it is green like my robe. You may recall this contest, Sir Gawain, as you journey among famous princes; and for chivalrous knights this girdle will serve as a token of the adventure of the Green Chapel. You must come again to my house this New Year. We shall revel very pleasantly during the remainder of the noble festival." The lord urged him to come, saying: "I think we can make your peace with my wife, who was your bitter foe!"

"Nay, forsooth," quoth the knight, seizing his helmet and courteously removing it, while he thanked 10 the nobleman. "I have stayed long enough. Happiness be yours! May He Who is the author of all honor reward you! Commend me to that gracious lady, your lovely wife, both to her and to the other, my honored ladies, who have so adroitly beguiled their knight by their trick. It is no wonder though a fool behave with folly and be brought to grief by the wiles of women, for so was Adam deceived by one during his life and Solomon by many, and Samson in turn was brought to his doom by Delilah, 20 and David afterwards was deluded by Bathsheba and suffered much sorrow. Now these men were brought to disaster by the wiles of women. It were altogether best, if a man could, to love them well and believe them not. For these men were the noblest of old, and all of them followed wisdom beyond all other men under heaven who have given themselves to thought; yet were they all deceived by the women they knew. Though I have been deluded, it seems to me I may be excused.

30 "But your girdle! God give you thanks! I will keep it with good will, not for the beautiful gold, or the barrings, or the silk, or the long pendants, for neither the richness nor the honor nor the lovely ornament; but in token of my wrong-doing I shall look at it often when I ride forth in splendor, thus recalling to my mind the frailty and faultiness of

the perverse flesh, how liable it is to the stain of impurity. Thus, when pride shall stir me on account of prowess in arms, looking on this love-token will humble my heart. But one thing I would pray you, if you will not be displeased by my asking. Since you are lord of yonder region where I have been honorably entertained by you—may the Lord, Who upholds heaven and sits on high, reward you for it!—what is your right name? I ask no more."

10 "I will tell you truly," quoth the other then. "I am called Bercilak de Hautdesert in this land. Morgan la Fay, who dwells in my house, has acquired many of the arts of Merlin through the power and skill of her learning, and has learned his magic well, for she has had pleasant passages of love of old with that excellent clerk, who knows all your knights at home. Therefore she is called Morgan the Goddess. No one has such lofty pride that she cannot tame him. She sent me in this guise to your delight-

20 ful hall, in order to test the pride and the truth of the great renown of the Round Table. She arranged this marvel to take away your wits; to grieve Guenevere and cause her to die with terror of that man—the phantom who spoke with his head in his hand before the high table. She is the ancient dame at home, and she is your aunt, too, Arthur's half-sister, the daughter of the Duchess of Tintagel, by whom noble Uther afterward had the now glorious Arthur. Therefore I beg you, sir knight, to

30 come to your aunt and make merry in my house. The people in my court love you, and for your great fidelity I love you as well as any man under God, by my honor."

But Gawain refused him. He would in no wise do it. They embraced, and kissed, and commended each other to the Prince of Paradise, and parted

straightway with regret. Gawain on his fair steed rode boldly towards the castle of the king, and the knight all in green whithersoever he would. Now Gawain, having won the grace of his life, rode Gringolet by wild ways through the world. Often he lodged indoors and often outside, had many adventures by the way, and gained so many victories that I do not intend to recount them now. The hurt he had received in his neck was made whole; and he
10 wore the gleaming belt bound slantwise like a baldric by his side and tied with a knot under his left arm, in token of the spot of wrong-doing by which he had been overcome. Thus in sound health the knight reached the court. Joy awoke in the house when the great king heard that Gawain had come. He was glad and kissed the knight, as did the queen also, and afterward many brave knights came to embrace him and ask him about his fortune. He told the marvels of it, re-
20 counting all the hardships he had experienced, the adventure of the Chapel, the behavior of the knight, the lady's love-making, and at last the story of the girdle. Although he suffered agony when he had to tell of it, and groaned with sorrow and mortification, he bared his neck to show the little cut he had received at the lord's hands as a rebuke for his disloyalty. His face flushed with shame as he showed the mark.

"Lo, my lord," quoth the knight, and touched
30 the girdle, "this is the symbol of the fault for which my neck is scarred, of the hurt and damage I have received, of the cowardice and covetousness with which I was there overcome. This is the token of the disloyalty in which I was caught. I must needs wear it while I live, for none may conceal his wrong-

doing without harm coming of it, since where wrong-doing has fastened itself it will never depart."
The king comforted the knight, and all the court laughed loud at the tale. Then the lords and ladies of the Table courteously agreed that each man of the brotherhood should wear a band of bright green slantwise about him like a baldric, and this on account of that knight and in imitation of him. The Round Table gave the baldric renown, and ever
10 after he who wore it was honored, as is told in the best books of romance. Thus in Arthur's day this adventure took place, and the Bruts bear witness to it. Since the bold warrior Brutus first came hither, after the siege and assault of Troy had come to an end, many such adventures have occurred. Now He Who wore the crown of thorns bring us to joy with Him! Amen.

HONI SOYT QUI MAL PENCE

GEOFFREY CHAUCER

"CHAUCER," says Professor Manly, "is securely placed as one of the three greatest poets who have ever written in English." This challenging statement is far less likely to be attacked than it would have been a generation ago, since appreciation of his genius has steadily increased as his poems have been more carefully studied. He is seen to be not merely the genial and humorous observer of the surfaces of human life, but a poet with a wide-ranging and powerful imagination, acute of mind and very wise, whose mastery of every detail of his art was so perfect that careless readers have sometimes failed to recognize it as art at all.

Born about 1340, he was very fortunately placed in the social scale. His father was a vintner in London, presumably wealthy and certainly prominent, whose relations with the court of Edward III enabled him to give Geoffrey every advantage by way of education and experience that a young nobleman could have enjoyed. At the same time, since the Chaucers belonged to the merchant class, he would have had opportunities of knowing men and women of every degree. While still in his 'teens, he was attached to the train of a royal duchess and saw service with the king's army in France. His life thereafter was that of a successful courtier and public servant. He was sent on missions to France and Italy, had a long tenure of an important office in the customs, had charge of numerous royal estates and buildings, sat in parliament as a knight of the shire from Kent, and served as justice of the peace in the same county, where he must have held land. His wife, like himself, was connected with the court, being a lady-in-waiting to the queen at the time he married her. Until the middle of 1391 he was almost constantly in one service or another—so actively, indeed, that one wonders how he found time to write so much verse and prose as he left behind him at his death on October 25, 1400, even though two important works were still incomplete. His interment in Westminster Abbey was a happy chance. Ten months before, he had taken a long lease of a house close by, and was thus entitled to burial within the Abbey like any other distinguished citizen of the neighborhood.

Chaucer's successful career as a man of affairs was important, in a number of ways, with reference to his infinitely greater career as a poet. It brought him into contact with men and women of every kind, gave him the opportunity of knowing intimately many parts of England as well as London, and by good fortune took him to Italy at a time when Dante's fame was still fresh and Boccaccio and Petrarch still lived. His imagination was fed by his experience of men as well as books; it was fired and directed, unquestionably, by reading the great Italian poets. Though no man's disciple, he absorbed everything his French and Italian predecessors had to give him, and in mature middle age produced his masterpieces, which are still unrivalled in their kind.

Probably he did his early experimenting in French, since French was the language of the court and of polite literature when he grew up. His first work that can be dated was an allegorical elegy, *The Book of the Duchess*, which must have followed soon after the death of John of Gaunt's wife in 1369. Before this time he had probably worked at a translation of *The Romance of the Rose,* of which we possess a fragment only. Of his other more ambitious poems, only one, *The House of Fame,* was written before his fortieth year. *The Parliament of Birds* was composed in 1381 or 1382; and *Troilus and Criseyde,* representing the work of three or four years, must have been completed in 1385 or 1386. At about that time he began *The Legend of Good Women,* which he never finished; and not later than 1387 he embarked on his most ambitious project of all, *The Canterbury Tales.* That he did not live to write the sixty-odd tales he planned is a misfortune, but it does not keep us from admiring the general dramatic scheme as well as the completed sections. He went far enough with his plan to make what we have one of the great stories of all time.

Apart from the brilliant *Prologue,* which pictures a representative group of mediæval men and women, the collection includes specimens of every type of story current in the Middle Ages. Of those printed below, *The Nun's Priest's Tale* is perhaps the best fable ever written; *The Pardoner's Tale* is really a mock sermon delivered by a slightly tipsy seller of relics and pardons, but it contains a superbly told narrative which in bare outline is one of the exempla wherewith preachers pointed their homilies; *The Second Nun's Tale* is a saint's legend, retold by Chaucer with exquisite art; and *The Franklin's Tale* is a lay, or short romance. Each deserves study as a specimen of what a many-sided genius can do with short stories in verse. It must be remembered that in *Troilus and Criseyde* Chaucer had already brought to completion a long narrative poem with a tragic theme and a serious purpose, though it has plenty of humor also. The range of his art in story-telling was limited to no one form, to no one mood, to no one length. His interest in human nature was inexhaustible, and equal to it was his resourcefulness as a poet.

THE CANTERBURY TALES

THE PROLOGUE

WHAN that Aprille with his shoures sote
The droghte of Marche hath perced to the rote,

Sote, sweet.

And bathed every veyne in swich licour,
Of which vertu engendred is the flour;
Whan Zephirus eek with his swete breeth
Inspired hath in every holt and heeth
The tendre croppes, and the yonge sonne
Hath in the Ram his halfe cours y-ronne,
And smale fowles maken melodye,
That slepen al the night with open yë,
(So priketh hem nature in hir corages):
10 That longen folk to goon on pilgrimages
(And palmers for to seken straunge strondes)
To ferne halwes, couthe in sondry londes;
And specially, from every shires ende
Of Engelond, to Caunterbury they wende,
The holy blisful martir for to seke,
That hem hath holpen, whan that they were seke.
  Bifel that, in that seson on a day,
In Southwerk at the Tabard as I lay
Redy to wenden on my pilgrimage
20 To Caunterbury with ful devout corage,
At night was come in-to that hostelrye
Wel nyne and twenty in a companye,
Of sondry folk, by aventure y-falle
In felawshipe, and pilgrims were they alle,
That toward Caunterbury wolden ryde;
The chambres and the stables weren wyde,

Swich licour, such moisture. *Holt*, wood.
Inspired hath, has quickened. *Croppes*, shoots.
Ram, Aries, *i.e.*, April 11 is past.
So priketh, etc., So nature awakens their desires.
Hem is Chaucer's form for *them*.
Palmers, perpetual pilgrims.
Ferne halwes, distant shrines.
Blisful martir, Thomas Becket, Archbishop of Canterbury, assassinated in 1170. His tomb became a shrine almost at once.
Tabard, a coat ornamented with armorial bearings, but in Chaucer's day the name for a smock. Here used as the sign for the inn.
Corage, heart.

And wel we weren esed atte beste.
And shortly, whan the sonne was to reste,
So hadde I spoken with hem everichon,
That I was of hir felawshipe anon,
And made forward erly for to ryse,
To take our wey, ther as I yow devyse.
But natheles, whyl I have tyme and space,
Er that I ferther in this tale pace,
Me thinketh it acordaunt to resoun,
10 To telle yow al the condicioun
Of ech of hem, so as it semed me,
And whiche they weren, and of what degree;
And eek in what array that they were inne:
And at a knight than wol I first biginne.
A KNIGHT ther was, and that a worthy man,
That fro the tyme that he first bigan
To ryden out, he loved chivalrye,
Trouthe and honour, fredom and curteisye.
Ful worthy was he in his lordes werre,
20 And therto hadde he riden (no man ferre)
As wel in Cristendom as hethenesse,
And ever honoured for his worthinesse.
At Alisaundre he was, whan it was wonne;
Ful ofte tyme he hadde the bord bigonne
Aboven alle naciouns in Pruce.
In Lettow hadde he reysed and in Ruce,
No Cristen man so ofte of his degree.
In Gernade at the sege eek hadde he be
Of Algezir, and riden in Belmarye.
30 At Lyeys was he, and at Satalye,

Forward, agreement. Worthy, of good repute.
Devyse, tell. Ryden out, serve as soldier.
Condicioun, circumstances. Fredom, liberality.
Alisaundre, etc., places at the eastern end of the Mediterranean,
fighting Turks, at the western, fighting Moors, and on the Baltic.
The bord bigonne, sat at the head of the table.
Reysed, made war.

Whan they were wonne; and in the Grete See
At many a noble armee hadde he be.
At mortal batailles hadde he been fiftene,
And foughten for our feith at Tramissene
In listes thryes, and ay slayn his fo.
This ilke worthy knight had been also
Somtyme with the lord of Palatye,
Ageyn another hethen in Turkye:
And evermore he hadde a sovereyn prys.
10 And though that he were worthy, he was wys,
And of his port as meke as is a mayde.
He never yet no vileinye ne sayde
In al his lyf, un-to no maner wight.
He was a verray parfit gentil knight.
But for to tellen yow of his array,
His hors were gode, but he was nat gay.
Of fustian he wered a gipoun
Al bismotered with his habergeoun;
For he was late y-come from his viage,
20 And wente for to doon his pilgrimage.
   With him ther was his sone, a yong SQUYER,
A lovyere, and a lusty bacheler,
With lokkes crulle, as they were leyd in presse.
Of twenty yeer of age he was, I gesse.
Of his stature he was of evene lengthe,
And wonderly deliver, and greet of strengthe.
And he had been somtyme in chivachye,
In Flaundres, in Artoys, and Picardye,
And born him wel, as of so litel space,
30 In hope to stonden in his lady grace.
Embrouded was he, as it were a mede
Al ful of fresshe floures, whyte and rede.

Armee, military expedition.   *Vileinye,* rudeness.
Hors, horses.   *Gipoun,* doublet of coarse cloth.
Crulle, curly. *Deliver,* agile. *Bismotered,* soiled by his hauberk.
Evene lengthe, moderate height.   *Chivachye,* military raid.
Embrouded, embroidered.

Singinge he was, or floytinge, al the day;
He was as fresh as is the month of May.
Short was his goune, with sleves longe and wyde.
Wel coude he sitte on hors, and faire ryde.
He coude songes make and wel endyte,
Juste and eek daunce, and wel purtreye and wryte.
So hote he lovede, that by nightertale
He sleep namore than dooth a nightingale.
Curteys he was, lowly, and servisable,
10 And carf biforn his fader at the table.
  A YEMAN hadde he, and servaunts namo
At that tyme, for him liste ryde so;
And he was clad in cote and hood of grene;
A sheef of pecok-arwes brighte and kene
Under his belt he bar ful thriftily;
(Wel coude he dresse his takel yemanly:
His arwes drouped noght with fetheres lowe),
And in his hand he bar a mighty bowe.
A not-heed hadde he, with a broun visage.
20 Of wode-craft wel coude he al the usage.
Upon his arm he bar a gay bracer,
And by his syde a swerd and a bokeler,
And on that other syde a gay daggere,
Harneised wel, and sharp as point of spere;
A Cristofre on his brest of silver shene.
An horn he bar, the bawdrik was of grene;
A forster was he, soothly, as I gesse.
  Ther was also a Nonne, a PRIORESSE,
That of hir smyling was ful simple and coy:
30 Hir gretteste ooth was but by sëynt Loy;

Floytinge, fluting.   *Songes make,* compose tunes.
Endyte, compose words for songs. *Purtreye,* draw.
Carf, carving being a gentleman's accomplishment.
Thriftily, carefully.   *Not-heed,* closely cropped.
Bracer, guard in archery.
Christofre, St. Christopher being patron of foresters.
Bawdrik, baldric.   *Coy,* quiet.   *Sëynt Loy,* Eligius.

And she was cleped madame Eglentyne.
Ful wel she song the service divyne,
Entuned in hir nose ful semely;
And Frensh she spak ful faire and fetisly,
After the scole of Stratford atte Bowe,
For Frensh of Paris was to hir unknowe.
At mete wel y-taught was she with-alle;
She leet no morsel from hir lippes falle,
Ne wette hir fingres in hir sauce depe.
10 Wel coude she carie a morsel, and wel kepe,
That no drope ne fille up-on hir brest.
In curteisye was set ful muche hir lest.
Hir over lippe wyped she so clene,
That in hir coppe was no ferthing sene
Of grece, whan she dronken hadde hir draughte.
Ful semely after hir mete she raughte,
And sikerly she was of greet disport,
And ful plesaunt, and amiable of port,
And peyned hir to countrefete chere
20 Of court, and been estatlich of manere,
And to ben holden digne of reverence.
But, for to speken of hir conscience,
She was so charitable and so pitous,
She wolde wepe, if that she sawe a mous
Caught in a trappe, if it were deed or bledde.
Of smale houndes had she, that she fedde
With rosted flesh, or milk and wastel-breed,
But sore weep she if oon of hem were deed,
Or if men smoot it with a yerde smerte:
30 And al was conscience and tendre herte.
Ful semely hir wimpel pinched was;
Hir nose tretys; hir eyen greye as glas;

Fetisly, gracefully.   *Scole of Stratford, i.e.,* London French.
Lest, desire, delight.   *Ferthing,* trace.   *Raughte,* reached.
Digne, worthy.   *Wastel-breed,* fine white bread.
Wimpel pinched, headdress pleated.
Tretys, well formed.   *Greye,* probably blue.

Hir mouth ful smal, and ther-to softe and reed;
But sikerly she hadde a fair forheed;
It was almost a spanne brood, I trowe;
For, hardily, she was nat undergrowe.
Ful fetis was hir cloke, as I was war.
Of smal coral aboute hir arm she bar
A peire of bedes, gauded al with grene;
And ther-on heng a broche of gold ful shene,
On which ther was first write a crowned A,
10 And after, *Amor vincit omnia.*
Another NONNE with hir hadde she,
That was hir chapeleyne, and PREESTES THREE.
A MONK ther was, a fair for the maistrye,
An out-rydere, that lovede venerye;
A manly man, to been an abbot able.
Ful many a deyntee hors hadde he in stable:
And, whan he rood, men mighte his brydel here
Ginglen in a whistling wind as clere,
And eek as loude as dooth the chapel-belle
20 Ther as this lord was keper of the celle.
The reule of seint Maure or of seint Beneit,
By-cause that it was old and som-del streit,
This ilke monk leet olde thinges pace,
And held after the newe world the space.
He yaf nat of that text a pulled hen,
That seith, that hunters been nat holy men;
Ne that a monk, whan he is cloisterlees,
Is lykned til a fish that is waterlees;
This is to seyn, a monk out of his cloistre.
30 But thilke text held he nat worth an oistre;

Undergrowe, small.   *Peire of bedes,* rosary.
Chapeleyne, nun acting as assistant.
Out-rydere, appointed to care of monastery's estates.
Venerye, hunting.
Keper of the celle, head of branch of a monastery.
Streit, strict.   *The space,* meanwhile.   *Pulled,* plucked.

And I seyde, his opinioun was good.
What sholde he studie, and make himselven wood,
Upon a book in cloistre alwey to poure,
Or swinken with his handes, and laboure,
As Austin bit? How shal the world be served?
Lat Austin have his swink to him reserved.
Therefore he was a pricasour aright;
Grehoundes he hadde, as swifte as fowel in flight;
Of priking and of hunting for the hare
10 Was al his lust, for no cost wolde he spare.
I seigh his sleves purfiled at the hond
With grys, and that the fyneste of a lond;
And, for to festne his hood under his chin,
He hadde of gold y-wroght a curious pin:
A love-knotte in the gretter ende ther was.
His heed was balled, that shoon as any glas,
And eek his face, as he had been anoint.
He was a lord ful fat and in good point;
His eyen stepe, and rollinge in his heed,
20 That stemed as a forneys of a leed;
His botes souple, his hors in greet estat.
Now certeinly he was a fair prelat;
He was nat pale as a for-pyned goost.
A fat swan loved the best of any roost.
His palfrey was as broun as is a berye.
    A FRERE ther was, a wantown and a merye,
A limitour, a ful solempne man.
In alle the ordres foure is noon that can
So muche of daliaunce and fair langage.
30 He hadde maad ful many a mariage

What sholde, Why should.   *Wood,* mad.
Swinken, work.   *Pricasour,* hard rider.
Purfiled, edged with fur.   *Grys,* costly gray fur.
In good point, see *embonpoint.*   *Stepe,* prominent.
Forneys of a leed, fire under a cauldron. *For-pyned,* tormented.
Limitour, having right to a district for his own begging.
Ordres four, Dominicans, Franciscans, Carmelites, Austins.

Of yonge wommen, at his owne cost.
Un-to his ordre he was a noble post.
Ful wel biloved and famulier was he
With frankeleyns over-al in his contree,
And eek with worthy wommen of the toun:
For he had power of confessioun,
As seyde him-self, more than a curat,
For of his ordre he was licentiat.
Ful swetely herde he confessioun,
10 And plesaunt was his absolucioun;
He was an esy man to yeve penaunce
Ther as he wiste to han a good pitaunce;
For unto a povre ordre for to yive
Is signe that a man is wel y-shrive.
For if he yaf, he dorste make avaunt,
He wiste that a man was repentaunt.
For many a man so hard is of his herte,
He may nat wepe al-thogh him sore smerte.
Therefore, in stede of weping and preyeres,
20 Men moot yeve silver to the povre freres.
His tipet was ay farsed ful of knyves
And pinnes, for to yeven faire wyves.
And certeinly he hadde a mery note;
Wel coude he singe and pleyen on a rote.
Of yeddinges he bar utterly the prys.
His nekke whyt was as the flour-de-lys;
Ther-to he strong was as a champioun.
He knew the tavernes wel in every toun,
And everich hostiler and tappestere
30 Bet than a lazar or a beggestere;
For un-to swich a worthy man as he
Acorded nat, as by his facultee,

Pitaunce, gift.   *Tipet,* loose hood *farsed* or stuffed.
Rote, stringed instrument.   *Yeddinges,* songs.   *Tappestere,* barmaid.
Lazar, leper.

To have with seke lazars aqueyntaunce.
It is nat honest, it may nat avaunce
For to delen with no swich poraille,
But al with riche and sellers of vitaille.
And over-al, ther as profit sholde aryse,
Curteys he was, and lowly of servyse.
Ther nas no man no-wher so vertuous.
He was the beste beggere in his hous;
For thogh a widwe hadde noght a sho,
10 So plesaunt was his 'In principio,'
Yet wolde he have a ferthing, er he wente.
His purchas was wel bettre than his rente.
And rage he coude, as it were right a whelpe.
In love-dayes ther coude he muchel helpe.
For there he was nat lyk a cloisterer,
With a thredbar cope, as is a povre scoler,
But he was lyk a maister or a pope.
Of double worsted was his semi-cope,
That rounded as a belle out of the presse.
20 Somwhat he lipsed, for his wantownesse,
To make his English swete up-on his tonge;
And in his harping, whan that he had songe,
His eyen twinkled in his heed aright,
As doon the sterres in the frosty night.
This worthy limitour was cleped Huberd.
    A MARCHANT was ther with a forked berd,
In mottelee, and hye on horse he sat,
Up-on his heed a Flaundrish bever hat;
His botes clasped faire and fetisly.
30 His resons he spak ful solempnely,
Souninge alway th'encrees of his winning.
He wolde the see were kept for any thing

Poraille, scum.   In principio, John i, 1.
Purchas, gettings, in contrast to regular income or rente.
Love-dayes, for settling differences out of court.
Semi-cope, short cape.   Mottelee, figured cloth.
Resons, opinions.   Souninge, discussing.

Bitwixe Middelburgh and Orewelle.
Wel coude he in eschaunge sheeldes selle.
This worthy man ful wel his wit bisette;
Ther wiste no wight that he was in dette,
So estatly was he of his governaunce,
With his bargaynes, and with his chevisaunce.
For sothe he was a worthy man with-alle,
But sooth to seyn, I noot how men him calle.
　A CLERK ther was of Oxenford also,
10 That un-to logik hadde longe y-go.
As lene was his hors as is a rake,
And he nas nat right fat, I undertake;
But loked holwe, and ther-to soberly.
Ful thredbar was his overest courtepy;
For he had geten him yet no benefyce,
Ne was so worldly for to have offyce.
For him was lever have at his beddes heed
Twenty bokes, clad in blak or reed,
Of Aristotle and his philosophye,
20 Than robes riche, or fithele, or gay sautrye.
But al be that he was a philosophre,
Yet hadde he but litel gold in cofre;
But al that he mighte of his freendes hente,
On bokes and on lerninge he it spente,
And bisily gan for the soules preye
Of hem that yaf him wher-with to scoleye.
Of studie took he most cure and most hede.
Noght o word spak he more than was nede,
And that was seyd in forme and reverence,
30 And short and quik, and ful of hy sentence.
Souninge in moral vertu was his speche,
And gladly wolde he lerne, and gladly teche.

Middelburgh, in Flanders.　　　　*Orewelle,* near Harwich.
Sheeldes, gold coins.　　　*Chevisaunce,* financial dealings.
Longe y-go, because logic was studied early in curriculum.
Courtepy, coat.　　　*Fithele,* fiddle.　　*Scoleye,* study.
Sentence, meaning, content.　　*Souninge in,* tending to.

A SERGEANT OF THE LAWE, war and wys,
That often hadde been at the parvys,
Ther was also, ful riche of excellence.
Discreet he was, and of greet reverence:
He semed swich, his wordes weren so wyse.
Justyce he was ful often in assyse,
By patente, and by pleyn commissioun;
For his science, and for his heigh renoun
Of fees and robes hadde he many oon.
10 So greet a purchasour was no-wher noon.
Al was fee simple to him in effect,
His purchasing mighte nat been infect.
No-wher so bisy a man as he ther nas,
And yet he semed bisier than he was.
In termes hadde he caas and domes alle,
That from the tyme of king William were falle.
Therto he coude endyte, and make a thing,
Ther coude no wight pinche at his wryting;
And every statut coude he pleyn by rote.
20 He rood but hoomly in a medlee cote
Girt with a ceint of silk, with barres smale;
Of his array telle I no lenger tale.
  A FRANKELEYN was in his companye;
Whyt was his berd, as is the dayesye.
Of his complexioun he was sangwyn.
Wel loved he by the morwe a sop in wyn.
To liven in delyt was ever his wone,
For he was Epicurus owne sone,
That heeld opinioun, that pleyn delyt
30 Was verraily felicitee parfyt.

Sergeant, belonging to highest rank of lawyers.
Parvys, perhaps instructing law students.
Assyse, county court.   *Purchasour,* conveyancer.
Caas and domes, cases and decisions. *Medlee,* woven in **stripes.**
Ceint, girdle.   *Frankeleyn,* country gentleman of **estate.**

An housholdere, and that a greet, was he;
Seint Julian he was in his contree.
His breed, his ale, was alwey after oon;
A bettre envyned man was no-wher noon.
With-oute bake mete was never his hous,
Of fish and flesh, and that so plentevous,
It snewed in his hous of mete and drinke,
Of alle deyntees that men coude thinke.
After the sondry sesons of the yeer,
10 So chaunged he his mete and his soper.
Ful many a fat partrich hadde he in mewe,
And many a breem and many a luce in stewe.
Wo was his cook, but-if his sauce were
Poynaunt and sharp, and redy al his gere.
His table dormant in his halle alway
Stood redy covered al the longe day.
At sessiouns ther was he lord and sire;
Ful ofte tyme he was knight of the shire.
An anlas and a gipser al of silk
20 Heng at his girdel, whyt as morne milk.
A shirreve hadde he been, and a countour;
Was no-wher such a worthy vavasour.
    An HABERDASSHER and a CARPENTER,
A WEBBE, a DYERE, and a TAPICER,
Were with us eek, clothed in o liveree,
Of a solempne and greet fraternitee.
Ful fresh and newe hir gere apyked was;
Hir knyves were y-chaped noght with bras,

Julian, patron of hospitality.   *Envyned,* supplied with wines.
Luce in stewe, pike in his fish-pond.
Table dormant, not set away between meals.
Knight of the shire, in parliament.
Anlas and a gipser, dagger and a small bag.
Countour, auditor of county finances.
Vavasour, vassal holding from a vassal; used of franklins.
Haberdassher, etc., rich tradesmen belonging to same gild.
Y-chaped, mounted.

But al with silver, wroght ful clene and weel,
Hir girdles and hir pouches every-deel.
Wel semed ech of hem a fair burgeys,
To sitten in a yeldhalle on a deys.
Everich, for the wisdom that he can,
Was shaply for to been an alderman.
For catel hadde they y-nogh and rente,
And eek hir wyves wolde it wel assente;
And elles certein were they to blame.
10 It is ful fair to been y-clept 'ma dame,'
And goon to vigilyës al bifore,
And have a mantel royalliche y-bore.
A Cook they hadde with hem for the nones,
To boille the chiknes with the marybones,
And poudre-marchant tart, and galingale.
Wel coude he knowe a draughte of London ale.
He coude roste, and sethe, and broille, and frye,
Maken mortreux, and wel bake a pye.
But greet harm was it, as it thoughte me,
20 That on his shine a mormal hadde he;
For blankmanger, that made he with the beste.
A Shipman was ther, woning fer by weste:
For aught I woot, he was of Dertemouthe.
He rode up-on a rouncy, as he couthe,
In a gowne of falding to the knee.
A daggere hanging on a laas hadde he
Aboute his nekke under his arm adoun.
The hote somer had maad his hewe al broun;
And, certeinly, he was a good felawe.
30 Ful many a draughte of wyn had he y-drawe

Shaply, suited.	*Catel,* property.
For the nones, for the occasion.	
Poudre-marchant, powder for flavoring.	
Galingale, a spice.	*Mortreux,* stews.
Mormal, sore.	*Blankmanger,* minced capon.
Rouncy, strong horse.	*Falding,* coarse serge.

From Burdeux-ward, whyl that the chapman sleep.
Of nyce conscience took he no keep.
If that he faught, and hadde the hyer hond,
By water he sente hem hoom to every lond.
But of his craft to rekene wel his tydes,
His stremes and his daungers him bisydes,
His herberwe and his mone, his lode-menage,
Ther nas noon swich from Hulle to Cartage.
Hardy he was, and wys to undertake;
10 With many a tempest hadde his berd been shake
He knew wel alle the havenes, as they were,
From Gootlond to the cape of Finistere,
And every cryke in Britayne and in Spayne;
His barge y-cleped was the Maudelayne.

    With us ther was a DOCTOUR OF PHISYK,
In al this world ne was ther noon him lyk
To speke of phisik and of surgerye;
For he was grounded in astronomye.
He kept his pacient a ful greet del
20 In houres, by his magik naturel.
Wel coude he fortunen the ascendent
Of his images for his pacient.
He knew the cause of everich maladye,
Were it of hoot or cold, or moiste, or drye,
And where engendred, and of what humour;
He was a verrey parfit practisour.
The cause y-knowe, and of his harm the rote,
Anon he yaf the seke man his bote.
Ful redy hadde he his apothecaries,
30 To sende him drogges and his letuaries,

Chapman, merchant.   *Nyce*, delicate.
Herberwe, harborage.   *Lode-menage*, navigation.
Astronomye, because astrology, a part of the science, was used in medical practice.
Fortunen, etc., make astronomical figures when planetary influences were right.
Hoot or cold, etc., because diseases came from excess of one of the four elements.   *Bote*, cure.   *Letuaries*, medicinal syrups.

For ech of hem made other for to winne;
Hir frendschipe nas nat newe to biginne.
Wel knew he th'olde Esculapius,
And Deiscorides, and eek Rufus,
Old Ypocras, Haly, and Galien;
Serapion, Razis, and Avicen;
Averrois, Damascien, and Constantyn;
Bernard, and Gatesden, and Gilbertyn.
Of his diete mesurable was he,
10 For it was of no superfluitee,
But of greet norissing and digestible.
His studie was but litel on the Bible.
In sangwin and in pers he clad was al,
Lyned with taffata and with sendal;
And yet he was but esy of dispence;
He kepte that he wan in pestilence.
For gold in phisik is a cordial,
Therefore he lovede gold in special.
A good WYF was ther of bisyde BATHE,
20 But she was som-del deef, and that was scathe.
Of clooth-making she hadde swiche an haunt,
She passed hem of Ypres and of Gaunt.
In al the parisshe wyf ne was ther noon
That to the offring bifore hir sholde goon;
And if ther dide, certeyn, so wrooth was she,
That she was out of alle charitee.
Hir coverchiefs ful fyne were of ground;
I dorste swere they weyeden ten pound
That on a Sonday were upon hir heed.
30 Hir hosen weren of fyn scarlet reed,
Ful streite y-teyd, and shoos ful moiste and newe.
Bold was hir face, and fair, and reed of hewe.

Esculapius, etc., doctors from Greek times down to 14th century.
Sangwin and in pers, red and blue.
Sendal, thin silk.   *Esy of dispence,* moderate in spending.
Gold, regarded as valuable in medicine.
Scathe, a pity.   *Haunt,* skill.

She was a worthy womman al hir lyve,
Housbondes at chirche-dore she hadde fyve,
Withouten other companye in youthe;
But thereof nedeth nat to speke as nouthe.
And thryes hadde she been at Jerusalem;
She hadde passed many a straunge streem;
At Rome she hadde been, and at Boloigne,
In Galice at seint Jame, and at Coloigne.
She coude muche of wandring by the weye:
10 Gat-tothed was she, soothly for to seye.
Up-on an amblere esily she sat,
Y-wimpled wel, and on hir heed an hat
As brood as is a bokeler or a targe;
A foot-mantel aboute hir hipes large,
And on hir feet a paire of spores sharpe.
In felawschip wel coude she laughe and carpe.
Of remedyes of love she knew perchaunce,
For she coude of that art the olde daunce.
A good man was ther of religioun,
20 And was a povre PERSOUN of a toun;
But riche he was of holy thoght and werk.
He was also a lerned man, a clerk,
That Cristes gospel trewely wolde preche;
His parisshens devoutly wolde he teche.
Benigne he was, and wonder diligent,
And in adversitee ful pacient;
And swich he was y-preved ofte sythes.
Ful looth were him to cursen for his tythes.

Chirche-dore, where marriages were celebrated.
Nouthe, now.
Boloigne, Boulogne, where there was a wonder-working image of the Virgin.
Galice, shrine of St. James at Compostella in northwestern Spain.
Coloigne, with shrines of Three Magi and St. Ursula.
Gat-tothed, with wide-set teeth.
Bokeler or a targe, small round shields.
Carpe, talk.
Sythes, times.
Cursen, excommunicate to get his tithes or fixed dues.

But rather wolde he yeven, out of doute,
Un-to his povre parisshens aboute
Of his offring, and eek of his substaunce.
He coude in litel thing han suffisaunce.
Wyd was his parisshe, and houses fer a-sonder,
But he ne lafte nat, for reyn ne thonder,
In siknes nor in meschief, to visyte
The ferreste in his parisshe, muche and lyte,
Up-on his feet, and in his hand a staf.
10 This noble ensample to his sheep he yaf,
That first he wroghte, and afterward he taughte;
Out of the gospel he tho wordes caughte;
And this figure he added eek ther-to,
That if gold ruste, what shal iren do?
For if a preest be foul, on whom we truste,
No wonder is a lewed man to ruste;
And shame it is, if a preest take keep,
A shiten shepherde and a clene sheep.
Wel oghte a preest ensample for to yive,
20 By his clennesse, how that his sheep shold live.
He sette nat his benefice to hyre,
And leet his sheep encombred in the myre,
And ran to London, unto sëynt Poules,
To seken him a chaunterie for soules,
Or with a bretherhed to been withholde;
But dwelte at hoom, and kepte wel his folde,
So that the wolf ne made it nat miscarie;
He was a shepherde and no mercenarie.
And though he holy were, and vertuous,
30 He was to sinful man nat despitous,
Ne of his speche daungerous ne digne,
But in his teching discreet and benigne.

Lewed, ignorant.
Chaunterie, an endowed chapel in a large church, often part of
a tomb.
Despitous, scornful.
Daungerous ne digne, haughty or pompous.

To drawen folk to heven by fairnesse
By good ensample, was his bisinesse:
But it were any persone obstinat,
What-so he were, of heigh or lowe estat,
Him wolde he snibben sharply for the nones.
A bettre preest, I trowe that nowher noon is.
He wayted after no pompe and reverence,
Ne maked him a spyced conscience,
But Cristes lore, and his apostles twelve,
10 He taughte, and first he folwed it himselve.
   With him ther was a PLOWMAN, was his brother,
That hadde y-lad of dong ful many a fother,
A trewe swinker and a good was he,
Livinge in pees and parfit charitee.
God loved he best with al his hole herte
At alle tymes, thogh him gamed or smerte,
And thanne his neighebour right as himselve.
He wolde thresshe, and ther-to dyke and delve,
For Cristes sake, for every povre wight,
20 Withouten hyre, if it lay in his might.
His tythes payed he ful faire and wel,
Bothe of his propre swink and his catel.
In a tabard he rood upon a mere.
   Ther was also a Reve and a Millere,
A Somnour and a Pardoner also,
A Maunciple, and my-self; ther were namo.
   The MILLER was a stout carl, for the nones,
Ful big he was of braun, and eek of bones;
That proved wel, for over-al ther he cam,
30 At wrastling he wolde have alwey the ram.

Snibben, reprove.
Spyced conscience, one stiff, careful about non-essentials.
Fother, load.
Swinker, worker.
Mere, since only the humble rode mares.
Carl, fellow.
Ram, a common prize for wrestling.

He was short-sholdred, brood, a thikke knarre,
Ther was no dore that he nolde heve of harre,
Or breke it, at a renning, with his heed.
His berd as any sowe or fox was reed,
And ther-to brood, as though it were a spade.
Up-on the cop right of his nose he hade
A werte, and ther-on stood a tuft of heres,
Reed as the bristles of a sowes eres;
His nose-thirles blake were and wyde.
10 A swerd and bokeler bar he by his syde;
His mouth as greet was as a greet forneys.
He was a janglere and a goliardeys,
And that was most of sinne and harlotryes.
Wel coude he stelen corn, and tollen thryes;
And yet he hadde a thombe of gold, pardee.
A why cote and a blew hood wered he.
A baggepype wel coude he blowe and sowne,
And ther-with-al he broghte us out of towne.
    A gentil MAUNCIPLE was ther of a temple,
20 Of which achatours mighte take exemple
For to be wyse in bying of vitaille
For whether that he payde, or took by taille,
Algate he wayted so in his achat,
That he was ay biforn and in good stat.
Now is nat that of God a ful fair grace,
That swich a lewed mannes wit shal pace
The wisdom of an heep of lerned men?
Of maistres hadde he mo than thryes ten,
That were of lawe expert and curious;
30 Of which ther were a doseyn in that hous

Knarre, thickset fellow.
Harre, hinge.   *Goliardeys,* loose story-teller.
Cop, top.   *Tollen thryes,* take triple pay.
    Thombe of gold, referring to the ironical proverb, that honest
millers have golden thumbs.
    Maunciple, steward of one of the inns of court.
    Achatours, purchasers.   *Algate,* at all events.

Worthy to been stiwardes of rente and lond
Of any lord that is in Engelond,
To make him live by his propre good,
In honour dettelees, but he were wood,
Or live as scarsly as him list desire;
And able for to helpen al a shire
In any cas that mighte falle or happe;
And yit this maunciple sette hir aller cappe.
   The REVE was a sclendre colerik man,
10 His berd was shave as ny as ever he can.
His heer was by his eres round y-shorn.
His top was dokked lyk a preest biforn.
Ful longe were his legges, and ful lene,
Y-lyk a staf, ther was no calf y-sene.
Wel coude he kepe a gerner and a binne;
Ther was noon auditour coude on him winne.
Wel wiste he, by the droghte, and by the reyn,
The yelding of his seed, and of his greyn.
His lordes sheep, his neet, his dayerye,
30 His swyn, his hors, his stoor, and his pultrye,
Was hoolly in this reves governing,
And by his covenaunt yaf the rekening,
Sin that his lord was twenty yeer of age;
Ther coude no man bringe him in arrerage.
Ther nas baillif, ne herde, ne other hyne,
That he ne knew his sleighte and his covyne;
They were adrad of him, as of the deeth.
His woning was ful fair up-on an heeth,
With grene treës shadwed was his place.
20 He coude bettre than his lord purchace.
Ful riche he was astored prively,
His lord wel coude he plesen subtilly,

Aller cappe, duped all of them.
Reve, bailiff in direct charge of an estate.
Dokked, cut short.   *Neet,* cattle.
Stoor, provisions.   *Hyne,* hind, man on the estate.
Covyne, trickery.   *Woning,* dwelling.

To yeve and lene him of his owne good,
And have a thank, and yet a cote and hood.
In youthe he lerned hadde a good mister;
He was a wel good wrighte, a carpenter.
This reve sat up-on a ful good stot,
That was al pomely grey, and highte Scot.
A long surcote of pers up-on he hade,
And by his syde he bar a rusty blade.
Of Northfolk was this reve, of which I telle,
10 Bisyde a toun men clepen Baldeswelle.
Tukked he was, as is a frere, aboute,
And ever he rood the hindreste of our route.
   A SOMNOUR was ther with us in that place
That hadde a fyr-reed cherubinnes face,
For sawcefleem he was, with eyen narwe.
As hoot he was, and lecherous, as a sparwe;
With scalled browes blake, and piled berd;
Of his visage children were aferd.
Ther nas quik-silver, litarge, ne brimstoon,
20 Boras, ceruce, ne oille of tartre noon,
Ne oynement that wolde clense and byte,
That him mighte helpen of his whelkes whyte,
Nor of the knobbes sittinge on his chekes.
Wel loved he garleek, oynons, and eek lekes,
And for to drinken strong wyn, reed as blood.
Than wolde he speke, and crye as he were wood.
And whan that he wel dronken hadde the wyn,
Than wolde he speke no word but Latyn.
A fewe termes hadde he, two or three,
30 That he had lerned out of som decree;

Mister, trade.   *Stot,* stallion.
Tukked, with coat tucked into girdle.
Somnour, constable attached to an ecclesiastical court.
Cherubinnes, like that of cherubs in wall-paintings.
Sawcefleem, pimpled.   *Scalled,* scabby.   *Piled,* scanty.
Litarge, white lead.   *Ceruce,* lead carbonate. *Whelkes,* pimples.

No wonder is, he herde it al the day;
And eek ye knowen wel, how that a jay
Can clepen 'Watte,' as well as can the pope.
But who-so coude in other thing him grope,
Thanne hadde he spent al his philosophye;
Ay 'Questio quid iuris' wolde he crye.
He was a gentil harlot and a kinde;
A bettre felawe sholde men noght finde.
He wolde suffre, for a quart of wyn,
10 A good felawe to have his concubyn
A twelf-month, and excuse him atte fulle:
Ful prively a finch eek coude he pulle.
And if he fond o-wher a good felawe,
He wolde techen him to have non awe,
In swich cas, of the erchedeknes curs,
But-if a mannes soule were in his purs;.
For in his purs he sholde y-punisshed be.
'Purs is the erchedeknes helle,' seyde he.
But wel I woot he lyed right in dede;
20 Of cursing oghte ech gilty man him drede—
For curs wol slee, right as assoilling saveth—
And also war him of a significavit.
In daunger hadde he at his owne gyse
The yonge girles of the diocyse,
And knew hir counseil, and was al hir reed.
A gerland hadde he set up-on his heed,
As greet as it were for an ale-stake;
A bokeler hadde he maad him of a cake.
    With him ther rood a gentil PARDONER
30 Of Rouncival, his freend and his compeer,
That streight was comen fro the court of Rome.
Ful loude he song, 'Com hider, love, to me.'

Questio quid iuris, what is the law?   Harlot, rascal.
Daunger, control.   Girles, youth of both sexes.
Ale-stake, bush or garland was set on a pole as a tavern sign.
Pardoner, dispenser of indulgences.
Rouncival, a conventual house at Charing Cross.

This somnour bar to him a stif burdoun,
Was never trompe of half so greet a soun.
This pardoner hadde heer as yelow as wex,
But smothe it heng, as dooth a strike of flex;
By ounces henge his lokkes that he hadde,
And ther-with he his shuldres overspradde;
But thinne it lay, by colpons oon and oon;
But hood, for jolitee, ne wered he noon,
For it was trussed up in his walet.
10 Him thoughte, he rood al of the newe jet;
Dischevele, save his cappe, he rood al bare.
Swiche glaringe eyen hadde he as an hare.
A vernicle hadde he sowed on his cappe.
His walet lay biforn him in his lappe,
Bret-ful of pardoun come from Rome all hoot.
A voys he hadde as smal as hath a goot.
No berd hadde he, ne never sholde have,
As smothe it was as it were late y-shave;
I trowe he were a gelding or a mare.
20 But of his craft, fro Berwik into Ware,
Ne was ther swich another pardoner.
For in his male he hadde a pilwe-beer,
Which that, he seyde, was our lady veyl:
He seyde, he hadde a gobet of the seyl
That sëynt Peter hadde, whan that he wente
Up-on the see, til Jesu Crist him hente.
He hadde a croys of latoun, ful of stones,
And in a glas he hadde pigges bones.
But with thise relikes, whan that he fond
30 A povre person dwelling up-on lond,

Burdoun, bass accompaniment.   *Strike of flex,* hank of flax.
Ounces, small bunches.   *Colpons,* shreds.   *Jet,* fashion.
Vernicle, copy of handkerchief on which Christ was said to have
wiped his face, preserved by St. Veronica.   A portrait was im-
printed on it.   *Bret-ful,* brimfull.   *Smal,* thin.
Male, bag.   *Pilwe-beer,* pillow case.   *Latoun,* a cheap alloy.

Up-on a day he gat him more moneye
Than that the person gat in monthes tweye.
And thus, with feyned flaterye and japes,
He made the person and the peple his apes.
But trewely to tellen, atte laste,
He was in chirche a noble ecclesiaste.
Wel coude he rede a lessoun or a storie,
But alderbest he song an offertorie;
For wel he wiste, whan that song was songe
10 He moste preche, and wel affyle his tonge,
To winne silver, as he ful wel coude;
Therefore he song so meriely and loude.
   Now have I told you shortly, in a clause,
Th'estat, th'array, the nombre, and eek the cause
Why that assembled was this companye
In Southwerk, at this gentil hostelrye,
That highte the Tabard, faste by the Belle.
But now is tyme to yow for to telle
How that we baren us that ilke night,
20 Whan we were in that hostelrye alight.
And after wol I telle of our viage,
And all the remenaunt of our pilgrimage.
But first I pray yow, of your curteisye,
That ye n'arette it nat my vileinye,
Thogh that I pleynly speke in this matere,
To telle yow hir wordes and hir chere;
Ne thogh I speke hir wordes properly.
For this ye knowen al-so wel as I,
Who-so shal telle a tale after a man,
30 He moot reherce, as ny as ever he can,
Everich a word, if it be in his charge,
Al speke he never so rudeliche and large;
Or elles he moot telle his tale untrewe,
Or feyne thing, or finde wordes newe.

Large, broadly.

He may nat spare, al-thogh he were his brother;
He moot as wel seye o word as another.
Crist spak him-self ful brode in holy writ,
And wel ye woot, no vileinye is it.
Eek Plato seith, who-so that can him rede,
The wordes mote be cosin to the dede.
Also I prey yow to foryeve it me,
Al have I nat set folk in hir degree
Here in this tale, as that they sholde stonde;
10 My wit is short, ye may wel understonde.
  Greet chere made our hoste us everichon,
And to the soper sette us anon;
And served us with vitaille at the beste.
Strong was the wyn, and wel to drinke us leste.
A semely man our hoste was with-alle
For to han been a marshal in an halle;
A large man he was with eyen stepe,
A fairer burgeys is ther noon in Chepe:
Bold of his speche, and wys, and wel y-taught,
20 And of manhod him lakkede right naught.
Eek thereto he was right a mery man,
And after soper pleyen he bigan,
And spak of mirthe amonges othere thinges,
Whan that we hadde maad our rekeninges;
And seyde thus: 'Now, lordinges, trewely,
Ye been to me right welcome hertely:
For by my trouthe, if that I shal not lye,
I ne saugh this yeer so mery a companye
At ones in this herberwe as is now.
30 Fayn wolde I doon yow mirthe, wiste I how.
And of a mirthe I am right now bithoght,
To doon yow ese, and it shal coste noght.
  Ye goon to Caunterbury; God yow spede,
The blisful martir quyte yow your mede.
And wel I woot, as ye goon by the weye,
Ye shapen yow to talen and to pleye;

Leste, it pleased.   *Herberwe,* lodging, inn.

For trewely, confort ne mirthe is noon
To ryde by the weye doumb as a stoon;
And therfore wol I maken yow disport,
As I seyde erst, and doon yow som confort.
And if yow lyketh alle, by oon assent,
Now for to stonden at my jugement,
And for to werken as I shal yow seye,
To-morwe, whan ye ryden by the weye,
Now, by my fader soule, that is deed,
10 But ye be merye, I wol yeve yow myn heed.
Hold up your hond, withouten more speche.'
    Our counseil was nat longe for to seche;
Us thoughte it was noght worth to make it wys,
And graunted him withouten more avys,
And bad him seye his verdit, as him leste.
    'Lordinges,' quod he, 'now herkneth for the beste,
But tak it not, I prey yow, in desdeyn;
This is the poynt, to speken short and pleyn,
That ech of yow, to shorte with your weye,
20 In this viage, shal telle tales tweye,
To Caunterbury-ward, I mene it so,
And hom-ward he shal tellen othere two,
Of aventures that whylom han bifalle.
And which of yow that bereth him best of alle,
That is to seyn, that telleth in this cas
Tales of best sentence and most solas,
Shal have a soper at our aller cost
Here in this place, sitting by this post,
Whan that we come agayn fro Caunterbury.
30 And for to make yow the more mery,
I wol my-selven gladly with yow ryde,
Right at myn owne cost, and be your gyde.

Make it wys, deliberate.
Tales tweye, the plan to tell two tales on both the outward and homeward journeys was later cut down by half.
Sentence, solid content.

And who-so wol my jugement withseye
Shal paye al that we spenden by the weye.
And if ye vouche-sauf that it be so,
Tel me anon, with-outen wordes mo,
And I wol erly shape me therfore.'
This thing was graunted, and our othes swore
With ful glad herte, and preyden him also
That he wold vouche-sauf for to do so,
And that he wolde been our governour,
10 And of our tales juge and reportour,
And sette a soper at a certeyn prys;
And we wold reuled been at his devys,
In heigh and lowe; and thus, by oon assent,
We been acorded to his jugement.
And there-up-on the wyn was fet anon;
We dronken, and to reste wente echon,
With-outen any lenger taryinge.
A-morwe, whan that day bigan to springe,
Up roos our host, and was our aller cok,
20 And gadrede us togidre, alle in a flok,
And forth we riden, a litel more than pas,
Un-to the watering of seint Thomas.
And there our host bigan his hors areste,
And seyde; 'Lordinges, herkneth, if yow leste.
Ye woot your forward, and I it yow recorde.
If even-song and morwe-song acorde,
Lat see now who shal telle the firste tale.
As ever mote I drinke wyn or ale,
Who-so be rebel to my jugement
30 Shal paye for al that by the weye is spent.
Now draweth cut, er that we ferrer twinne;
He which that hath the shortest shal biginne.

Aller cok, the cock to waken all of us.
Watering of seint Thomas, a mile and a half from the Tabard.
Forward, agreement.
Twinne, proceed.

Sire knight,' quod he, 'my maister and my lord,
Now draweth cut, for that is myn acord.
Cometh neer,' quod he, 'my lady prioresse;
And ye, sir clerk, lat be your shamfastnesse,
Ne studieth noght; ley hond to, every man.'
Anon to drawen every wight bigan,
And shortly for to tellen, as it was,
Were it by aventure, or sort, or cas,
The sothe is this, the cut fil to the knight,
10 Of which ful blythe and glad was every wight;
And telle he moste his tale, as was resoun,
By forward and by composicioun,
As ye han herd; what nedeth wordes mo?
And whan this gode man saugh it was so,
As he that wys was and obedient
To kepe his forward by his free assent,
He seyde: 'Sin I shal beginne the game,
What, welcome be the cut, a Goddes name!
Now lat us ryde, and herkneth what I seye.'
20 And with that word we riden forth our weye;
And he bigan with right a mery chere
His tale anon, and seyde in this manere.

THE NUN'S PRIEST'S TALE

THAN spak our host, with rude speche and bold,
And seyde un-to the Nonnes Preest anon,
'Com neer, thou preest, com hider, thou sir John,
Tel us swich thing as may our hertes glade,
Be blythe, though thou ryde up-on a jade.
What though thyn hors be bothe foule and lene,
If he wol serve thee, rekke nat a bene;

Cometh neer, come nearer. *Sothe,* truth.
Sort, or cas, chance or circumstance.
Composicioun, arrangement.
Spak our host, after ten tales have been told.

Look that thyn herte be mery evermo.'
'Yis, sir,' quod he, 'yis, host, so mote I go,
But I be mery, y-wis, I wol be blamed :'—
And right anon his tale he hath attamed,
And thus he seyde un-to us everichon,
This swete preest, this goodly man, sir John.

A POVRE widwe, somdel stape in age,
Was whylom dwelling in a narwe cotage,
Bisyde a grove, stonding in a dale.
10 This widwe, of which I telle yow my tale,
Sin thilke day that she was last a wyf,
In pacience ladde a ful simple lyf,
For litel was hir catel and hir rente;
By housbondrye, of such as God hir sente,
She fond hir-self, and eek hir doghtren two.
Three large sowes hadde she, and namo,
Three kyn, and eek a sheep that highte Malle.
Ful sooty was hir bour, and eek hir halle,
In which she eet ful many a sclendre meel.
20 Of poynaunt sauce hir neded never a deel.
No deyntee morsel passed thurgh hir throte;
Hir dyete was accordant to hir cote.
Repleccioun ne made hir never syk;
Attempree dyete was al hir phisyk,
And exercyse, and hertes suffisaunce.
The goute lette hir no-thing for to daunce,
N'apoplexye shente nat hir heed;
No wyn ne drank she, neither whyt ne reed;
Hir bord was served most with whyt and blak,
30 Milk and broun breed, in which she fond no lak,
Seynd bacoun, and somtyme an ey or tweye,
For she was as it were a maner deye.

Attamed, begun.   *Stape,* advanced.
Lette hir no-thing, prevented her in no way.   *Shente,* hurt.
Seynd, broiled.   *Ey,* egg.   *Deye,* dairywoman.

A yerd she hadde, enclosed al aboute
With stikkes, and a drye dich with-oute,
In which she hadde a cok, hight Chauntecleer,
In al the land of crowing nas his peer.
His vois was merier than the mery orgon
On messe-dayes that in the chirche gon;
Wel sikerer was his crowing in his logge,
Than is a clokke, or an abbey orlogge.
By nature knew he ech ascencioun
10 Of equinoxial in thilke toun;
For whan degrees fiftene were ascended,
Thanne crew he, that it mighte nat ben amended.
His comb was redder than the fyn coral,
And batailed, as it were a castel-wal.
His bile was blak, and as the jeet it shoon;
Lyk asur were his legges, and his toon;
His nayles whytter than the lilie flour,
And lyk the burned gold was his colour.
This gentil cok hadde in his governaunce
20 Sevene hennes, for to doon al his plesaunce,
Whiche were his sustres and his paramours,
And wonder lyk to him, as of colours.
Of whiche the faireste hewed on hir throte
Was cleped faire damoysele Pertelote.
Curteys she was, discreet, and debonaire,
And compaignable, and bar hir-self so faire,
Sin thilke day that she was seven night old,
That trewely she hath the herte in hold
Of Chauntecleer loken in every lith;
30 He loved hir so, that wel was him therwith.
But such a joye was it to here hem singe,
Whan that the brighte sonne gan to springe,

Sikerer, more surely on time.
Batailed, battlemented, the whole description being mock heroic.
Lith, limb.

In swete accord, 'my lief is faren in londe.'
For thilke tyme, as I have understonde,
Bestes and briddes coude speke and singe.
And so bifel, that in a daweninge,
As Chauntecleer among his wyves alle
Sat on his perche, that was in the halle,
And next him sat this faire Pertelote,
This Chauntecleer gan gronen in his throte,
As man that in his dreem is drecched sore.
10 And whan that Pertelote thus herde him rore,
She was agast, and seyde, 'O herte dere,
What eyleth yow, to grone in this manere?
Ye been a verray sleper, fy for shame!'
And he answerde and seyde thus, 'madame,
I pray yow, that ye take it nat a-grief:
By god, me mette I was in swich meschief
Right now, that yet myn herte is sore afright.
Now god,' quod he, 'my swevene recche aright,
And keep my body out of foul prisoun!
20 Me mette, how that I romed up and doun
Withinne our yerde, wher-as I saugh a beste,
Was lyk an hound, and wolde han maad areste
Upon my body, and wolde han had me deed.
His colour was bitwixe yelwe and reed;
And tipped was his tail, and bothe his eres,
With blak, unlyk the remenant of his heres;
His snowte smal, with glowinge eyen tweye.
Yet of his look for fere almost I deye;
This caused me my groning, doutelees.'
30   'Avoy!' quod she, 'fy on yow, hertelees!
Allas!' quod she, 'for, by that god above,
Now han ye lost myn herte and al my love;
I can nat love a coward, by my feith.
For certes, what so any womman seith,

Drecched, disturbed.   *Me mette,* I dreamed.
Swevene recche, interpret my dream.   *Hertelees,* you coward!

We alle desyren, if it mighte be,
To han housbondes hardy, wyse, and free,
And secree, and no nigard, ne no fool,
Ne him that is agast of every tool,
Ne noon avauntour, by that god above!
How dorste ye seyn for shame unto your love,
That any thing mighte make yow aferd?
Have ye no mannes herte, and han a berd?
Allas! and conne ye been agast of swevenis?
10 No-thing, god wot, but vanitee, in sweven is.
Swevenes engendren of replecciouns,
And ofte of fume, and of complecciouns,
Whan humours been to habundant in a wight.
Certes this dreem, which ye han met to-night,
Cometh of the grete superfluitee
Of youre rede *colera,* pardee,
Which causeth folk to dreden in here dremes
Of arwes, and of fyr with rede lemes,
Of grete bestes, that they wol hem byte,
20 Of contek, and of whelpes grete and lyte;
Right as the humour of malencolye
Causeth ful many a man, in sleep, to crye,
For fere of blake beres, or boles blake,
Or elles, blake develes wole hem take.
Of othere humours coude I telle also,
That werken many a man in sleep ful wo;
But I wol passe as lightly as I can.
    Lo Catoun, which that was so wys a man,
Seyde he nat thus, ne do no fors of dremes?
30 Now, sire,' quod she, 'whan we flee fro the bemes,
For Goddes love, as tak some laxatyf;
Up peril of my soule, and of my lyf,

Free, liberal.   *Tool,* weapon.   *Avauntour,* braggart.
Fume, vapors supposed to get into cells of the brain.
Colera, one of the so-called humors or bodily fluids.
Lemes, flames.   *Contek,* violence.
Boles, bulls.   *Do no fors,* take no heed.

I counseille yow the beste, I wol nat lye,
That bothe of colere and of malencolye
Ye purge yow; and for ye shul nat tarie,
Though in this toun is noon apotecarie,
I shal my-self to herbes techen yow,
That shul ben for your hele, and for your prow;
And in our yerd tho herbes shal I finde,
The whiche han of hir propretee, by kinde,
To purgen yow binethe, and eek above.
10 Forget not this, for goddes owene love!
Ye been ful colerik of compleccioun.
Ware the sonne in his ascencioun
Ne fynde yow nat repleet of humours hote;
And if it do, I dar wel leye a grote,
That ye shul have a fevere terciane,
Or an agu, that may be youre bane.
A day or two ye shul have digestyves
Of wormes, er ye take your laxatyves,
Of lauriol, centaure, and fumetere,
20 Or elles of ellebor, that groweth there,
Of catapuce, or of gaytres beryis,
Of erbe yve, growing in our yerd, that mery is;
Pekke hem up right as they growe, and ete hem in.
Be mery, housbond, for your fader kin!
Dredeth no dreem; I can say yow na-more.'
    'Madame,' quod he, '*graunt mercy* of your lore.
But nathelees, as touching daun Catoun,
That hath of wisdom such a greet renoun,
Though that he bad no dremes for to drede,
30 By god, men may in olde bokes rede
Of many a man, more of auctoritee
Than ever Catoun was, so mote I thee,

Prow, help.   *By kinde,* by nature.
Lauriol, etc., medicinal herbs.
Mote I thee, may I thrive.

That al the revers seyn of his sentence,
And han wel founden by experience,
That dremes ben significaciouns,
As wel of joye as tribulaciouns
That folk enduren in this lyf present.
Ther nedeth make of this noon argument;
The verray preve sheweth it in dede.
   Oon of the gretteste auctours that men rede
Seith thus, that whylom two felawes wente
10 On pilgrimage, in a ful good entente;
And happed so, thay come into a toun,
Wher-as ther was swich congregacioun
Of peple, and eek so streit of herbergage
That they ne founde as muche as o cotage
In which they bothe mighte y-logged be.
Wherfor thay mosten, of necessitee,
As for that night, departen compaignye;
And ech of hem goth to his hostelrye,
And took his logging as it wolde falle.
20 That oon of hem was logged in a stalle,
Fer in a yerd, with oxen of the plough;
That other man was logged wel y-nough,
As was his aventure, or his fortune,
That us governeth alle as in commune.
   And so bifel, that, longe er it were day,
This man mette in his bed, ther-as he lay,
How that his felawe gan up-on him calle,
And seyde, "allas! for in an oxes stalle
This night I shal be mordred ther I lye.
30 Now help me, dere brother, er I dye;
In alle haste com to me," he sayde.
This man out of his sleep for fere abrayde;
But whan that he was wakned of his sleep,
He turned him, and took of this no keep;

Seyn, said.   *Verray preve,* true proof.
Streit of herbergage, lack of lodging.   *Abrayde,* started up.

Him thoughte his dreem nas but a vanitee.
Thus twyës in his sleping dremed he.
And atte thridde tyme yet his felawe
Cam, as him thoughte, and seide, "I am now slawe;
Bihold my blody woundes, depe and wyde!
Arys up erly in the morwe-tyde,
And at the west gate of the toun," quod he,
"A carte ful of dong ther shaltow see,
In which my body is hid ful prively;
10 Do thilke carte aresten boldely.
My gold caused my mordre, sooth to sayn";
And tolde him every poynt how he was slayn,
With a ful pitous face, pale of hewe.
And truste wel, his dreem he fond ful trewe;
For on the morwe, as sone as it was day,
To his felawes in he took the way;
And whan that he cam to this oxes stalle,
After his felawe he bigan to calle.
     The hostiler answered him anon,
20 And seyde, "sire, your felawe is agon,
As sone as day he wente out of the toun."
This man gan fallen in suspecioun,
Remembring on his dremes that he mette,
And forth he goth, no lenger wolde he lette,
Unto the west gate of the toun, and fond
A dong-carte, as it were to donge lond,
That was arrayed in the same wyse
As ye han herd the dede man devyse;
And with an hardy herte he gan to crye
30 Vengeaunce and justice of this felonye:—
"My felawe mordred is this same night,
And in this carte he lyth gapinge upright.
I crye out on the ministres," quod he,
"That sholden kepe and reulen this citee;
Harrow! allas! her lyth my felawe slayn!"
What sholde I more un-to this tale sayn?

The peple out-sterte, and caste the cart to grounde,
And in the middel of the dong they founde
The dede man, that mordred was al newe.
   O blisful god, that art so just and trewe!
Lo, how that thou biwreyest mordre alway!
Mordre wol out, that see we day by day.
Mordre is so wlatsom and abhominable
To god, that is so just and resonable,
That he ne wol nat suffre it heled be;
10 Though it abyde a yeer, or two, or three,
Mordre wol out, this my conclusioun.
And right anoon, ministres of that toun
Han hent the carter, and so sore him pyned,
And eek the hostiler so sore engyned,
That thay biknewe hir wikkednesse anoon,
And were an-hanged by the nekke-boon.
   Here may men seen that dremes been to drede.
And certes, in the same book I rede,
Right in the nexte chapitre after this,
20 (I gabbe nat, so have I joye or blis,)
Two men that wolde han passed over see,
For certeyn cause, in-to a fer contree,
If that the wind ne hadde been contrarie,
That made hem in a citee for to tarie,
That stood ful mery upon an haven-syde.
But on a day, agayn the even-tyde,
The wind gan chaunge, and blew right as hem leste.
Jolif and glad they wente un-to hir reste,
And casten hem ful erly for to saille;
30 But to that oo man fil a greet mervaille.
That oon of hem, in sleping as he lay,
Him mette a wonder dreem, agayn the day;

Biwreyest, revealest.	*Wlatsom,* loathsome.	
Heled, hidden.	*Hent,* seized.	*Pyned,* tortured.
Biknewe, confessed.	*Gabbe,* jest.	*Mery,* pleasant.

Him thoughte a man stood by his beddes syde,
And him comaunded, that he sholde abyde,
And seyde him thus, "if thou to-morwe wende,
Thou shalt be dreynt; my tale is at an ende."
He wook, and tolde his felawe what he mette,
And preyde him his viage for to lette;
As for that day, he preyde him to abyde.
His felawe, that lay by his beddes syde,
Gan for to laughe, and scorned him ful faste.
10 "No dreem," quod he, "may so myn herte agaste,
That I wol lette for to do my thinges.
I sette not a straw by thy dreminges,
For swevenes been but vanitees and japes.
Men dreme al-day of owles or of apes,
And eke of many a mase therwithal;
Men dreme of thing that never was ne shal.
But sith I see that thou wolt heer abyde,
And thus for-sleuthen wilfully thy tyde,
God wot it reweth me; and have good day."
20 And thus he took his leve, and wente his way.
But er that he hadde halfe his cours y-seyled,
Noot I nat why, ne what mischaunce it eyled,
But casuelly the shippes botme rente,
And ship and man under the water wente
In sighte of othere shippes it byside,
That with hem seyled at the same tyde.
And therfor, faire Pertelote so dere,
By swiche ensamples olde maistow lere,
That no man sholde been to recchelees
30 Of dremes, for I sey thee, doutelees,
That many a dreem ful sore is for to drede.
  Lo, in the lyf of seint Kenelm, I rede,

Dreynt, drowned.   *Japes,* tricks.
For-sleuthen, waste by sloth.   *Tyde,* time.
Noot I, I know not.   *Lere,* learn.
Kenelm, ninth century prince of Mercia, murdered by his aunt.

That was Kenulphus sone, the noble king
Of Mercenrike, how Kenelm mette a thing;
A lyte er he was mordred, on a day,
His mordre in his avisioun he say.
His norice him expouned every del
His sweven, and bad him for to kepe him wel
For traisoun; but he nas but seven yeer old,
And therfore litel tale hath he told
Of any dreem, so holy was his herte.
10 By god, I hadde lever than my sherte
That ye had rad his legende, as have I.
Dame Pertelote, I sey yow trewely,
Macrobeus, that writ th'avisioun
In Affrike of the worthy Cipioun,
Affermeth dremes, and seith that they been
Warning of thinges that men after seen.
And forther-more, I pray yow loketh wel
In th'olde testament, of Daniel,
If he held dremes any vanitee.
20 Reed eek of Joseph, and ther shul ye see
Wher dremes ben somtyme (I sey nat alle)
Warning of thinges that shul after falle.
Loke of Egipt the king, daun Pharao,
His bakere and his boteler also,
Wher they ne felte noon effect in dremes.
Who-so wol seken actes of sondry remes,
May rede of dremes many a wonder thing.
Lo Cresus, which that was of Lyde king,
Mette he nat that he sat upon a tree,
30 Which signified he sholde anhanged be?
Lo heer Andromacha, Ectores wyf,
That day that Ector sholde lese his lyf,

Say, saw.   *Norice,* nurse.   *Tale,* attention.
Macrobeus, Macrobius wrote a commentary on Cicero's *Somnium Scipionis.*

She dremed on the same night biforn,
How that the lyf of Ector sholde be lorn,
If thilke day he wente in-to bataille;
She warned him, but it mighte nat availle;
He wente for to fighte nathelees,
But he was slayn anoon of Achilles.
But thilke tale is al to long to telle,
And eek it is ny day, I may nat dwelle.
Shortly I seye, as for conclusioun,
10 That I shal han of th's avisioun
Adversitee; and I seye forther-more,
That I ne telle of laxatyves no store,
For they ben venimous, I woot it wel;
I hem defye, I love hem never a del.
      Now let us speke of mirthe, and stinte al this;
Madame Pertelote, so have I blis,
Of o thing god hath sent me large grace;
For whan I see the beautee of your face,
Ye ben so scarlet-reed about your yën,
20 It maketh al my drede for to dyen;
For, also siker as *In principio,*
Mulier est hominis confusio;
Madame, the sentence of this Latin is—
Womman is mannes joye and al his blis.
For whan I fele a-night your softe syde,
Al-be-it that I may nat on you ryde,
For that our perche is maad so narwe, alas!
I am so ful of joye and of solas
That I defye bothe sweven and dreem.'
30 And with that word he fley doun fro the beem,
For it was day, and eek his hennes alle;
And with a chuk he gan hem for to calle,

Telle . . . no store, make no account.
In principio, a mediæval Latin jest, which Chaunticleer mis-translates.
Sentence, meaning.

For he had founde a corn, lay in the yerd.
Royal he was, he was namore aferd;
He fethered Pertelote twenty tyme,
And trad as ofte, er that it was pryme.
He loketh as it were a grim leoun;
And on his toos he rometh up and doun,
Him deyned not to sette his foot to grounde.
He chukketh, whan he hath a corn y-founde,
And to him rennen thanne his wyves alle.
10 Thus royal, as a prince is in his halle,
Leve I this Chauntecleer in his pasture;
And after wol I telle his aventure.
      Whan that the month in which the world bigan,
That highte March, whan god first maked man,
Was complet, and [y]-passed were also,
Sin March bigan, thritty dayes and two,
Bifel that Chauntecleer, in al his pryde,
His seven wyves walking by his syde,
Caste up his eyen to the brighte sonne,
20 That in the signe of Taurus hadde y-ronne
Twenty degrees and oon, and somwhat more;
And knew by kynde, and by noon other lore,
That it was pryme, and crew with blisful stevene.
'The sonne,' he sayde, 'is clomben up on hevene
Fourty degrees and oon, and more, y-wis.
Madame Pertelote, my worldes blis,
Herkneth thise blisful briddes how they singe,
And see the fresshe floures how they springe;
Ful is my herte of revel and solas.'
30 But sodeinly him fil a sorweful cas;
For ever the latter ende of joye is wo.
God woot that worldly joye is sone ago;
And if a rethor coude faire endyte,
He in a cronique saufly mighte it wryte,

Pryme, six to nine a.m.   *Stevene,* voice.
Rethor . . . endyte, rhetorician . . . compose.

As for a sovereyn notabilitee.
Now every wys man, lat him herkne me;
This storie is al-so trewe, I undertake,
As is the book of Launcelot de Lake,
That wommen holde in ful gret reverence.
Now wol I torne agayn to my sentence.
A col-fox, ful of sly iniquitee,
That in the grove hadde woned yeres three,
By heigh imaginacioun forn-cast,
10 The same night thurgh-out the hegges brast
Into the yerd, ther Chauntecleer the faire
Was wont, and eek his wyves, to repaire;
And in a bed of wortes stille he lay,
Til it was passed undern of the day,
Wayting his tyme on Chauntecleer to falle,
As gladly doon thise homicydes alle,
That in awayt liggen to mordre men.
O false mordrer, lurking in thy den!
O newe Scariot, newe Genilon!
20 False dissimilour, O Greek Sinon,
That broghtest Troye al outrely to sorwe!
O Chauntecleer, acursed be that morwe,
That thou into that yerd flough fro the bemes:
Thou were ful wel y-warned by thy dremes,
That thilke day was perilous to thee.
But what that god forwoot mot nedes be,
After the opinioun of certeyn clerkis.
Witnesse on him, that any perfit clerk is,
That in scole is gret altercacioun
30 In this matere, and greet disputisoun,
And hath ben of an hundred thousand men.
But I ne can not bulte it to the bren,

Sentence, matter.
Heigh imaginacioun forn-cast, predestined by divine foresight.
Wortes, herbs.   *Undern,* nine a.m.   *Scariot,* Judas.
Genilon, Ganelon, who betrayed Roland at Roncesvaux.
Sinon, who made the wooden horse at Troy.
Bulte it to the bren, sift it to the bran.

As can the holy doctour Augustyn,
Or Boëce, or the bishop Bradwardyn,
Whether that goddes worthy forwiting
Streyneth me nedely for to doon a thing,
(Nedely clepe I simple necessitee) ;
Or elles, if free choys be graunted me
To do that same thing, or do it noght,
Though god forwoot it, er that it was wroght;
Or if his witing streyneth nevere a del
10 But by necessitee condicionel.
I wol not han to do of swich matere;
My tale is of a cok, as ye may here,
That took his counseil of his wyf, with sorwe,
To walken in the yerd upon that morwe
That he had met the dreem, that I yow tolde.
Wommennes counseils been ful ofte colde;
Wommannes counseil broghte us first to wo,
And made Adam fro paradys to go,
Ther-as he was ful mery, and wel at ese.—
20 But for I noot, to whom it mighte displese,
If I counseil of wommen wolde blame,
Passe over, for I seyde it in my game.
Rede auctours, wher they trete of swich matere,
And what thay seyn of wommen ye may here.
Thise been the cokkes wordes, and nat myne;
I can noon harm of no womman divyne.—
  Fair in the sond, to bathe hir merily,
Lyth Pertelote, and alle hir sustres by,
Agayn the sonne; and Chauntecleer so free
30 Song merier than the mermayde in the see;
For Phisiologus seith sikerly,
How that they singen wel and merily.

Augustine, of Hippo, died 430.
Boëce, Boethius, author of Consolations of Philosophy, died 524.
Bradwardyn, died 1349, as Archbishop of Canterbury.
Worthy forwiting, noble foreknowledge.
Streyneth, compels.   Colde, fatal.

And so bifel that, as he caste his yë,
Among the wortes, on a boterflye,
He was war of this fox that lay ful lowe.
No-thing ne liste him thanne for to crowe,
But cryde anon, 'cok, cok,' and up he sterte,
As man that was affrayed in his herte.
For naturelly a beest desyreth flee
Fro his contrarie, if he may it see,
Though he never erst had seyn it with his yë.
10   This Chauntecleer, whan he gan him espye,
He wolde han fled, but that the fox anon
Seyde, 'Gentil sire, allas! wher wol ye gon?
Be ye affrayed of me that am your freend?
Now certes, I were worse than a feend,
If I to yow wolde harm or vileinye.
I am nat come your counseil for t'espye;
But trewely, the cause of my cominge
Was only for to herkne how that ye singe.
For trewely ye have as mery a stevene
20 As eny aungel hath, that is in hevene;
Therwith ye han in musik more felinge
Than hadde Boëce, or any that can singe.
My lord your fader (god his soule blesse!)
And eek your moder, of hir gentilesse,
Han in myn hous y-been, to my gret ese;
And certes, sire, ful fayn wolde I yow plese.
But for men speke of singing, I wol saye,
So mote I brouke wel myn eyen tweye,
Save yow, I herde never man so singe,
30 As dide your fader in the morweninge;
Certes, it was of herte, al that he song.
And for to make his voys the more strong,
He wolde so peyne him, that with bothe his yën
He moste winke, so loude he wolde cryen,
Brouke, enjoy.

And stonden on his tiptoon ther-with-al,
And strecche forth his nekke long and smal.
And eek he was of swich discrecioun,
That ther nas no man in no regioun
That him in song or wisdom mighte passe.
I have wel rad in daun Burnel the Asse,
Among his vers, how that ther was a cok,
For that a preestes sone yaf him a knok
Upon his leg, whyl he was yong and nyce,
10 He mad him for to lese his benefyce.
But certeyn, ther nis no comparisoun
Bitwix the wisdom and discrecioun
Of youre fader, and of his subtiltee.
Now singeth, sire, for seinte Charitee,
Let see, conne ye your fader countrefete?'
This Chauntecleer his winges gan to bete,
As man that coude his tresoun nat espye,
So was he ravisshed with his flaterye.
    Allas! ye lordes, many a fals flatour
20 Is in your courtes, and many a losengeour,
That plesen yow wel more, by my feith,
Than he that soothfastnesse unto yow seith.
Redeth Ecclesiaste of flaterye;
Beth war, ye lordes, of hir trecherye.
    This Chauntecleer stood hye up-on his toos,
Strecching his nekke, and heeld his eyen cloos,
And gan to crowe loude for the nones;
And daun Russel the fox sterte up at ones,
And by the gargat hente Chauntecleer,
30 And on his bak toward the wode him beer,
For yet ne was ther no man that him sewed.
O destinee, that mayst nat been eschewed!

Smal, thin.
Daun Burnel, referring to a book by Nigel Wireker from end of
12th century.   *Nyce,* foolish.   *Losengeour,* like *flatour,* flatterer.
    Gargat hente, throat seized.   *Sewed,* pursued.

Allas, that Chauntecleer fleigh fro the bemes!
Allas, his wyf ne roghte nat of dremes!
And on a Friday fil al this meschaunce.
O Venus, that art goddesse of plesaunce,
Sin that thy servant was this Chauntecleer,
And in thy service dide al his poweer,
More for delyt, than world to multiplye,
Why woldestow suffre him on thy day to dye?
O Gaufred, dere mayster soverayn,
10 That, whan thy worthy king Richard was slayn
With shot, compleynedest his deth so sore,
Why ne hadde I now thy sentence and thy lore,
The Friday for to chyde, as diden ye?
(For on a Friday soothly slayn was he.)
Than wolde I shewe yow how that I coude pleyne
For Chauntecleres drede, and for his peyne.
    Certes, swich cry ne lamentacioun
Was never of ladies maad, whan Ilioun
Was wonne, and Pirrus with his streite swerd,
20 Whan he hadde hent king Priam by the berd,
And slayn him (as saith us *Eneydos*),
As maden alle the hennes in the clos,
Whan they had seyn of Chauntecleer the sighte.
But sovereynly dame Pertelote shrighte,
Ful louder than dide Hasdrubales wyf,
Whan that hir housbond hadde lost his lyf,
And that the Romayns hadde brend Cartage;
She was so ful of torment and of rage,
That wilfully into the fyr she sterte,
30 And brende hir-selven with a stedfast herte.
O woful hennes, right so cryden ye,
As, whan that Nero brende the citee

Roghte, cared.
Gaufred, Geoffrey de Vinsauf in his *Nova Poetria,* written soon
after Richard I died.   *Brend,* burned.

Of Rome, cryden senatoures wyves,
For that hir housbondes losten alle hir lyves;
Withouten gilt this Nero hath hem slayn.
Now wol I torne to my tale agayn:—
   This sely widwe, and eek hir doghtres two,
Herden thise hennes crye and maken wo,
And out at dores sterten they anoon,
And syen the fox toward the grove goon,
And bar upon his bak the cok away;
10 And cryden, 'Out! harrow! and weylaway!
Ha, ha, the fox!' and after him they ran,
And eek with staves many another man;
Ran Colle our dogge, and Talbot, and Gerland,
And Malkin, with a distaf in hir hand;
Ran cow and calf, and eek the verray hogges
So were they fered for berking of the dogges
And shouting of the men and wimmen eke,
They ronne so, hem thoughte hir herte breke.
They yelleden as feendes doon in helle;
20 The dokes cryden as men wolde hem quelle;
The gees for fere flowen over the trees;
Out of the hyve cam the swarm of bees;
So hidous was the noyse, a! *benedicite!*
Certes, he Jakke Straw, and his meynee,
Ne made never shoutes half so shrille,
Whan that they wolden any Fleming kille,
As thilke day was maad upon the fox.
Of bras thay broghten bemes, and of box,
Of horn, of boon, in whiche they blewe and pouped,
30 And therwithal thay shryked and they houped;
It seemed as that heven sholde falle.
Now, gode men, I pray yow herkneth alle!

   Sely, simple.   *Quelle,* kill.
   Jakke Straw and his meynee, Jack Straw and his crew, in
Peasants' Revolt of 1381.
   Bemes, trumpets.

Lo, how fortune turneth sodeinly
The hope and pryde eek of hir enemy!
This cok, that lay upon the foxes bak,
In al his drede, un-to the fox he spak,
And seyde, 'sire, if that I were as ye,
Yet sholde I seyn (as wis god helpe me),
Turneth agayn, ye proude cherles alle!
A verray pestilence up-on yow falle!
Now am I come un-to this wodes syde,
10 Maugree your heed, the cok shal heer abyde;
I wol him ete in feith, and that anon.'—
The fox answerde, 'in feith, it shal be don,'—
And as he spak that word, al sodeinly
This cok brak from his mouth deliverly,
And heighe up-on a tree he fleigh anon.
And whan the fox saugh that he was y-gon,
'Allas!' quod he, 'O Chauntecleer, allas!
I have to yow,' quod he, 'y-doon trespas,
In-as-muche as I maked yow aferd,
20 Whan I yow hente, and broghte out of the yerd;
But, sire, I dide it in no wikke entente;
Com doun, and I shal telle yow what I mente.
I shal seye sooth to yow, god help me so.'
'Nay than,' quod he, 'I shrewe us bothe two,
And first I shrewe my-self, bothe blood and bones,
If thou bigyle me ofter than ones.
Thou shalt na-more, thurgh thy flaterye,
Do me to singe and winke with myn yë.
For he that winketh, whan he sholde see,
30 Al wilfully, god lat him never thee!'
'Nay,' quod the fox, 'but god yeve him meschaunce,
That is so undiscreet of governaunce,
That jangleth whan he sholde holde his pees.'
Lo, swich it is for to be recchelees,

Maugree, in spite of.   *Deliverly,* nimbly.
Shrewe, curse.   *Thee,* thrive.

And necligent, and truste on flaterye.
But ye that holden this tale a folye,
As of a fox, or of a cok and hen,
Taketh the moralitee, good men.
For seint Paul seith, that al that writen is,
To our doctryne it is y-write, y-wis.
Taketh the fruyt, and lat the chaf be stille.
  Now, gode god, if that it be thy wille,
As seith my lord, so make us alle good men;
10 And bringe us to his heighe blisse. Amen.

THE PARDONER'S TALE

  'Thou bel amy, thou Pardoner,' he seyde,
'Tel us som mirthe or japes right anon.'
'It shall be doon,' quod he, 'by seint Ronyon!
But first,' quod he, 'heer at this ale-stake
I wol both drinke, and eten of a cake.'
  But right anon thise gentils gonne to crye,
'Nay! lat him telle us of no ribaudye;
Tel us som moral thing, that we may lere
Som wit, and thanne wol we gladly here.'
20 'I graunte, y-wis,' quod he, 'but I mot thinke
Up-on som honest thing, whyl that I drinke.'

  *Radix malorum est Cupiditas: Ad Thimotheum,
sexto.*

  'LORDINGS,' quod he, 'in chirches whan I preche,
I peyne me to han an hauteyn speche,
And ringe it out as round as gooth a belle,
For I can al by rote that I telle.

  Thou bel amy, the Host is speaking after the *Physician's Tale*
has ended.
  Heer at this ale-stake, referring to the garland on the head of the
Summoner, who also was carrying a cake like a buckler.
  Y-wis, to be sure.

My theme is alwey oon, and ever was—
"*Radix malorum est Cupiditas.*"
First I pronounce whennes that I come,
And than my bulles shewe I, alle and somme.
Our lige lordes seel on my patente,
That shewe I first, my body to warente,
That no man be so bold, ne preest ne clerk,
Me to destourbe of Cristes holy werk;
And after that than telle I forth my tales.
10 Bulles of popes and of cardinales,
Of patriarkes, and bishoppes I shewe;
And in Latyn I speke a wordes fewe,
To saffron with my predicacioun,
And for to stire men to devocioun.
Than shewe I forth my longe cristal stones,
Y-crammed ful of cloutes and of bones;
Reliks been they, as wenen they echoon.
Than have I in latoun a sholder-boon
Which that was of an holy Jewes shepe.
20 "Good men," seye I, "tak of my wordes kepe;
If that this boon be wasshe in any welle,
If cow, or calf, or sheep, or oxe swelle
That any worm hath ete, or worm y-stonge,
Tak water of that welle, and wash his tonge,
And it is hool anon; and forthermore,
Of pokkes and of scabbe, and every sore
Shal every sheep be hool, that of this welle
Drinketh a draughte; tak kepe eek what I telle.
If that the good-man, that the bestes oweth,
30 Wol every wike, er that the cok him croweth,
Fastinge, drinken of this welle a draughte,
As thilke holy Jewe our eldres taughte,

My theme, text. He starts a sermon on avarice, but in his
befuddled state frequently wanders.
Lige lordes, the bishop's seal.
Bulles of popes, etc., a drunken expansion. *Saffron,* flavor.
Cristal stones, glass receptacles. *Oweth,* owns.

His bestes and his stoor shal multiplye.
And, sirs, also it heleth jalousye;
For, though a man be falle in jalous rage,
Let maken with this water his potage,
And never shal he more his wyf mistriste,
Though he the sooth of hir defaute wiste;
Al had she taken preestes two or three.
  Heer is a miteyn eek, that ye may see.
He that his hond wol putte in this miteyn,
10 He shal have multiplying of his greyn,
Whan he hath sowen, be it whete or otes,
So that he offre pens, or elles grotes.
  Good men and wommen, o thing warne I **yow,**
If any wight be in this chirche now,
That hath doon sinne horrible, that he
Dar nat, for shame, of it y-shriven be,
Or any womman, be she yong or old,
That hath y-maad hir housbond cokewold,
Swich folk shul have no power ne no **grace**
20 To offren to my reliks in this place.
And who-so findeth him out of swich blame,
He wol com up and offre in goddes name,
And I assoille him by the auctoritee
Which that by bulle y-graunted was to me."
  By this gaude have I wonne, yeer by **yeer,**
An hundred mark sith I was Pardoner.
I stonde lyk a clerk in my pulpet,
And whan the lewed peple is doun **y-set,**
I preche, so as ye han herd bifore,
30 And telle an hundred false japes more.
Than peyne I me to strecche forth the **nekke,**
And est and west upon the peple I **bekke,**
As doth a dowve sitting on a berne.
Myn hondes and my tonge goon so **yerne,**

Gaude, trickery.   *Assoille,* absolve.
Japes, falsities.   *Bekke,* nod.   *Yerne,* quickly.

That it is joye to see my bisinesse.
Of avaryce and of swich cursednesse
Is al my preching, for to make hem free
To yeve her pens, and namely un-to me.
For my entente is nat but for to winne,
And no-thing for correccioun of sinne.
I rekke never, whan that they ben beried,
Though that her soules goon a-blakeberied!
For certes, many a predicacioun
10 Comth ofte tyme of yvel entencioun;
Som for plesaunce of folk and flaterye,
To been avaunced by ipocrisye,
And som for veyne glorie, and som for hate.
For, whan I dar non other weyes debate,
Than wol I stinge him with my tonge smerte
In preching, so that he shal nat asterte
To been defamed falsly, if that he
Hath trespased to my brethren or to me.
For, though I telle noght his propre name,
20 Men shal wel knowe that it is the same
By signes and by othere circumstances.
Thus quyte I folk that doon us displesances;
Thus spitte I out my venim under hewe
Of holynesse, to seme holy and trewe.
  But shortly myn entente I wol devyse;
I preche of no-thing but for coveityse.
Therfor my theme is yet, and ever was—
"*Radix malorum est cupiditas.*"
Thus can I preche agayn that same vyce
30 Which that I use, and that is avaryce.
But, though my-self be gilty in that sinne,
Yet can I maken other folk to twinne
From avaryce, and sore to repente.
But that is nat my principal entente.

A-blakeberied, blackberrying, probably current slang.
Asterte, escape.   *Devyse,* tell.   *Twinne,* depart.

I preche no-thing but for coveityse;
Of this matere it oughte y-nogh suffyse.
Than telle I hem ensamples many oon
Of olde stories, longe tyme agoon:
For lewed peple loven tales olde;
Swich thinges can they wel reporte and holde.
What? trowe ye, the whyles I may preche,
And winne gold and silver for I teche,
That I wol live in povert wilfully?
10 Nay, nay, I thoghte it never trewely!
For I wol preche and begge in sondry londes;
I wol not do no labour with myn hondes,
Ne make baskettes, and live therby,
Because I wol nat beggen ydelly.
I wol non of the apostles counterfete;
I wol have money, wolle, chese, and whete,
Al were it yeven of the povrest page,
Or of the povrest widwe in a village,
Al sholde hir children sterve for famyne.
20 Nay! I wol drinke licour of the vyne,
And have a joly wenche in every toun.
But herkneth, lordings, in conclusioun;
Your lyking is that I shal telle a tale.
Now, have I dronke a draughte of corny ale,
By god, I hope I shal yow telle a thing
That shal, by resoun, been at your lyking.
For, though myself be a ful vicious man,
A moral tale yet I yow telle can,
Which I am wont to preche, for to winne.
30 Now holde your pees, my tale I wol beginne.

In Flaundres whylom was a companye
Of yonge folk, that haunteden folye,

Ensamples, examples, illustrative stories, were an ordinary part
of sermons.   *Sterve*, die.

As ryot, hasard, stewes, and tavernes,
Wher-as, with harpes, lutes, and giternes,
They daunce and pleye at dees bothe day and night,
And ete also and drinken over hir might,
Thurgh which they doon the devel sacrifyse
With-in that develes temple, in cursed wyse,
By superfluitee abhominable;
Hir othes been so grete and so dampnable,
That it is grisly for to here hem swere;
10 Our blissed lordes body they to-tere;
Hem thoughte Jewes rente him noght y-nough;
And ech of hem at otheres sinne lough.
And right anon than comen tombesteres
Fetys and smale, and yonge fruytesteres,
Singers with harpes, baudes, wafereres,
Whiche been the verray develes officeres
To kindle and blowe the fyr of lecherye,
That is annexed un-to glotonye;
The holy writ take I to my witnesse,
20 That luxurie is in wyn and dronkenesse.
  Lo, how that dronken Loth, unkindely,
Lay by his doghtres two, unwitingly;
So dronke he was, he niste what he wroghte.
  Herodes, (who-so wel the stories soghte,)
Whan he of wyn was replet at his feste,
Right at his owene table he yaf his heste
To sleen the Baptist John ful giltelees.
  Senek seith eek a good word doutelees;
He seith, he can no difference finde
30 Bitwix a man that is out of his minde
And a man which that is dronkelewe,
But that woodnesse, y-fallen in a shrewe,

Giternes, cithern, like a guitar.   *Lough,* laughed.
Tombesteres, female acrobats.
Fetys and smale, graceful and slender.
Wafereres, cake-makers. *Luxurie,* lust. *Heste,* command.
Dronkelewe, drunken.   *Woodnesse,* insanity.

Persevereth lenger than doth dronkenesse.
O glotonye, ful of cursednesse,
O cause first of our confusioun,
O original of our dampnacioun,
Til Crist had boght us with his blood agayn!
Lo, how dere, shortly for to sayn,
Aboght was thilke cursed vileinye;
Corrupt was al this world for glotonye!
Adam our fader, and his wyf also,
10 Fro Paradys to labour and to wo
Were driven for that vyce, it is no drede;
For whyl that Adam fasted, as I rede,
He was in Paradys; and whan that he
Eet of the fruyt defended on the tree,
Anon he was out-cast to wo and peyne.
O glotonye, on thee wel oghte us pleyne!
O, wiste a man how many maladyes
Folwen of excesse and of glotonyes,
He wolde been the more mesurable
20 Of his diete, sittinge at his table.
Allas! the shorte throte, the tendre mouth,
Maketh that, Est and West, and North and South,
In erthe, in eir, in water men to-swinke
To gete a glotoun deyntee mete and drinke!
Of this matere, o Paul, wel canstow trete,
'Mete un-to wombe, and wombe eek un-to mete,
Shal god destroyen bothe,' as Paulus seith.
Allas! a foul thing is it, by my feith,
To seye this word, and fouler is the dede,
30 Whan man so drinketh of the whyte and rede,
That of his throte he maketh his privee,
Thurgh thilke cursed superfluitee.
The apostel weping seith ful pitously,
'Ther walken many of whiche yow told have I,

No drede, no doubt.   Defended, forbidden.
Apostel weping, a good example of drunken histrionic fervor.

I seye it now weping with pitous voys,
[That] they been enemys of Cristes croys,
Of whiche the ende is deeth, wombe is her god.'
O wombe! O bely! O stinking cod,
Fulfild of donge and of corrupcioun!
At either ende of thee foul is the soun.
How greet labour and cost is thee to finde!
Thise cokes, how they stampe, and streyne, and
    grinde,
And turnen substaunce in-to accident,
10 To fulfille al thy likerous talent!
Out of the harde bones knokke they
The mary, for they caste noght a-wey
That may go thurgh the golet softe and swote;
Of spicerye, of leef, and bark, and rote
Shal been his sauce y-maked by delyt,
To make him yet a newer appetyt.
But certes, he that haunteth swich delyces
Is deed, whyl that he liveth in tho vyces.
    A lecherous thing is wyn, and dronkenesse
20 Is ful of stryving and of wrecchednesse.
O dronke man, disfigured is thy face,
Sour is thy breeth, foul artow to embrace,
And thurgh thy dronke nose semeth the soun
As though thou seydest ay 'Sampsoun, Sampsoun';
And yet, god wot, Sampsoun drank never no wyn.
Thou fallest, as it were a stiked swyn;
Thy tonge is lost, and al thyn honest cure;
For dronkenesse is verray sepulture
Of mannes wit and his discrecioun.
30 In whom that drinke hath dominacioun,
He can no conseil kepe, it is no drede.
Now kepe yow fro the whyte and fro the rede,

To finde, provide for.
Substaunce, etc., a travesty on the scholastic theory of reality.
Likerous talent, wanton appetite.
Stiked swyn, stuck pig.   *Honest cure,* care for decency.

And namely fro the whyte wyn of Lepe,
That is to selle in Fish-strete or in Chepe.
This wyn of Spayne crepeth subtilly
In othere wynes, growing faste by,
Of which ther ryseth swich fumositee,
That whan a man hath dronken draughtes three,
And weneth that he be at hoom in Chepe,
He is in Spayne, right at the toune of Lepe,
Nat at the Rochel, ne at Burdeux toun;
10 And thanne wol he seye, 'Sampsoun, Sampsoun.'
But herkneth, lordings, o word, I yow preye,
That alle the sovereyn actes, dar I seye,
Of victories in th' olde testament,
Thurgh verray god, that is omnipotent,
Were doon in abstinence and in preyere;
Loketh the Bible, and ther ye may it lere.
Loke, Attila, the grete conquerour,
Deyde in his sleep, with shame and dishonour,
Bledinge ay at his nose in dronkenesse;
20 A capitayn shoulde live in sobrenesse.
And over al this, avyseth yow right wel
What was comaunded un-to Lamuel—
Nat Samuel, but Lamuel, seye I—
Redeth the Bible, and finde it expresly
Of wyn-yeving to hem that han justyse.
Na-more of this, for it may wel suffyse.
And now that I have spoke of glotonye,
Now wol I yow defenden hasardrye.
Hasard is verray moder of lesinges,
30 And of deceite, and cursed forsweringes,
Blaspheme of Crist, manslaughtre, and wast also
Of catel and of tyme; and forthermo,

Lepe, near Cadiz.   *Chepe,* Cheapside.
Fumositee, vaporous fumes.
Attila, whose story is not in the Bible, as in soberer moments
the Pardoner knew.   *Wyn-yeving,* see *Proverbs* xxxi, 4, 5.
Defenden hasardrye, speak against gaming.   *Lesinges,* lies.

It is repreve and contrarie of honour
For to ben holde a commune hasardour.
And ever the hyër he is of estaat,
The more is he holden desolaat.
If that a prince useth hasardrye,
In alle governaunce and policye
He is, as by commune opinioun,
Y-holde the lasse in reputacioun.
 Stilbon, that was a wys embassadour,
10 Was sent to Corinthe, in ful greet honour,
Fro Lacidomie, to make hir alliaunce.
And whan he cam, him happede, par chaunce,
That alle the grettest that were of that lond,
Pleyinge atte hasard he hem fond.
For which, as sone as it mighte be,
He stal him hoom agayn to his contree,
And seyde, 'ther wol I nat lese my name;
Ne I wol nat take on me so greet defame,
Yow for to allye un-to none hasardours.
20 Sendeth othere wyse embassadours;
For, by my trouthe, me were lever dye,
Than I yow sholde to hasardours allye.
For ye that been so glorious in honours
Shul nat allyen yow with hasardours
As by my wil, ne as by my tretee.'
This wyse philosophre thus seyde he.
 Loke eek that, to the king Demetrius
The king of Parthes, as the book seith us,
Sente him a paire of dees of gold in scorn,
30 For he hadde used hasard ther-biforn;
For which he heeld his glorie or his renoun
At no value or reputacioun.
Lordes may finden other maner pley
Honeste y-nough to dryve the day awey.

Repreve, reproach.
Stilbon, Chaucer's mistake for Chilon.

Now wol I speke of othes false and grete
A word or two, as olde bokes trete.
Gret swering is a thing abhominable,
And false swering is yet more reprevable.
The heighe god forbad swering at al,
Witnesse on Mathew; but in special
Of swering seith the holy Jeremye,
'Thou shalt seye sooth thyn othes, and nat lye,
And swere in dome, and eek in rightwisnesse;'
10 But ydel swering is a cursednesse.
Bihold and see, that in the firste table
Of heighe goddes hestes honurable,
How that the seconde heste of him is this—
'Tak nat my name in ydel or amis.'
Lo, rather he forbedeth swich swering
Than homicyde or many a cursed thing;
I seye that, as by ordre, thus it stondeth;
This knowen, that his hestes understondeth,
How that the second heste of god is that.
20 And forther over, I wol thee telle al plat,
That vengeance shal nat parten from his hous,
That of his othes is to outrageous.
'By goddes precious herte, and by his nayles,
And by the blode of Crist, that it is in Hayles,
Seven is my chaunce, and thyn is cink and treye;
By goddes armes, if thou falsly pleye,
This dagger shal thurgh-out thyn herte go'—
This fruyt cometh of the bicched bones two,

In dome, with soberness.
Firste table . . . hestes, since the Ten Commandments were divided into two sets, one referring to duties to God, the other to men.   *Rather,* earlier, sooner.   *Plat,* flatly.
   Nayles, referring either to the nails that pierced hands and feet, or to Christ's own nails.   Both oaths were used.
   Hayles, the Abbey of Hales in Gloucestershire, given some of the blood in the 13th century.
   Seven is my chaunce, etc., refers to hazard, the ancestor of craps.
Bicched bones, cursed dice.

Forswering, ire, falsnesse, homicyde.
Now, for the love of Crist that for us dyde,
Leveth your othes, bothe grete and smale;
But, sirs, now wòl I telle forth my tale.

THISE ryotoures three, of whiche I telle,
Longe erst er pryme rong of any belle,
Were set hem in a taverne for to drinke;
And as they satte, they herde a belle clinke
Biforn a cors, was caried to his grave;
10 That oon of hem gan callen to his knave,
'Go bet,' quod he, 'and axe redily,
What cors is this that passeth heer forby;
And look that thou reporte his name wel.'
'Sir,' quod this boy, 'it nedeth never-a-del.
It was me told, er ye cam heer, two houres;
He was, pardee, an old felawe of youres;
And sodeynly he was y-slayn to-night,
For-dronke, as he sat on his bench upright;
Ther cam a privee theef, men clepeth Deeth,
20 That in this contree al the peple sleeth,
And with his spere he smoot his herte a-two,
And wente his wey with-outen wordes mo.
He hath a thousand slayn this pestilence:
And, maister, er ye come in his presence,
Me thinketh that it were necessarie
For to be war of swich an adversarie:
Beth redy for to mete him evermore.
Thus taughte me my dame, I sey na-more.'
'By seinte Marie,' seyde this taverner,
30 'The child seith sooth, for he hath slayn this yeer,
Henne over a myle, with-in a greet village,
Both man and womman, child and hyne, and page.

Erst er pryme rong, before nine o'clock.
Knave, boy, servant.   *Go bet,* go quickly.
Pardee, truly.   *To-night,* last night.
Henne over, more than a mile hence.   *Hyne,* laborer.

I trowe his habitacioun be there;
To been avysed greet wisdom it were,
Er that he dide a man a dishonour.'
'Ye, goddes armes,' quod this ryotour,
'Is it swich peril with him for to mete?
I shal him seke by wey and eek by strete,
I make avow to goddes digne bones!
Herkneth, felawes, we three been al ones;
Lat ech of us holde up his hond til other,
10 And ech of us bicomen otheres brother,
And we wol sleen this false traytour Deeth;
He shal be slayn, which that so many sleeth,
By goddes dignitee, er it be night.'
　Togidres han thise three her trouthes plight,
To live and dyen ech of hem for other,
As though he were his owene y-boren brother.
And up they sterte al dronken, in this rage,
And forth they goon towardes that village,
Of which the taverner had spoke biforn,
20 And many a grisly ooth than han they sworn,
And Cristes blessed body they to-rente—
'Deeth shal be deed, if that they may him hente.'
　Whan they han goon nat fully half a myle,
Right as they wolde han troden over a style,
An old man and a povre with hem mette.
This olde man ful mekely hem grette,
And seyde thus, 'now, lordes, god yow see!'
The proudest of thise ryotoures three
Answerde agayn, 'what? carl, with sory grace,
30 Why artow al forwrapped save thy face?
Why livestow so longe in so greet age?'
　This olde man gan loke in his visage,

Al ones, in agreement.
Otheres brother, the oath of brotherhood being a most sacred one.
God yow see! God preserve you.
Carl, with sory grace, as if to say, "Damn it, man!"

And seyde thus, 'for I ne can nat finde
A man, though that I walked in-to Inde,
Neither in citee nor in no village,
That wolde chaunge his youthe for myn age;
And therfore moot I han myn age stille,
As longe time as it is goddes wille.
   Ne deeth, allas! ne wol nat han my lyf;
Thus walke I, lyk a restelees caityf,
And on the ground, which is my modres gate,
10 I knokke with my staf, bothe erly and late,
And seye, "leve moder, leet me in!
Lo, how I vanish, flesh, and blood, and skin!
Allas! whan shul my bones been at reste?
Moder, with yow wolde I chaunge my cheste,
That in my chambre longe tyme hath be,
Ye! for an heyre clout to wrappe me!"
But yet to me she wol nat do that grace,
For which ful pale and welked is my face.
   But, sirs, to yow it is no curteisye
20 To speken to an old man vileinye,
But he trespasse in worde, or elles in dede.
In holy writ ye may your-self wel rede,
"Agayns an old man, hoor upon his heed,
Ye sholde aryse;" wherfor I yeve yow reed,
Ne dooth un-to an old man noon harm now,
Na-more than ye wolde men dide to yow
In age, if that ye so longe abyde;
And god be with yow, wher ye go or ryde.
I moot go thider as I have to go.'
30   'Nay, olde cherl, by god, thou shalt nat so,'
Seyde this other hasardour anon;
'Thou partest nat so lightly, by seint John!

Caityf, wretch.
Cheste, box for clothes, *etc.,* which he would exchange for a
shroud of hair-cloth.
Welked, withered.   *Reed,* advice.

Thou spak right now of thilke traitour Deeth,
That in this contree alle our frendes sleeth.
Have heer my trouthe, as thou art his aspye,
Tel wher he is, or thou shalt it abye,
By god, and by the holy sacrament!
For soothly thou art oon of his assent,
To sleen us yonge folk, thou false theef!'
   'Now, sirs,' quod he, 'if that yow be so leef
To finde Deeth, turne up this croked wey,
10 For in that grove I lafte him, by my fey,
Under a tree, and ther he wol abyde;
Nat for your boost he wol him no-thing hyde.
See ye that ook? right ther ye shul him finde.
God save yow, that boghte agayn mankinde,
And yow amende!'—thus seyde this olde man.
And everich of thise ryotoures ran,
Til he cam to that tree, and ther they founde
Of florins fyne of golde y-coyned rounde
Wel ny an eighte busshels, as hem thoughte.
20 No lenger thanne after Deeth they soughte,
But ech of hem so glad was of that sighte,
For that the florins been so faire and brighte,
That doun they sette hem by this precious hord.
The worste of hem he spake the firste word.
   'Brethren,' quod he, 'tak kepe what I seye;
My wit is greet, though that I bourde and pleye.
This tresor hath fortune un-to us yiven,
In mirthe and jolitee our lyf to liven,
And lightly as it comth, so wol we spende.
30 Ey! goddes precious dignitee! who wende
To-day, that we sholde han so fair a grace?
But mighte this gold be caried fro this place
Hoom to myn hous, or elles un-to youres—
For wel ye woot that al this gold is oures—

Thilke, this same.	*Abye,* pay for it.	*Fey,* faith.
Bourde, jest.	*Wende,* thought.	

Than were we in heigh felicitee.
But trewely, by daye it may nat be;
Men wolde seyn that we were theves stronge,
And for our owene tresor doon us honge.
This tresor moste y-caried be by nighte
As wysly and as slyly as it mighte.
Wherfore I rede that cut among us alle
Be drawe, and lat see wher the cut wol falle;
And he that hath the cut with herte blythe
10 Shal renne to the toune, and that ful swythe,
And bringe us breed and wyn ful prively.
And two of us shul kepen subtilly
This tresor wel; and, if he wol nat tarie,
Whan it is night, we wol this tresor carie
By oon assent, wher-as us thinketh best.'
That oon of hem the cut broughte in his fest,
And bad hem drawe, and loke wher it wol falle;
And it fil on the yongeste of hem alle;
And forth toward the toun he wente anon.
20 And al-so sone as that he was gon,
That oon of hem spak thus un-to that other,
'Thou knowest wel thou art my sworne brother,
Thy profit wol I telle thee anon.
Thou woost wel that our felawe is agon;
And heer is gold, and that ful greet plentee,
That shal departed been among us three.
But natheles, if I can shape it so
That it departed were among us two,
Hadde I nat doon a freendes torn to thee?'
30 That other answerde, 'I noot how that may be;
He woot how that the gold is with us tweye.
What shal we doon, what shal we to him seye?'
    'Shal it be conseil?' seyde the firste shrewe,
'And I shal tellen thee, in wordes fewe,

Swythe, quickly.   *Shrewe,* rascal.

What we shal doon, and bringe it wel aboute.'
'I graunte,' quod that other, 'out of doute,
That, by my trouthe, I wol thee nat biwreye.'
'Now,' quod the firste, 'thou woost wel we be tweye,
And two of us shul strenger be than oon.
Look whan that he is set, and right anoon
Arys, as though thou woldest with him pleye;
And I shal ryve him thurgh the sydes tweye
Whyl that thou strogelest with him as in game,
10 And with thy dagger look thou do the same;
And than shal al this gold departed be,
My dere freend, bitwixen me and thee;
Than may we bothe our lustes al fulfille,
And pleye at dees right at our owene wille.'
And thus acorded been thise shrewes tweye
To sleen the thridde, as ye han herd me seye.
    This yongest, which that wente un-to the toun,
Ful ofte in herte he rolleth up and doun
The beautee of thise florins newe and brighte.
20 'O lord!' quod he, 'if so were that I mighte
Have al this tresor to my-self allone,
Ther is no man that liveth under the trone
Of god, that sholde live so mery as I!'
And atte laste the feend, our enemy,
Putte in his thought that he shold poyson beye,
With which he mighte sleen his felawes tweye;
For-why the feend fond him in swich lyvinge,
That he had leve him to sorwe bringe,
For this was outrely his fulle entente
30 To sleen hem bothe, and never to repente.
And forth he gooth, no lenger wolde he tarie,
Into the toun, un-to a pothecarie,
And preyed him, that he him wolde selle
Som poyson, that he mighte his rattes quelle;

Ryve, stab.   *Outrely,* utterly.

And eek ther was a polcat in his hawe,
That, as he seyde, his capouns hadde y-slawe,
And fayn he wolde wreke him, if he mighte,
On vermin, that destroyed him by nighte.
   The pothecarie answerde, 'and thou shalt have
A thing that, al-so god my soule save,
In al this world ther nis no creature,
That ete or dronke hath of this confiture
Noght but the mountance of a corn of whete,
10 That he ne shal his lyf anon forlete;
Ye, sterve he shal, and that in lasse whyle
Than thou wolt goon a paas nat but a myle;
This poyson is so strong and violent.'
   This cursed man hath in his hond y-hent
This poyson in a box, and sith he ran
In-to the nexte strete, un-to a man,
And borwed [of] him large botels three;
And in the two his poyson poured he;
The thridde he kepte clene for his drinke.
20 For al the night he shoop him for to swinke
In caryinge of the gold out of that place.
And whan this ryotour, with sory grace,
Had filled with wyn his grete botels three,
To his felawes agayn repaireth he.
   What nedeth it to sermone of it more?
For right as they had cast his deeth bifore,
Right so they han him slayn, and that anon.
And whan that this was doon, thus spak that oon,
'Now lat us sitte and drinke, and make us merie,
30 And afterward we wol his body berie.'
And with that word it happed him, par cas,
To take the botel ther the poyson was,

Hawe, yard.	*Destroyed,* troubled.
Al-so, as.	*Confiture,* mixture.
Forlete, lose.	*Sterve,* die.
A paas nat but, at a walk no more than.	
Shoop, planned.	*Cast,* planned.

And drank, and yaf his felawe drinke also,
For which anon they storven bothe two.
    But, certes, I suppose that Avicen
Wroot never in no canon, ne in no fen,
Mo wonder signes of empoisoning
Than hadde thise wrecches two, er hir ending.
Thus ended been thise homicydes two,
And eek the false empoysoner also.

    O cursed sinne, ful of cursednesse!
10 O traytours homicyde, o wikkednesse!
O glotonye, luxurie, and hasardrye!
Thou blasphemour of Crist with vileinye
And othes grete, of usage and of pryde!
Allas! mankinde, how may it bityde,
That to thy creatour which that thee wroughte,
And with his precious herte-blood thee boghte,
Thou art so fals and so unkinde, allas!
    Now, goode men, god forgeve yow your trespas,
And ware yow fro the sinne of avaryce.
20 Myn holy pardoun may yow alle waryce,
So that ye offre nobles or sterlinges,
Or elles silver broches, spones, ringes.
Boweth your heed under this holy bulle!
Cometh up, ye wyves, offreth of your wolle!
Your name I entre heer in my rolle anon;
In-to the blisse of hevene shul ye gon;
I yow assoile, by myn heigh power,
Yow that wol offre, as clene and eek as cleer
As ye were born; and, lo, sirs, thus I preche.
30 And Jesu Crist, that is our soules leche,
So graunte yow his pardon to receyve;
For that is best; I wol yow nat deceyve.

Avicen, Avicenna, the Arab physician, who used *canon* in sense
of rule of practice, and *fen* for a division of his book.
    Waryce, cure.   *Nobles or sterlinges,* silver coins.

But sirs, o word forgat I in my tale,
I have relikes and pardon in my male,
As faire as any man in Engelond,
Whiche were me yeven by the popes hond.
If any of yow wol, of devocioun,
Offren, and han myn absolucioun,
Cometh forth anon, and kneleth heer adoun,
And mekely receyveth my pardoun:
Or elles, taketh pardon as ye wende,
10 Al newe and fresh, at every tounes ende,
So that ye offren alwey newe and newe
Nobles and pens, which that be gode and trewe.
It is an honour to everich that is heer,
That ye mowe have a suffisant pardoneer
T'assoille yow, in contree as ye ryde,
For aventures which that may bityde.
Peraventure ther may falle oon or two
Doun of his hors, and breke his nekke atwo.
Look which a seuretee is it to yow alle
20 That I am in your felaweship y-falle,
That may assoille yow, bothe more and lasse,
Whan that the soule shal fro the body passe.
I rede that our hoste heer shal biginne,
For he is most envoluped in sinne.
Com forth, sir hoste, and offre first anon,
And thou shalt kisse the reliks everichon,
Ye, for a grote! unbokel anon thy purs.'

THE FRANKLIN'S TALE

'In feith, Squier, thou hast thee wel y-quit,
And gentilly I preise wel thy wit,'

Male, bag.
Squier, who had just been telling a story left unfinished by
Chaucer.

Quod the Frankeleyn, 'considering thy youthe,
So feelingly thou spekest, sir, I allow the!
As to my doom, there is non that is here
Of eloquence that shal be thy pere,
If that thou live; god yeve thee good chaunce,
And in vertu sende thee continuaunce!
For of thy speche I have greet deyntee.
I have a sone, and, by the Trinitee,
I hadde lever than twenty pound worth lond,
10 Though it right now were fallen in myn hond,
He were a man of swich discrecioun
As that ye been! fy on possessioun
But-if a man be vertuous with-al.
I have my sone snibbed, and yet shal,
For he to vertu listeth nat entende;
But for to pleye at dees, and to despende,
And lese al that he hath, is his usage.
And he hath lever talken with a page
Than to comune with any gentil wight
20 Ther he mighte lerne gentillesse aright.'
    'Straw for your gentillesse,' quod our host;
'What, frankeleyn? pardee, sir, wel thou wost
That eche of yow mot tellen atte leste
A tale or two, or breken his biheste.'
    'That knowe I wel, sir,' quod the frankeleyn;
'I prey yow, haveth me nat in desdeyn
Though to this man I speke a word or two.'
    'Telle on thy tale with-outen wordes mo.'
'Gladly, sir host,' quod he, 'I wol obeye
30 Un-to your wil; now herkneth what I seye.
I wol yow nat contrarien in no wyse
As fer as that my wittes wol suffyse;
I prey to god that it may plesen yow,
Than woot I wel that it is good y-now.'

Allow the, commend thee.　　　*Doom,* judgment.
Deyntee, pleasure.　　　*Snibbed,* reproved.

Thise olde gentil Britons in hir dayes
Of diverse aventures maden layes,
Rymeyed in hir firste Briton tonge;
Which layes with hir instruments they songe,
Or elles redden hem for hir plesaunce;
And oon of hem have I in remembraunce,
Which I shal seyn with good wil as I can.
But, sires, by-cause I am a burel man,
At my biginning first I yow biseche
10 Have me excused of my rude speche;
I lerned never rethoryk certeyn;
Thing that I speke, it moot be bare and pleyn.
I sleep never on the mount of Pernaso,
Ne lerned Marcus Tullius Cithero,
Colours ne knowe I none, with-outen drede,
But swiche colours as growen in the mede,
Or elles swiche as men dye or peynte.
Colours of rethoryk ben me to queynte;
My spirit feleth noght of swich matere.
20 But if yow list, my tale shul ye here.

In Armorik, that called is Britayne,
Ther was a knight that loved and dide his payne
To serve a lady in his beste wyse;
And many a labour, many a greet empryse
He for his lady wroghte, er she were wonne.
For she was oon, the faireste under sonne,
And eek therto come of so heigh kinrede,
That wel unnethes dorste this knight, for drede,
Telle hir his wo, his peyne, and his distresse.
30 But atte laste, she, for his worthinesse,
And namely for his meke obeysaunce,
Hath swich a pitee caught of his penaunce,

Burel, rude and uneducated.   Colours, rhetorical figures
Queynte, strange.   Armorik, Brittany.
Empryse, undertaking.   Wel uhnethes, scarcely.

That prively she fil of his accord
To take him for hir housbonde and hir lord,
Of swich lordshipe as men han over hir wyves;
And for to lede the more in blisse hir lyves,
Of his free wil he swoor hir as a knight,
That never in al his lyf he, day ne night,
Ne sholde up-on him take no maistrye
Agayn hir wil, ne kythe hir jalousye,
But hir obeye, and folwe hir wil in al
10 As any lovere to his lady shal;
Save that the name of soveraynetee,
That wolde he have for shame of his degree.
She thanked him, and with ful greet humblesse
She seyde, 'sire, sith of your gentillesse
Ye profre me to have so large a reyne,
Ne wolde never god bitwixe us tweyne,
As in my gilt, were outher werre or stryf.
Sir, I wol be your humble trewe wyf,
Have heer my trouthe, til that myn herte breste.'
20 Thus been they bothe in quiete and in reste.
For o thing, sires, saufly dar I seye,
That frendes everich other moot obeye,
If they wol longe holden companye.
Love wol nat ben constreyned by maistrye;
Whan maistrie comth, the god of love anon
Beteth hise winges, and farewel! he is gon!
Love is a thing as any spirit free;
Wommen of kinde desiren libertee,
And nat to ben constreyned as a thral;
30 And so don men, if I soth seyen shal.
Loke who that is most pacient in love,
He is at his avantage al above.
Pacience is an heigh vertu certeyn;
For it venquisseth, as thise clerkes seyn,

Kythe, show.   *As in my gilt,* through my fault.
Of kinde, by nature.

Thinges that rigour sholde never atteyne.
For every word men may nat chyde or pleyne.
Lerneth to suffre, or elles, so moot I goon,
Ye shul it lerne, wher-so ye wole or noon.
For in this world, certein, ther no wight is,
That he ne dooth or seith som-tyme amis.
Ire, siknesse, or constellacioun,
Wyn, wo, or chaunginge of complexioun
Causeth ful ofte to doon amis or speken.
10 On every wrong a man may nat be wreken;
After the tyme, moste be temperaunce
To every wight that can on governaunce.
And therfore hath this wyse worthy knight,
To live in ese, suffrance hir bihight,
And she to him ful wisly gan to swere
That never sholde ther be defaute in here.
Heer may men seen an humble wys accord;
Thus hath she take hir servant and hir lord,
Servant in love, and lord in mariage;
20 Than was he bothe in lordship and servage;
Servage? nay, but in lordshipe above,
Sith he hath bothe his lady and his love;
His lady, certes, and his wyf also,
The which that lawe of love acordeth to.
And whan he was in this prosperitee,
Hoom with his wyf he gooth to his contree,
Nat fer fro Penmark, ther his dwelling was,
Wher-as he liveth in blisse and in solas.
Who coude telle, but he had wedded be,
30 The joye, the ese, and the prosperitee
That is bitwixe an housbonde and his wyf?
A yeer and more lasted this blisful lyf,
Til that the knight of which I speke of thus,
That of Kayrrud was cleped Arveragus,

Complexioun, temperament.   *Wreken,* avenged.
Can on governaunce, knows how to rule.

Shoop him to goon, and dwelle a yeer or tweyne
In Engelond, that cleped was eek Briteyne,
To seke in armes worship and honour;
For al his lust he sette in swich labour;
And dwelled ther two yeer, the book seith thus.
    Now wol I stinte of this Arveragus,
And speken I wole of Dorigene his wyf,
That loveth hir housebonde as hir hertes lyf.
For his absence wepeth she and syketh,
10 As doon thise noble wyves whan hem lyketh.
She moorneth, waketh, wayleth, fasteth, pleyneth;
Desyr of his presence hir so distreyneth,
That al this wyde world she sette at noght.
Hir frendes, whiche that knewe hir hevy thoght,
Conforten hir in al that ever they may;
They prechen hir, they telle hir night and day,
That causelees she sleeth hir-self, allas!
And every confort possible in this cas
They doon to hir with al hir bisinesse,
20 Al for to make hir leve hir hevinesse.
    By proces, as ye knowen everichoon,
Men may so longe graven in a stoon,
Til some figure ther-inne emprented be.
So longe han they conforted hir, til she
Receyved hath, by hope and by resoun,
Th'emprenting of hir consolacioun,
Thurgh which hir grete sorwe gan aswage;
She may nat alwey duren in swich rage.
    And eek Arveragus, in al this care,
30 Hath sent hir lettres hoom of his welfare,
And that he wol come hastily agayn;
Or elles hadde this sorwe hir herte slayn.
    Hir freendes sawe hir sorwe gan to slake,
And preyede hir on knees, for goddes sake,

Syketh, sighs.   *Distreyneth,* troubles.

To come and romen hir in companye,
Awey to dryve hir derke fantasye.
And finally, she graunted that requeste;
For wel she saugh that it was for the beste.
Now stood hir castel faste by the see,
And often with hir freendes walketh she
Hir to disporte up-on the bank an heigh,
Wher-as she many a ship and barge seigh
Seilinge hir cours, wher-as hem liste go;
10 But than was that a parcel of hir wo.
For to hir-self ful ofte 'allas!' seith she,
'Is ther no ship, of so manye as I see,
Wol bringen hom my lord? than were myn herte
Al warisshed of his bittre peynes smerte.'
Another tyme ther wolde she sitte and thinke,
And caste hir eyen dounward fro the brinke.
But whan she saugh the grisly rokkes blake,
For verray fere so wolde hir herte quake,
That on hir feet she mighte hir noght sustene.
20 Than wolde she sitte adoun upon the grene,
And pitously in-to the see biholde,
And seyn right thus, with sorweful sykes colde:
'Eterne god, that thurgh thy purveyaunce
Ledest the world by certein governaunce,
In ydel, as men seyn, ye no-thing make;
But, lord, thise grisly feendly rokkes blake,
That semen rather a foul confusioun
Of werk than any fair creacioun
Of swich a parfit wys god and a stable,
30 Why han ye wroght this werk unresonable?
For by this werk, south, north, ne west, ne eest,
Ther nis y-fostred man, ne brid, ne beest;
It dooth no good, to my wit, but anoyeth.
See ye nat, lord, how mankinde it destroyeth?

Warisshed, cured.   *Sykes colde,* mournful sighs.

An hundred thousand bodies of mankinde
Han rokkes slayn, al be they nat in minde,
Which mankinde is so fair part of thy werk
That thou it madest lyk to thyn owene merk.
Than seemed it ye hadde a greet chiertee
Toward mankinde; but how than may it be
That ye swiche menes make it to destroyen,
Whiche menes do no good, but every anoyen?
I woot wel clerkes wol seyn, as hem leste,
10 By arguments, that al· is for the beste,
Though I ne can the causes nat y-knowe.
But thilke god, that made wind to blowe,
As kepe my lord! this my conclusioun;
To clerkes lete I al disputisoun.
But wolde god that alle thise rokkes blake
Were sonken in-to helle for his sake!
Thise rokkes sleen myn herte for the fere.'
Thus wolde she seyn, with many a pitous tere.

Hir freendes sawe that it was no disport
20 To romen by the see, but disconfort;
And shopen for to pleyen somwher elles.
They leden hir by riveres and by welles,
And eek in othere places delitables;
They dauncen, and they pleyen at ches and tables.

So on a day, right in the morwe-tyde,
Un-to a gardin that was ther bisyde,
In which that they had maad hir ordinaunce
Of vitaille and of other purveyaunce,
They goon and pleye hém al the longe day.
30 And this was on the sixte morwe of May,
Which May had peynted with his softe shoures
This gardin ful of leves and of floures;

Owene merk, own likeness.   *Chiertee,* love.
Shopen, arranged.   *Tables,* backgammon.
Hir ordinaunce of vitaille, their provision of food.

And craft of mannes hand so curiously
Arrayed hadde this gardin, trewely,
That never was ther gardin of swich prys,
But-if it were the verray paradys.
Th' odour of floures and the fresshe sighte
Wolde han maad any herte for to lighte
That ever was born, but-if to gret siknesse,
Or to gret sorwe helde it in distresse;
So ful it was of beautee with pleasaunce.
10 At-after diner gonne they to daunce,
And singe also, save Dorigen allone,
Which made alwey hir compleint and hir mone;
For she ne saugh him on the daunce go,
That was hir housbonde and hir love also.
But nathelees she moste a tyme abyde,
And with good hope lete hir sorwe slyde.

   Up-on this daunce, amonges othere men,
Daunced a squyer biforen Dorigen,
That fressher was and jolyer of array,
20 As to my doom, than is the monthe of May.
He singeth, daunceth, passinge any man
That is, or was, sith that the world bigan.
Ther-with he was, if men sholde him discryve,
Oon of the beste faringe man on-lyve;
Yong, strong, right vertuous, and riche and wys,
And wel biloved, and holden in gret prys.
And shortly, if the sothe I tellen shal,
Unwiting of this Dorigen at al,
This lusty squyer, servant to Venus,
30 Which that y-cleped was Aurelius,
Had loved hir best of any creature
Two yeer and more, as was his aventure,
But never dorste he telle hir his grevaunce;
With-outen coppe he drank al his penaunce.

Prys, excellence.   *Beste faringe,* most handsome.
Prys, esteem.   *With-outen coppe,* in full measure.

He was despeyred, no-thing dorste he seye,
Save in his songes somwhat wolde he wreye
His wo, as in a general compleyning;
He seyde he lovede, and was biloved no-thing.
Of swich matere made he manye layes,
Songes, compleintes, roundels, virelayes,
How that he dorste nat his sorwe telle,
But languissheth, as a furie dooth in helle;
And dye he moste, he seyde, as dide Ekko
10 For Narcisus, that dorste nat telle hir wo.
In other manere than ye here me seye,
Ne dorste he nat to hir his wo biwreye;
Save that, paraventure, som-tyme at daunces,
Ther yonge folk kepen hir observaunces,
It may wel be he loked on hir face
In swich a wyse, as man that asketh grace;
But no-thing wiste she of his entente.
Nathelees, it happed, er they thennes wente,
By-cause that he was hir neighebour,
20 And was a man of worship and honour,
And hadde y-knowen him of tyme yore,
They fille in speche; and forth more and more
Un-to his purpos drough Aurelius,
And whan he saugh his tyme, he seyde thus:
    'Madame,' quod he, 'by god that this world made,
So that I wiste it mighte your herte glade,
I wolde, that day that your Arveragus
Wente over the see, that I, Aurelius,
Had went ther never I sholde have come agayn;
30 For wel I woot my service is in vayn.
My guerdon is but bresting of myn herte;
Madame, reweth upon my peynes smerte;
For with a word ye may me sleen or save,
Heer at your feet god wolde that I were grave!

Wreye, expressed.   _Service,_ wooing.   _Grave,_ buried.

I ne have as now no leyser more to seye;
Have mercy, swete, or ye wol do me deye!'
    She gan to loke up-on Aurelius:
'Is this your wil,' quod she, 'and sey ye thus?
Never erst,' quod she, 'ne wiste I what ye mente.
But now, Aurelie, I knowe your entente,
By thilke god that yaf me soule and lyf,
Ne shal I never been untrewe wyf
In word ne werk, as fer as I have wit:
10 I wol ben his to whom that I am knit;
Tak this for fynal answer as of me.'
But after that in pley thus seyde she:
    'Aurelie,' quod she, 'by heighe god above,
Yet wolde I graunte yow to been your love,
Sin I yow see so pitously complayne;
Loke what day that, endelong Britayne,
Ye remoeve alle the rokkes, stoon by stoon,
That they ne lette ship ne boot to goon—
I seye, whan ye han maad the coost so clene
20 Of rokkes, that ther nis no stoon y-sene,
Than wol I love yow best of any man;
Have heer my trouthe in al that ever I can.'
'Is ther non other grace in yow?' quod he.
'No, by that lord,' quod she, 'that maked me!
For wel I woot that it shal never bityde.
Lat swiche folies out of your herte slyde.
What deyntee sholde a man han in his lyf
For to go love another mannes wyf,
That hath hir body whan so that him lyketh?'
30   Aurelius ful ofte sore syketh;
Wo was Aurelie, whan that he this herde,
And with a sorweful herte he thus answerde:
    'Madame,' quod he, 'this were an inpossible!
Than moot I dye of sodein deth horrible.'
    Trouthe, promise.

And with that word he turned him anoon.
Tho come hir othere freendes many oon,
And in the aleyes romeden up and doun,
And no-thing wiste of this conclusioun,
But sodeinly bigonne revel newe
Til that the brighte sonne loste his hewe;
For th'orisonte hath reft the sonne his light;
This is as muche to seye as it was night.
And hoom they goon in joye and in solas,
10 Save only wrecche Aurelius, allas!
He to his hous is goon with sorweful herte;
He seeth he may nat fro his deeth asterte.
Him semed that he felte his herte colde;
Up to the hevene his handes he gan holde,
And on his knowes bare he sette him doun,
And in his raving seyde his orisoun.
For verray wo out of his wit he breyde.
He niste what he spak, but thus he seyde;
With pitous herte his pleynt hath he bigonne
20 Un-to the goddes, and first un-to the sonne:
    He seyde, 'Appollo, god and governour
Of every plaunte, herbe, tree and flour,
That yevest, after thy declinacioun,
To ech of hem his tyme and his sesoun,
As thyn herberwe chaungeth lowe or hye,
Lord Phebus, cast thy merciable yë
On wrecche Aurelie, which that am but lorn.
Lo, lord! my lady hath my deeth y-sworn
With-oute gilt, but thy benignitee
30 Upon my dedly herte have som pitee!
For wel I woot, lord Phebus, if yow lest,
Ye may me helpen, save my lady, best.

Orisoun, prayer.   *Breyde,* started.
After thy declinacioun, according to the sun's distance from the celestial equator.
Herberwe, position.   *Dedly,* death-struck.

Now voucheth sauf that I may yow devyse
How that I may been holpe and in what wyse.
Your blisful suster, Lucina the shene,
That of the see is chief goddesse and quene,
Though Neptunus have deitee in the see,
Yet emperesse aboven him is she:
Ye knowen wel, lord, that right as hir desyr
Is to be quiked and lightned of your fyr,
For which she folweth yow ful bisily,
10 Right so the see desyreth naturelly
To folwen hir, as she that is goddesse
Bothe in the see, and riveres more and lesse.
Wherfore, lord Phebus, this is my requeste—
Do this miracle, or do myn herte breste—
That now, next at this opposicioun,
Which in the signe shal be of the Leoun,
As preyeth hir so greet a flood to bringe,
That fyve fadme at the leeste it overspringe
The hyeste rokke in Armorik Briteyne;
20 And lat this flood endure yeres tweyne;
Than certes to my lady may I seye:
"Holdeth your heste, the rokkes been aweye."
Lord Phebus, dooth this miracle for me;
Preye hir she go no faster cours than ye;
I seye, preyeth your suster that she go
No faster cours than ye thise yeres two.
Than shal she been evene atte fulle alway,
And spring-flood laste bothe night and day.
And, but she vouche-sauf in swiche manere
30 To graunte me my sovereyn lady dere,
Prey hir to sinken every rok adoun
In-to hir owene derke regioun
Under the ground, ther Pluto dwelleth inne,
Or never-mo shal I my lady winne.

Lucina the shene, the shining moon.   *Heste,* promise.

Thy temple in Delphos wol I barefoot seke;
Lord Phebus, see the teres on my cheke,
And of my peyne have som compassioun.'
And with that word in swowne he fil adoun,
And longe tyme he lay forth in a traunce.
    His brother, which that knew of his penaunce,
Up caughte him and to bedde he hath him broght.
Dispeyred in this torment and this thoght
Lete I this woful creature lye;
10 Chese he, for me, whether he wol live or dye.
    Arveragus, with hele and greet honour,
As he that was of chivalrye the flour,
Is comen hoom, and othere worthy men.
O blissful artow now, thou Dorigen,
That hast thy lusty housbonde in thyne armes,
The fresshe knight, the worthy man of armes,
That loveth thee, as his owene hertes lyf.
No-thing list him to been imaginatyf
If any wight had spoke, whyl he was oute,
20 To hire of love; he hadde of it no doute.
He noght entendeth to no swich matere,
But daunceth, justeth, maketh hir good chere;
And thus in joye and blisse I lete hem dwelle,
And of the syke Aurelius wol I telle.
    In langour and in torment furious
Two yeer and more lay wrecche Aurelius,
Er any foot he might on erthe goon;
Ne confort in this tyme hadde he noon,
Save of his brother, which that was a clerk;
30 He knew of al this wo and al this werk.
For to non other creature certeyn
Of this matere he dorste no word seyn.
Under his brest he bar it more secree

Chese he, for me, let him choose, as far as I am concerned.
Hele, prosperity.   Imaginatyf, suspicious.
Doute, fear.   Entendeth, pays attention.

Than ever dide Pamphilus for Galathee.
His brest was hool, with-oute for to sene,
But in his herte ay was the arwe kene.
And wel ye knowe that of a sursanure
In surgerye is perilous the cure,
But men mighte touche the arwe, or come thereby.
His brother weep and wayled prively,
Til atte laste him fil in remembraunce,
That whyl he was at Orliens in Fraunce,
10 As yonge clerkes, that been likerous
To reden artes that been curious,
Seken in every halke and every herne
Particuler sciences for to lerne,
He him remembred that, upon a day,
At Orliens in studie a book he say
Of magik naturel, which his felawe,
That was that tyme a bacheler of lawe,
Al were he ther to lerne another craft,
Had prively upon his desk y-laft;
20 Which book spak muchel of the operaciouns,
Touchinge the eighte and twenty mansiouns
That longen to the mone, and swich folye,
As in our dayes is nat worth a flye;
For holy chirches feith in our bileve
Ne suffreth noon illusion us to greve.
And whan this book was in his remembraunce,
Anon for joye his herte gan to daunce,
And to him-self he seyde prively:
'My brother shal be warisshed hastily;
30 For I am siker that ther be sciences,
By whiche men make diverse apparences

Pamphilus, referring to a Latin poem of the 13th century.
Sursanure, a wound superficially healed.
Likerous, desirous.
Halke . . . herne, nook . . . corner.
Mansiouns, the parts into which the moon's course was divided.
Siker, sure.

Swiche as thise subtile tregetoures pleye.
For ofte at festes have I wel herd seye,
That tregetours, with-inne an halle large,
Have maad come in a water and a barge,
And in the halle rowen up and doun.
Som tyme hath semed come a grim leoun;
And somtyme floures springe as in a mede;
Somtyme a vyne, and grapes whyte and rede;
Somtyme a castel, al of lym and stoon;
10 And whan hem lyked, voyded it anoon.
Thus semed it to every mannes sighte.
    Now than conclude I thus, that if I mighte
At Orliens som old felawe y-finde,
That hadde this mones mansions in minde,
Or other magik naturel above,
He sholde wel make my brother han his love.
For with an apparence a clerk may make
To mannes sighte, that alle the rokkes blake
Of Britaigne weren y-voyded everichon,
20 And shippes by the brinke comen and gon,
And in swich forme endure a day or two;
Than were my brother warisshed of his wo.
Than moste she nedes holden hir biheste,
Or elles he shal shame hir atte leste.'
    What sholde I make a lenger tale of this?
Un-to his brotheres bed he comen is,
And swich confort he yaf him for to gon
To Orliens, that he up stirte anon,
And on his wey forthward thanne is he fare,
30 In hope for to ben lissed of his care.
    Whan they were come almost to that citee,
But-if it were a two furlong or three,
A yong clerk rominge by him-self they mette,
Which that in Latin thriftily hem grette,

Tregetoures, magicians.   *Lissed,* relieved.   *Thriftily,* politely.

And after that he seyde a wonder thing:
'I knowe,' quod he, 'the cause of your coming';
And er they ferther any fote wente,
He tolde hem al that was in hir entente.
This Briton clerk him asked of felawes
The whiche that he had knowe in olde dawes;
And he answerde him that they dede were,
For which he weep ful ofte many a tere.
Doun of his hors Aurelius lighte anon,
10 And forth with this magicien is he gon
Hoom to his hous, and made hem wel at ese.
Hem lakked no vitaille that might hem plese;
So wel arrayed hous as ther was oon
Aurelius in his lyf saugh never noon.
He shewed him, er he wente to sopeer,
Forestes, parkes ful of wilde deer;
Ther saugh he hertes with hir hornes hye,
The gretteste that ever were seyn with yë.
He saugh of hem an hondred slayn with houndes,
20 And somme with arwes blede of bittre woundes.
He saugh, whan voided were thise wilde deer,
This fauconers upon a fair river,
That with hir haukes han the heron slayn.
Tho saugh he knightes justing in a playn;
And after this, he dide him swich plesaunce,
That he him shewed his lady on a daunce
On which him-self he daunced, as him thoughte.
And whan this maister, that this magik wroughte,
Saugh it was tyme, he clapte his handes two,
30 And farewel! al our revel was ago.
And yet remoeved they never out of the hous,
Whyl they saugh al this sighte merveillous,
But in his studie, ther-as his bookes be,
They seten stille, and no wight but they three.
   Fair river, fair river-bank.

To him this maister called his squyer,
And seyde him thus: 'is redy our soper?
Almost an houre it is, I undertake,
Sith I yow bad our soper for to make,
Whan that thise worthy men wenten with me
In-to my studie, ther-as my bookes be.'
'Sire,' quod this squyer, 'whan it lyketh yow,
It is al redy, though ye wol right now.'
'Go we than soupe,' quod he, 'as for the beste;
10 This amorous folk som-tyme mote han reste.'
At-after soper fille they in tretee,
What somme sholde this maistres guerdon be,
To remoeven alle the rokkes of Britayne,
And eek from Gerounde to the mouth of Sayne.
He made it straunge, and swoor, so god him save,
Lasse than a thousand pound he wolde nat have,
Ne gladly for that somme he wolde nat goon.
Aurelius, with blisful herte anoon,
Answerde thus, 'fy on a thousand pound!
20 This wyde world, which that men seye is round,
I wolde it yeve, if I were lord of it.
This bargayn is ful drive, for we ben knit.
Ye shal be payed trewely, by my trouthe!
But loketh now, for no necligence or slouthe,
Ye tarie us heer no lenger than to-morwe.'
'Nay,' quod this clerk, 'have heer my feith to
       borwe.'
To bedde is goon Aurelius whan him leste,
And wel ny al that night he hadde his reste;
What for his labour and his hope of blisse,
30 His woful herte of penaunce hadde a lisse.
Upon the morwe, whan that it was day,
To Britaigne toke they the righte way,

Undertake, declare.　　　　　*Guerdon,* recompense.
Made it straunge, seemed reluctant.
Borwe, surety.　　　　　*Lisse,* relief.

Aurelius, and this magicien bisyde,
And been descended ther they wolde abyde;
And this was, as the bokes me remembre,
The colde frosty seson of Decembre.
Phebus wex old, and hewed lyk latoun,
That in his hote declinacioun
Shoon as the burned gold with stremes brighte;
But now in Capricorn adoun he lighte,
Wher-as he shoon ful pale, I dar wel seyn.
10 The bittre frostes, with the sleet and reyn,
Destroyed hath the grene in every yerd.
Janus sit by the fyr, with double berd,
And drinketh of his bugle-horn the wyn.
Biforn him stant braun of the tusked swyn,
And 'Nowel' cryeth every lusty man.
Aurelius, in al that ever he can,
Doth to his maister chere and reverence,
And preyeth him to doon his diligence
To bringen him out of his peynes smerte,
20 Or with a swerd that he wolde slitte his herte.
This subtil clerk swich routhe had of this man,
That night and day he spedde him that he can,
To wayte a tyme of his conclusioun;
This is to seye, to make illusioun,
By swich an apparence or jogelrye,
I ne can no termes of astrologye,
That she and every wight sholde wene and seye,
That of Britaigne the rokkes were aweye,
Or elles they were sonken under grounde.
30 So atte laste he hath his tyme y-founde
To maken his japes and his wrecchednesse
Of swich a supersticious cursednesse.

Latoun, cheap alloy, like brass.
Conclusioun, exercise in astrological magic.
Japes, tricks.

His tables Toletanes forth he broght,
Ful wel corrected, ne ther lakked noght,
Neither his collect ne his expans yeres,
Ne his rotes ne his othere geres,
As been his centres and his arguments,
And his proporcionels convenients
For his equacions in every thing.
And, by his eighte spere in his wirking,
He knew ful wel how fer Alnath was shove
10 Fro the heed of thilke fixe Aries above
That in the ninthe speere considered is;
Ful subtilly he calculed al this.

    Whan he had founded his firste mansioun,
He knew the remenant by proporcioun;
And knew the arysing of his mone weel,
And in whos face, and terme, and every-deel;
And knew ful weel the mones mansioun
Acordaunt to his operacioun,
And knew also his othere observaunces
20 For swiche illusiouns and swiche meschaunces
As hethen folk used in thilke dayes;
For which no lenger maked he delayes,
But thurgh his magik, for a wyke or tweye,
It seemed that alle the rokkes were aweye.

    Aurelius, which that yet despeired is
Wher he shal han his love or fare amis,
Awaiteth night and day on this miracle;
And whan he knew that ther was noon obstacle,
That voided were thise rokkes everichon,
Doun to his maistres feet he fil anon,

Tables Toletanes, astronomical tables, calculated for Toledo.
Collect and *expans yeres* indicated additions to be made to the rote or position of a planet at birth of Christ.
Centres, planetary centres.
Arguments, angle or arc as basis for calculation.
Eighte spere, sphere of the fixed stars.

And seyde, 'I woful wrecche, Aurelius,
Thanke yow, lord, and lady myn Venus,
That me han holpen fro my cares colde':
And to the temple his wey forth hath he holde,
Wher-as he knew he sholde his lady see.
And whan he saugh his tyme, anon-right he,
With dredful herte and with ful humble chere,
Salewed hath his sovereyn lady dere:
'My righte lady,' quod this woful man,
10 'Whom I most drede and love as I best can,
And lothest were of al this world displese,
Nere it that I for yow have swich disese,
That I moste dyen heer at your foot anon,
Noght wolde I telle how me is wo bigon;
But certes outher moste I dye or pleyne;
Ye slee me giltelees for verray peyne.
But of my deeth, thogh that ye have no routhe,
Avyseth yow, er that ye breke your trouthe.
Repenteth yow, for thilke god above,
20 Er ye me sleen by-cause that I yow love.
For, madame, wel ye woot what ye han hight;
Nat that I chalange any thing of right
Of yow my sovereyn lady, but your grace;
But in a gardin yond, at swich a place,
Ye woot right wel what ye bihighten me;
And in myn hand your trouthe plighten ye
To love me best, god woot, ye seyde so,
Al be that I unworthy be therto.
Madame, I speke it for the honour of yow,
30 More than to save myn hertes lyf right now;
I have do so as ye comanded me;
And if ye vouche-sauf, ye may go see.

Dredful, afraid.   *Salewed,* greeted.

Doth as yow list, have your biheste in minde,
For quik or deed, right ther ye shul me finde;
In yow lyth al, to do me live or deye;—
But wel I woot the rokkes been aweye!'
He taketh his leve, and she astonied stood,
In all hir face nas a drope of blood;
She wende never han come in swich a trappe:
'Allas!' quod she, 'that ever this sholde happe!
For wende I never, by possibilitee,
10 That swich a monstre or merveille mighte be!
It is agayns the proces of nature':
And hoom she gooth a sorweful creature.
For verray fere unnethe may she go,
She wepeth, wailleth, al a day or two,
And swowneth, that it routhe was to see;
But why it was, to no wight tolde she;
For out of toune was goon Arveragus.
But to hir-self she spak, and seyde thus,
With face pale and with ful sorweful chere,
20 In hir compleynt, as ye shul after here:
'Allas,' quod she, 'on thee, Fortune, I pleyne,
That unwar wrapped hast me in thy cheyne;
For which, t'escape, woot I no socour
Save only deeth or elles dishonour;
Oon of thise two bihoveth me to chese.
But nathelees, yet have I lever to lese
My lyf than of my body have a shame,
Or knowe my-selven fals, or lese my name,
And with my deth I may be quit, y-wis.
30 Hath ther nat many a noble wyf, er this,
And many a mayde y-slayn hir-self, allas!
Rather than with hir body doon trespas?
Yis, certes, lo, thise stories beren witnesse;
Whan thretty tyraunts, ful of cursednesse,
Had slayn Phidoun in Athenes, atte feste,
They comanded his doghtres for t'areste,

And bringen hem biforn hem in despyt
Al naked, to fulfille hir foul delyt,
And in hir fadres blood they made hem daunce
Upon the pavement, god yeve hem mischaunce!
For which thise woful maydens, ful of drede,
Rather than they wolde lese hir maydenhede,
They prively ben stirt in-to a welle,
And dreynte hem-selven, as the bokes telle.
   They of Messene lete enquere and seke
10 Of Lacedomie fifty maydens eke,
On whiche they wolden doon hir lecherye;
But was ther noon of al that companye
That she nas slayn, and with a good entente
Chees rather for to dye than assente
To been oppressed of hir maydenhede.
Why sholde I thanne to dye been in drede?
   Lo, eek, the tiraunt Aristoclides
That loved a mayden, heet Stimphalides,
Whan that hir fader slayn was on a night,
20 Un-to Dianes temple goth she right,
And hente the image in hir handes two,
Fro which image wolde she never go.
No wight ne mighte hir handes of it arace,
Til she was slayn right in the selve place.
Now sith that maydens hadden swich despyt
To been defouled with mannes foul delyt,
Wel oghte a wyf rather hir-selven slee
Than be defouled, as it thinketh me.
   What shal I seyn of Hasdrubales wyf,
30 That at Cartage birafte hir-self hir lyf?
For whan she saugh that Romayns wan the toun,
She took hir children alle, and skipte adoun
In-to the fyr, and chees rather to dye
Than any Romayn dide hir vileinye.

Arace, remove.   *Despyt,* insult, scorn.

Hath nat Lucresse y-slayn hir-self, allas!
At Rome, whanne she oppressed was
Of Tarquin, for hir thoughte it was a shame
To liven whan she hadde lost hir name?
The sevene maydens of Milesie also
Han slayn hem-self, for verray drede and wo,
Rather than folk of Gaule hem sholde oppresse.
Mo than a thousand stories, as I gesse,
Coude I now telle as touchinge this matere.
10 Whan Habradate was slayn, his wyf so dere
Hirselven slow, and leet hir blood to glyde
In Habradates woundes depe and wyde,
And seyde, 'my body, at the leeste way,
Ther shal no wight defoulen, if I may.'
What sholde I mo ensamples heer-of sayn,
Sith that so manye han hem-selven slayn
Wel rather than they wolde defouled be?
I wol conclude, that it is bet for me
To sleen my-self, than been defouled thus.
20 I wol be trewe un-to Arveragus,
Or rather sleen my-self in som manere,
As dide Demociones doghter dere,
By-cause that she wolde nat defouled be.
O Cedasus! it is ful greet pitee,
To reden how thy doghtren deyde, allas!
That slowe hem-selven for swich maner cas.
As greet a pitee was it, or wel more,
The Theban mayden, that for Nichanore
Hir-selven slow, right for swich maner wo.
30 Another Theban mayden dide right so;
For oon of Macedoine hadde hir oppressed,
She with hir deeth hir maydenhede redressed.
What shal I seye of Nicerates wyf,
That for swich cas birafte hir-self hir lyf?
How trewe eek was to Alcebiades
His love, that rather for to dyen chees

Than for to suffre his body unburied be!
Lo, which a wyf was Alcestè,' quod she.
'What seith Omer of gode Penalopee?
Al Grece knoweth of hir chastitee.
Pardee, of Laodomya is writen thus,
That whan at Troye was slayn Protheselaus,
No lenger wolde she live after his day.
The same of noble Porcia tell I may;
With-oute Brutus coude she nat live,
10 To whom she hadde al hool hir herte yive.
The parfit wyfhod of Arthemesye
Honoured is thurgh al the Barbarye.
O Teuta, queen! thy wyfly chastitee
To alle wyves may a mirour be.
The same thing I seye of Bilia,
Of Rodogone, and eek Valeria.'
Thus pleyned Dorigene a day or tweye,
Purposinge ever that she wolde deye.
But nathelees, upon the thridde night,
20 Home came Arveragus, this worthy knight,
And asked hir, why that she weep so sore?
And she gan wepen ever lenger the more.
'Allas!' quod she, 'that ever was I born!
Thus have I seyd,' quod she, 'thus have I sworn'—
And told him al as ye han herd bifore;
It nedeth nat reherce it yow na-more.
This housbond with glad chere, in freendly wyse,
Answerde and seyde as I shal yow devyse:
'Is ther oght elles, Dorigen, but this?'
30 'Nay, nay,' quod she, 'god help me so, as wis;
This is to muche, and it were goddes wille.'
'Ye, wyf,' quod he, 'lat slepen that is stille;
It may be wel, paraventure, yet to-day.
Ye shul your trouthe holden, by my fay!
Trouthe, pledged word.

For god so wisly have mercy on me,
I hadde wel lever y-stiked for to be,
For verray love which that I to yow have,
But-if ye sholde your trouthe kepe and save.
Trouthe is the hyeste thing that man may kepe':—
But with that word he brast anon to wepe,
And seyde, 'I yow forbede, up peyne of deeth,
That never, whyl thee lasteth lyf ne breeth,
To no wight tel thou of this aventure.
10 As I may best, I wol my wo endure,
Ne make no contenance of hevinesse,
That folk of yow may demen harm or gesse.'
    And forth he cleped a squyer and a mayde:
'Goth forth anon with Dorigen,' he sayde,
'And bringeth hir to swich a place anon.'
They take hir leve, and on hir wey they gon;
But they ne wiste why she thider wente.
He nolde no wight tellen his entente.
    Paraventure an heep of yow, y-wis,
20 Wol holden him a lewed man in this,
That he wol putte his wyf in jupartye;
Herkneth the tale, er ye up-on hir crye.
She may have bettre fortune than yow semeth;
And whan that ye han herd the tale, demeth.
    This squyer, which that highte Aurelius,
On Dorigen that was so amorous,
Of aventure happed hir to mete
Amidde the toun, right in the quikkest strete,
As she was boun to goon the wey forth-right
30 Toward the gardin ther-as she had hight.
And he was to the gardinward also;
For wel he spyed, whan she wolde go
Out of hir hous to any maner place.
But thus they mette, of aventure or grace;

Y-stiked, stabbed.   *Lewed,* base.   *Jupartye,* jeopardy.
Demeth, judge.   *Quikkest,* liveliest.   *Boun,* bound, on her way.

And he saleweth hir with glad entente,
And asked of hir whiderward she wente?
  And she answerde, half as she were mad,
'Un-to the gardin, as myn housbond bad,
My trouthe for to holde, allas! allas!'
  Aurelius gan wondren on this cas,
And in his herte had greet compassioun
Of hir and of hir lamentacioun,
And of Arveragus, the worthy knight,
10 That bad hir holden al that she had hight,
So looth him was his wyf sholde breke hir trouthe;
And in his herte he caughte of this greet routhe,
Consideringe the beste on every syde,
That fro his lust yet were him lever abyde
Than doon so heigh a cherlish wrecchednesse
Agyns franchyse and alle gentillesse;
For which in fewe wordes seyde he thus:
  'Madame, seyth to your lord Arveragus,
That sith I see his grete gentillesse
20 To yow, and eek I see wel your distresse,
That him were lever han shame (and that were
      routhe)
Than ye to me sholde, breke thus your trouthe,
I have wel lever ever to suffre wo
Than I departe the love bitwix yow two.
I yow relesse, madame, in-to your hond
Quit every surement and every bond,
That ye han maad to me as heer-biforn,
Sith thilke tyme which that ye were born.
My trouthe I plighte, I shal yow never repreve
30 Of no biheste, and here I take my leve,
As of the treweste and the beste wyf
That ever yet I knew in al my lyf.
But every wyf be-war of hir biheste,
On Dorigene remembreth atte leste.
  Franchyse, nobility of heart.

Thus can a squyer doon a gentil dede,
As well as can a knight, with-outen drede.'
 She thonketh him up-on hir knees al bare,
And hoom un-to hir housbond is she fare,
And tolde him al as ye han herd me sayd;
And be ye siker, he was so weel apayd,
That it were inpossible me to wryte;
What sholde I lenger of this cas endyte?
 Arveragus and Dorigene his wyf
10 In sovereyn blisse leden forth hir lyf.
Never eft ne was ther angre hem bitwene;
He cherisseth hir as though she were a quene;
And she was to him trewe for evermore.
Of thise two folk ye gete of me na-more.
 Aurelius, that his cost hath al forlorn,
Curseth the tyme that ever he was born:
'Allas,' quod he, 'allas! that I bihighte
Of pured gold a thousand pound of wighte
Un-to this philosophre! how shal I do?
20 I see na-more but that I am fordo.
Myn heritage moot I nedes selle,
And been a begger; heer may I nat dwelle,
And shamen al my kinrede in this place,
But I of him may gete bettre grace.
But nathelees, I wol of him assaye,
At certeyn dayes, yeer by yeer, to paye,
And thanke him of his grete curteisye;
My trouthe wol I kepe, I wol nat lye.'
 With herte soor he gooth un-to his cofre,
30 And broghte gold un-to this philosophre,
The value of fyve hundred pound, I gesse,
And him bisecheth, of his gentillesse,
To graunte him dayes of the remenaunt,
And seyde, 'maister, I dar wel make avaunt,

Apayd, pleased. *Forlorn,* lost. *Dayes,* credit.

I failled never of my trouthe as yit;
For sikerly my dette shal be quit
Towardes yow, how-ever that I fare
To goon a-begged in my kirtle bare.
But wolde ye vouche-sauf, up-on seurtee,
Two yeer or three for to respyten me,
Than were I wel; for elles moot I selle
Myn heritage; ther is na-more to telle.'
This philosophre sobrely answerde,
10 And seyde thus, whan he thise wordes herde:
'Have I nat holden covenant un-to thee?'
'Yes, certes, wel and trewely,' quod he.
'Hastow nat had thy lady as thee lyketh?'
'No, no,' quod he, and sorwefully he syketh.
'What was the cause? tel me if thou can.'
Aurelius his tale anon bigan,
And tolde him al, as ye han herd bifore;
It nedeth nat to yow reherce it more.
He seide, 'Arveragus, of gentillesse,
20 Had lever dye in sorwe and in distresse
Than that his wyf were of hir trouthe fals.'
The sorwe of Dorigen he tolde him als,
How looth hir was to been a wikked wyf,
And that she lever had lost that day hir lyf,
And that hir trouthe she swoor, thurgh innocence:
'She never erst herde speke of apparence;
That made me han of hir so greet pitee.
And right as frely as he sente hir me,
As frely sente I hir to him ageyn.
30 This al and som, ther is na-more to seyn.'
This philosophre answerde, 'leve brother,
Everich of yow dide gentilly til other.
Thou art a squyer, and he is a knight;
But god forbede, for his blisful might,

Kirtle, tunic.   Apparence, trick of illusion.

But-if a clerk coude doon a gentil dede
As wel as any of yow, it is no drede!
   Sire, I relesse thee thy thousand pound,
As thou right now were cropen out of the ground.
Ne never er now ne haddest knowen me.
For sire, I wol nat take a peny of thee
For al my craft, ne noght for my travaille.
Thou hast y-payed wel for my vitaille;
It is y-nogh, and farewel, have good day:'
10 And took his hors, and forth he gooth his way.
   Lordinges, this question wolde I aske now,
Which was the moste free, as thinketh yow?
Now telleth me, er that ye ferther wende.
   I can na-more, my tale is at an ende.

THE SECOND NUN'S TALE

The ministre and the norice un-to vyces,
Which that men clepe in English ydelnesse,
That porter of the gate is of delyces,
T'eschue, and by hir contrarie hir oppresse,
That is to seyn, by leveful bisinesse,
20 Wel oghten we to doon al our entente,
Lest that the feend thurgh ydelnesse us hente.

For he, that with his thousand cordes slye
Continuelly us waiteth to biclappe,
Whan he may man in ydelnesse espye,
He can so lightly cacche him in his trappe,
Til that a man be hent right by the lappe,
He nis nat war the feend hath him in honde;
Wel oughte us werche, and ydelnes withstonde.

Travaille, labor.   *Moste free,* most noble and generous.
  Rhyme royal is the name given to the stanza used in this poem.
Chaucer introduced it into English, as he did the heroic couplet,
and in the *Canterbury Tales* employed it when he wished to give a
lyrical tone to his work. *Delyces, pleasures.*   **Biclappe,** catch.

And though men dradden never for to dye,
Yet seen men wel by reson doutelees,
That ydelnesse is roten slogardye,
Of which ther never comth no good encrees;
And seen, that slouthe hir holdeth in a lees
Only to sleepe, and for to ete and drinke,
And to devouren al that othere swinke.

And for to putte us fro swich ydelnesse,
That cause is of so greet confusioun,
10 I have heer doon my feithful bisinesse,
After the legende, in translacioun
Right of thy glorious lyf and passioun,
Thou with thy gerland wroght of rose and lilie;
Thee mene I, mayde and martir, seint Cecilie!

Inuocacio ad Mariam.

AND thou that flour of virgines art alle,
Of whom that Bernard list so wel to wryte,
To thee at my biginning first I calle;
Thou comfort of us wrecches, do me endyte
Thy maydens deeth, that wan thurgh hir meryte
20 The eternal lyf, and of the feend victorie,
As man may after reden in hir storie.

Thou mayde and mooder, doghter of thy sone,
Thou welle of mercy, sinful soules cure,
In whom that god, for bountee, chees to wone,
Thou humble, and heigh over every creature,
Thou nobledest so ferforth our nature,

After the legende, just what Latin text Chaucer used is not yet
known. It is not that of the *Legenda Aurea* as printed.
Lees, leash.　　　*Bernard,* of Clairvaux.
Thou mayde and mooder, and following stanzas are adapted
freely from Dante's *Paradiso,* with many phrases recollected from
Latin hymns.
Bountee, goodness.　　　*Wone,* dwell.

That no desdeyn the maker hadde of kinde,
His sone in blode and flesh to clothe and winde.

Withinne the cloistre blisful of thy sydes
Took mannes shap the eternal love and pees,
That of the tryne compas lord and gyde is,
Whom erthe and see and heven, out of relees,
Ay herien; and thou, virgin wemmelees,
Bar of thy body, and dweltest mayden pure,
The creatour of every creature.

10 Assembled is in thee magnificence
With mercy, goodnesse, and with swich pitee
That thou, that art the sonne of excellence,
Nat only helpest hem that preyen thee,
But ofte tyme, of thy benignitee,
Ful frely, er that men thyn help biseche,
Thou goost biforn, and art hir lyves leche.

Now help, thou meke and blisful fayre mayde,
Me, flemed wrecche, in this desert of galle;
Think on the womman Cananee, that sayde
20 That whelpes eten somme of the crommes alle
That from hir lordes table been y-falle;
And though that I, unworthy sone of Eve,
Be sinful, yet accepte my bileve.

And, for that feith is deed with-outen werkes,
So for to werken yif me wit and space,
That I be quit fro thennes that most derk is!

Kinde, nature.
Tryne compas, triple world of earth, sea, and heaven.
Out of relees, ay herien, praise without ceasing.
Wemmelees, spotless.   *Leche,* physician.
Flemed wrecche . . . galle, banished outcast in this desert ot
bitterness.   *Womman Cananee, Matthew* xv, 22.
Unworthy sone, showing that Chaucer, in writing this, had
not the Second Nun in mind.

O thou, that art so fayr and ful of grace,
Be myn advocat in that heighe place
Ther-as withouten ende is songe 'Osanne,'
Thou Cristes mooder, doghter dere of Anne!

And of thy light my soule in prison lighte,
That troubled is by the contagioun
Of my body, and also by the wighte
Of erthly luste and fals affeccioun;
O haven of refut, o salvacioun
10 Of hem that been in sorwe and in distresse,
Now help, for to my werk I wol me dresse.

Yet preye I yow that reden that I wryte,
Foryeve me, that I do no diligence
This ilke storie subtilly to endyte;
For both have I the wordes and sentence
Of him that at the seintes reverence
The storie wroot, and folwe hir legende,
And prey yow, that ye wol my werk amende.

Interpretacio nominis Cecilie, quam ponit frater
Iacobus Ianuensis in Legenda Aurea.

FIRST wolde I yow the name of seint Cecilie
20 Expoune, as men may in hir storie see,
It is to seye in English 'hevenes lilie,'
For pure chastnesse of virginitee;
Or, for she whytnesse hadde of honestee,

Refut, refuge.
Reden, again showing that Chaucer did not write this for the Second Nun.
Wordes and sentence, words and meaning. That is, he would have thought it irreverent to alter a saint's legend, though he might abbreviate it.
Iacobus Ianuensis, James of Varragine, end of 13th century.
Expoune, elucidate, since fanciful etymologies of saints' names were usual.

And grene of conscience, and of good fame
The sote savour, 'lilie' was hir name.

Or Cecile is to seye 'the wey to blinde,'
For she ensample was by good techinge;
Or elles Cecile, as I writen finde,
Is joyned, by a maner conjoininge
Of 'hevene' and 'Lia'; and heer, in figuringe,
The 'heven' is set for thoght of holinesse,
And 'Lie' for hir lasting bisinesse.

10 Cecile may eek be seyd in this manere,
'Wanting of blindnesse,' for hir grete light
Of sapience, and for hir thewes clere;
Or elles, lo! this maydens name bright
Of 'hevene' and 'leos' comth, for which by right
Men mighte hir wel 'the heven of peple' calle,
Ensample of gode and wyse werkes alle.

For 'leos' 'peple' in English is to seye,
And right as men may in the hevene see
The sonne and mone and sterres every weye,
20 Right so men gostly, in this mayden free,
Seyen of feith the magnanimitee,
And eek the cleernesse hool of sapience,
And sondry werkes, brighte of excellence.

And right so as thise philosophres wryte
That heven is swift and round and eek brenninge,
Right so was fayre Cecilie the whyte
Ful swift and bisy ever in good werkinge,
And round and hool in good perseveringe,
And brenning ever in charitee ful brighte;
30 Now have I yow declared what she highte.

Sapience . . . thewes, wisdom . . . virtues.
Highte, was called.

THIS mayden bright Cecilie, as hir lyf seith,
Was comen of Romayns, and of noble kinde,
And from hir cradel up fostred in the feith
Of Crist, and bar his gospel in hir minde;
She never cessed, as I writen finde,
Of hir preyere, and god to love and drede,
Biseking him to keep hir maydenhede.

And when this mayden sholde unto a man
Y-wedded be, that was ful yong of age,
10 Which that y-cleped was Valerian,
And day was comen of hir mariage,
She, ful devout and humble in hir corage,
Under hir robe of gold, that sat ful fayre,
Had next hir flesh y-clad hir in an heyre.

And whyl the organs maden melodye,
To god alone in herte thus sang she;
'O lord, my soule and eek my body gye
Unwemmed, lest that I confounded be:'
And, for his love that deyde upon a tree,
20 Every seconde or thridde day she faste,
Ay biddinge in hir orisons ful faste.

The night cam, and to bedde moste she gon
With hir housbonde, as ofte is the manere,
And prively to him she seyde anon,
'O swete and wel biloved spouse dere,
Ther is a conseil, and ye wolde it here,
Which that right fain I wolde unto yow seye,
So that ye swere ye shul me nat biwreye.'

Corage, heart.
An heyre, a hair-shirt.
Gye, guide.
Biddinge, praying.
Conseil, secret.

Valerian gan faste unto hir swere,
That for no cas, ne thing that mighte be,
He sholde never-mo biwreyen here;
And thanne at erst to him thus seyde she,
'I have an angel which that loveth me,
That with greet love, wher-so I wake or slepe,
Is redy ay my body for to kepe.

And if that he may felen, out of drede,
That ye me touche or love in vileinye,
10 He right anon wol slee yow with the dede,
And in your yowthe thus ye shulden dye;
And if that ye in clene love me gye,
He wol yow loven as me, for your clennesse,
And shewen yow his joye and his brightnesse.'

Valerian, corrected as god wolde,
Answerde agayn, 'if I shal trusten thee,
Lat me that angel see, and him biholde;
And if that it a verray angel be,
Than wol I doon as thou hast preyed me;
20 And if thou love another man, for sothe
Right with this swerd than wol I slee yow bothe.'

Cecile answerde anon right in this wyse,
'If that yow list, the angel shul ye see,
So that ye trowe on Crist and yow baptyse.
Goth forth to Via Apia,' quod she,
'That fro this toun ne stant but myles three,
And, to the povre folkes that ther dwelle,
Sey hem right thus, as that I shal yow telle.

Telle hem that I, Cecile, yow to hem sente,
30 To shewen yow the gode Urban the olde,
For secree nedes and for good entente.

In vileinye, unbecomingly.   *Me gye,* keep me.
Secree nedes, secret but necessary business.

And whan that ye seint Urban han biholde,
Telle him the wordes whiche I to yow tolde;
And whan that he hath purged yow fro sinne,
Thanne shul ye see that angel, er ye twinne.'

Valerian is to the place y-gon,
And right as him was taught by his lerninge,
He fond this holy olde Urban anon
Among the seintes buriels lotinge.
And he anon, with-outen taryinge,
10 Dide his message; and whan that he it tolde,
Urban for joye his hondes gan up holde.

The teres from his yën leet he falle—
'Almighty lord, O Jesu Crist,' quod he,
'Sower of chast conseil, herde of us alle,
The fruit of thilke seed of chastitee
That thou hast sowe in Cecile, tak to thee!
Lo, lyk a bisy bee, with-outen gyle,
Thee serveth ay thyn owene thral Cecile!

For thilke spouse, that she took but now
20 Ful lyk a fiers leoun, she sendeth here,
As meke as ever was any lamb, to yow!'
And with that worde, anon ther gan appere
An old man, clad in whyte clothes clere,
That hadde a book with lettre of golde in honde,
And gan biforn Valerian to stonde.

Valerian as deed fil doun for drede
Whan he him saugh, and he up hente him tho,
And on his book right thus he gan to rede—
'Oo Lord, oo feith, oo god with-outen mo,
30 Oo Cristendom, and fader of alle also,

Buriels lotinge, burial places hiding.
Hente him, took him, lifted him.   *Oo Cristendom,* one baptism.

Aboven alle and over al everywhere'—
Thise wordes al with gold y-writen were.

Whan this was rad, than seyde this olde man,
'Levestow this thing or no? sey ye or nay.'
'I leve al this thing,' quod Valerian,
'For sother thing than this, I dar wel say,
Under the hevene no wight thinke may.'
Tho vanisshed th'olde man, he niste where,
And pope Urban him cristened right there.

10 Valerian goth hoom, and fint Cecilie
With-inne his chambre with an angel stonde;
This angel hadde of roses and of lilie
Corones two, the which he bar in honde;
And first to Cecile, as I understonde,
He yaf that oon, and after gan he take
That other to Valerian, hir make.

'With body clene and with unwemmed thoght
Kepeth ay wel thise corones,' quod he;
'Fro Paradys to yow have I hem broght,
20 Ne never-mo ne shal they roten be,
Ne lese her sote savour, trusteth me;
Ne never wight shal seen hem with his yë,
But he be chaast and hate vileinyë.

And thou, Valerian, for thou so sone
Assentedest to good conseil also,
Sey what thee list, and thou shalt han thy bone.'
'I have a brother,' quod Valerian tho,
'That in this world I love no man so.
I pray yow that my brother may han grace
30 To knowe the trouthe, as I do in this place.'

Levestow, do you believe. *Niste,* knew not. *Make,* mate.

The angel seyde, 'god lyketh thy requeste,
And bothe, with the palm of martirdom,
Ye shullen come unto his blisful feste.'
And with that word Tiburce his brother com.
And whan that he the savour undernom
Which that the roses and the lilies caste,
With-inne his herte he gan to wondre faste,

And seyde, 'I wondre, this tyme of the yeer,
Whennes that sote savour cometh so
10 Of rose and lilies that I smelle heer.
For though I hadde hem in myn hondes two,
The savour mighte in me no depper go.
The sote smel that in myn herte I finde
Hath chaunged me al in another kinde.'

Valerian seyde, 'two corones han we,
Snow-whyte and rose-reed, that shynen clere,
Whiche that thyn yën han no might to see;
And as thou smellest hem thurgh my preyere,
So shaltow seen hem, leve brother dere,
20 If it so be thou wolt, withouten slouthe,
Bileve aright and knowen verray trouthe.'

Tiburce answerde, 'seistow this to me
In soothnesse, or in dreem I herkne this?'
'In dremes,' quod Valerian, 'han we be
Unto this tyme, brother myn, y-wis.
But now at erst in trouthe our dwelling is.'
'How woostow this,' quod Tiburce, 'in what wyse?'
Quod Valerian, 'that shal I thee devyse.

The angel of god hath me the trouthe y-taught
30 Which thou shalt seen, if that thou wolt reneye
The ydoles and be clene, and elles naught.'—

   Undernom, perceived.   *Reneye,* give up.

And of the miracle of thise corones tweye
Seint Ambrose in his preface list to seye;
Solempnely this noble doctour dere
Commendeth it, and seith in this manere.

The palm of martirdom for to receyve,
Seinte Cecile, fulfild of goddes yifte,
The world and eek hir chambre gan she weyve;
Witnes Tyburces and Valerians shrifte,
To whiche god of his bountee wolde shifte
10 Corones two of floures wel smellinge,
And made his angel hem the corones bringe:

The mayde hath broght thise men to blisse above;
The world hath wist what it is worth, certeyn,
Devocioun of chastitee to love.—
Tho shewede him Cecile al open and pleyn
That alle ydoles nis but a thing in veyn;
For they been dombe, and therto they been deve,
And charged him his ydoles for to leve.

'Who so that troweth nat this, a beste he is,'
20 Quod tho Tiburce, 'if that I shal nat lye.'   ·
And she gan kisse his brest, that herde this,
And was ful glad he coude trouthe espye.
'This day I take thee for myn allye,'
Seyde this blisful fayre mayde dere;
And after that she seyde as ye may here:

'Lo, right so as the love of Crist,' quod she,
'Made me thy brotheres wyf, right in that wyse
Anon for myn allye heer take I thee,
Sin that thou wolt thyn ydoles despyse.
30 Go with thy brother now, and thee baptyse,

Weyve, renounce.   *Shrifte,* confession.

And make thee clene; so that thou mowe biholde
The angels face of which thy brother tolde.'

Tiburce answerde and seyde, 'brother dere,
First tel me whider I shal, and to what man?'
'To whom?' quod he, 'com forth with right good
 chere,
I wol thee lede unto the pope Urban.'
'Til Urban? brother myn Valerian,'
Quod tho Tiburce, 'woltow me thider lede?
10 Me thinketh that it were a wonder dede.

Ne menestow nat Urban,' quod he tho,
'That is so ofte dampned to be deed,
And woneth in halkes alwey to and fro,
And dar nat ones putte forth his heed?
Men sholde him brennen in a fyr so reed
If he were founde, or that men mighte him spye;
And we also, to bere him companye—

And whyl we seken thilke divinitee
That is y-hid in hevene prively,
20 Algate y-brend in this world shul we be!'
To whom Cecile answerde boldely,
'Men mighten dreden wel and skilfully
This lyf to lese, myn owene dere brother,
If this were livinge only and non other.

But ther is better lyf in other place,
That never shal be lost, ne drede thee noght,
Which goddes sone us tolde thurgh his grace;
That fadres sone hath alle thinges wroght;
And al that wroght is with a skilful thoght,
30 The goost, that fro the fader gan procede,
Hath sowled hem, withouten any drede.

Woneth in halkes, dwells in secret places.
Algate, nevertheless.   *Sowled,* given a soul.

By word and by miracle goddes sone,
Whan he was in this world, declared here
That ther was other lyf ther men may wone.'
To whom answerde Tiburce, 'O suster dere,
Ne seydestow right now in this manere,
Ther nis but o god, lord in soothfastnesse;
And now of three how maystow bere witnesse?'

'That shal I telle,' quod she, 'er I go.
Right as a man hath sapiences three,
10 Memorie, engyn, and intellect also,
So, in o being of divinitee,
Three persones may ther right wel be.'
Tho gan she him ful bisily to preche
Of Cristes come and of his peynes teche,

And many pointes of his passioun;
How goddes sone in this world was withholde,
To doon mankinde pleyn remissioun,
That was y-bounde in sinne and cares colde:
Al this thing she unto Tiburce tolde.
20 And after this Tiburce, in good entente,
With Valerian to pope Urban he wente,

That thanked god; and with glad herte and light
He cristned him, and made him in that place
Parfit in his lerninge, goddes knight.
And after this Tiburce gat swich grace,
That every day he saugh, in tyme and space,
The angel of god; and every maner bone
That he god axed, it was sped ful sone.

It were ful hard by ordre for to seyn
30 How many wondres Jesus for hem wroghte;
But atte laste, to tellen short and pleyn,

Engyn, Latin *ingenium,* natural capacity.
Pleyn, full.   *Bone,* boon, request.

The sergeants of the toun of Rome hem soghte,
And hem biforn Almache the prefect broghte,
Which hem apposed, and knew al hir entente,
And to the image of Jupiter hem sente,

And seyde, 'who so wol nat sacrifyse,
Swap of his heed, this is my sentence here.'
Anon thise martirs that I yow devyse,
Oon Maximus, that was an officere
Of the prefectes and his corniculere,
10 Hem hente; and whan he forth the seintes ladde,
Him-self he weep, for pitee that he hadde.

Whan Maximus had herd the seintes lore,
He gat him of the tormentoures leve,
And ladde hem to his hous withoute more;
And with hir preching, er that it were eve,
They gonnen fro the tormentours to reve,
And fro Maxime, and fro his folk echone
The false feith, to trowe in god allone.

Cecilie cam, wha it was woxen night,
20 With preestes that hem cristned alle y-fere;
And afterward, whan day was woxen light,
Cecile hem seyde with a ful sobre chere,
'Now, Cristes owene knightes leve and dere,
Caste alle awey the werkes of derknesse,
And armeth yow in armure of brightnesse.

Ye han for sothe y-doon a greet bataille,
Your cours is doon, your feith han ye conserved,
Goth to the corone of lyf that may nat faille;
The rightful juge, which that ye han served,
30 Shall yeve it yow, as ye han it deserved.'

Apposed, examined.   Swap, strike.   Corniculere, military aide.
Reve, take away.   Trowe, believe.   Y-fere, together.

And whan this thing was seyd as I devyse,
Men ladde hem forth to doon the sacrifyse.

But whan they weren to the place broght,
To tellen shortly the conclusioun,
They nolde encense ne sacrifice right noght,
But on hir knees they setten hem adoun
With humble herte and sad devocioun,
And losten bothe hir hedes in the place.
Hir soules wenten to the king of grace.

10 This Maximus, that saugh this thing bityde,
With pitous teres tolde it anon-right,
That he hir soules saugh to heven glyde
With angels ful of cleernesse and of light,
And with his word converted many a wight;
For which Almachius dide him so to-bete
With whippe of leed, til he his lyf gan lete.

Cecile him took and buried him anoon
By Tiburce and Valerian softely,
Withinne hir burying-place, under the stoon.
20 And after this Almachius hastily
Bad his ministres fecchen openly
Cecile, so that she mighte in his presence
Doon sacrifyce, and Jupiter encense.

But they, converted at hir wyse lore,
Wepten ful sore, and yaven ful credence
Unto hir word, and cryden more and more,
'Crist, goddes sone withouten difference,
Is verray god, this is al our sentence,
That hath so good a servant him to serve;
30 This with o voys we trowen, thogh we sterve!'

Sad, sober, earnest.   *Encense,* offer incense to.

Almachius, that herde of this doinge,
Bad fecchen Cecile, that he might hir see,
And alderfirst, lo! this was his axinge,
'What maner womman artow?' tho quod he.
'I am a gentil womman born,' quod she.
'I axe thee,' quod he, 'thogh it thee greve,
Of thy religioun and of thy bileve.'

'Ye han bigonne your question folily,'
Quod she, 'that wolden two answeres conclude
10 In oo demande; ye axed lewedly.'
Almache answerde unto that similitude,
'Of whennes comth thyn answering so rude?'
'Of whennes?' quod she, whan that she was freyned,
'Of conscience and of good feith unfeyned.'

Almachius seyde, 'ne takestow non hede
Of my power?' and she answerde him this—
'Your might,' quod she, 'ful litel is to drede;
For every mortal mannes power nis
But lyk a bladdre, ful of wind, y-wis.
20 For with a nedles poynt, whan it is blowe,
May al the boost of it be leyd ful lowe.'

'Ful wrongfully bigonne thou,' quod he,
'And yet in wrong is thy perseveraunce;
Wostow nat how our mighty princes free
Han thus comanded and maad ordinaunce,
That every Cristen wight shal han penaunce
But-if that he his Cristendom withseye,
And goon al quit, if he wol it reneye?'

Lewedly, ignorantly, because mixing up the question of rank and
religion.
Freyned, questioned.
Withseye, renounce, like *reneye.*

'Your princes erren, as your nobley dooth,'
Quod tho Cecile, 'and with a wood sentence
Ye make us gilty, and it is nat sooth ;
For ye, that knowen wel our innocence,
For as muche as we doon a reverence
To Crist, and for we bere a Cristen name,
Ye putte on us a cryme, and eek a blame.

But we that knowen thilke name so
For vertuous, we may it nat withseye.'
10 Almache answerde, 'chees oon of thise two,
Do sacrifyce, or Cristendom reneye,
That thou mowe now escapen by that weye.'
At which the holy blisful fayre mayde
Gan for to laughe, and to the juge seyde,

'O juge, confus in thy nycetee,
Woltow that I reneye innocence,
To make me a wikked wight?' quod she;
'Lo! he dissimuleth here in audience,
He stareth and woodeth in his advertence!'
20 To whom Almachius, 'unsely wrecche,
Ne woostow nat how far my might may strecche?

Han noght our mighty princes to me yeven,
Ye, bothe power and auctoritee
To maken folk to dyen or to liven?
Why spekestow so proudly than to me?'
'I speke noght but stedfastly,' quod she,
'Nat proudly, for I seye, as for my syde,
We haten deedly thilke vyce of pryde.

And if thou drede nat a sooth to here,
30 Than wol I shewe al openly, by right,
That thou hast maad a ful gret lesing here.

Nobley, nobility.	*Wood sentence,* foolish verdict.
Nycetee, folly.	*Advertence,* attention.
Unsely, unhappy.	*Lesing,* lie.

Thou seyst, thy princes han thee yeven might
Bothe for to sleen and for to quiken a wight;
Thou, that ne mayst but only lyf bireve,
Thou hast non other power ne no leve!

But thou mayst seyn, thy princes han thee maked
Ministre of deeth; for if thou speke of mo,
Thou lyest, for thy power is ful naked.'
'Do wey thy boldnes,' seyde Almachius tho,
'And sacrifyce to our goddes, er thou go;
10 I recche nat what wrong that thou me profre,
For I can suffre it as a philosophre;

For thilke wronges may I nat endure
That thou spekest of our goddes here,' quod he.
Cecile answerede, 'O nyce creature,
Thou seydest no word sin thou spak to me
That I ne knew therwith thy nycetee;
And that thou were, in every maner wyse,
A lewed officer and a veyn justyse.

Ther lakketh no-thing to thyn utter yën
20 That thou nart blind, for thing that we seen alle
That it is stoon, that men may wel espyen,
That ilke stoon a god thou wolt it calle.
I rede thee, lat thyn hand upon it falle,
And taste it wel, and stoon thou shalt it finde,
Sin that thou seest nat with thyn yën blinde.

It is a shame that the peple shal
So scorne thee, and laughe at thy folye;
For comunly men woot it wel overal,
That mighty god is in his hevenes hye,
30 And thise images, wel thou mayst espye,

Utter yën, bodily eyes.   *Taste,* try.

To thee ne to hem-self mowe nought profyte,
For in effect they been nat worth a myte.'

Thise wordes and swiche othere seyde she,
And he weex wroth, and bad men sholde hir lede
Hom til hir hous, 'and in hir hous,' quod he,
'Brenne hir right in a bath of flambes rede.'
And as he bad, right so was doon in dede;
For in a bath they gonne hir faste shetten,
And night and day greet fyr they under betten.

10 The longe night and eek a day also,
For al the fyr and eek the bathes hete,
She sat al cold, and felede no wo,
It made hir nat a drope for to swete.
But in that bath hir lyf she moste lete;
For he, Almachius, with ful wikke entente
To sleen hir in the bath his sonde sente.

Three strokes in the nekke he smoot hir tho,
The tormentour, but for no maner chaunce
He mighte noght smyte al hir nekke a-two;
20 And for ther was that tyme an ordinaunce,
That no man sholde doon man swich penaunce
The ferthe strook to smyten, softe or sore,
This tormentour ne dorste do na-more.

But half-deed, with hir nekke y-corven there,
He lefte hir lye, and on his wey is went.
The Cristen folk, which that aboute hir were,
With shetes han the blood ful faire y-hent.
Three dayes lived she in this torment,
And never cessed hem the feith to teche;
30 That she hadde fostred, hem she gan to preche;

Betten, kindled.
Sonde, message.

And hem she yaf hir moebles and hir thing,
And to the pope Urban bitook hem tho,
And seyde, 'I axed this at hevene king,
To han respyt three dayes and na-mo,
To recomende to yow, er that I go,
Thise soules, lo! and that I mighte do werche
Here of myn hous perpetuelly a cherche.'

Seint Urban, with his deknes, prively
The body fette, and buried it by nighte
10 Among his othere seintes honestly.
Hir hous the chirche of seint Cecilie highte;
Seint Urban halwed it, as he wel mighte;
In which, into this day, in noble wyse,
Men doon to Crist and to his seint servyse.

LYRICS

THAT our forefathers wrote songs and sang them must not be forgotten. A few specimens will serve to show the range of lyric poetry between the thirteen and fifteenth centuries.

SONG

Sing cuccu nu! Sing cuccu!
Sing cuccu! Sing cuccu nu!

Sumer is icumen in,
Lude sing cuccu;

Moebles, property.
Do werche, cause to be made.
Honestly, honorably.

Bitook hem, commended them.
Fette, fetched.
Halwed, consecrated.

Groweth sed and bloweth med
And springth the wude nu.
Sing cuccu!
Awe bleteth after lomb,
Lhouth after calve cu;
Bulluc sterteth, bucke verteth;
Murie sing cuccu.
Cuccu, cuccu,
Wel singes thu, cuccu,
10   Ne swik thu naver nu.
13th Century.

LADY FORTUNE

The lady Fortune is both friend and foe;
The poor she maketh rich, rich poor also;
She turneth woe to weal and weal to woe.
Trust thou no weal, her wheel she turneth so.
14th Century, modernized.

AGAINST MY WILL I TAKE MY LEAVE

Nou, bernes, buirdus, bolde and blythe,
To blessen ow her nou am I bounde;
I thonke you alle a thousend sithe,
And prei God save you hol and sounde;
Wherever ye go, on gras or grounde,
20   He· ow governe withouten greve.
For frendschipe that I here have founde,
Agein mi wille I take mi leve.

For frendschipe and for giftes goode,
For mete and drinke so gret plente,

Bloweth med, blossometh the meadow.   *Awe*, ewe.
Lhouth, lows.   *Verteth*, lurks in the green.   *Swik*, cease.
Bernes, buirdus, men, maidens.   *Ow*, you.   *Sithe*, times.

That Lord that raught was on the roode,
   He kepe thi comeli cumpanye;
On see or lond wher that ye be,
   He governe ow withouten greve.
So good disport ye han mad me,
   Agein my wille I take mi leve.

Agein mi wille althaugh I wende,
   I may not alwey dwellen here;
For everithing schal have an ende,
10   And frendes are not ay ifere;
Be we never so lef and dere,
   Out of this world al schul we meve;
And whon we buske unto ur bere,
   Agein ur wille we take ur leve.

And wende we schulle, I wot never whenne,
   Ne whoderward that we schul fare;
But endeles blisse or ay to brenne
   To everi mon is yarked yare.
Forthi I rede uch mon beware,
20   And lete ur werk ur wordes preve,
So that no sunne ur soule forfare
   Whon that ur lyf hath taken his leve.

Whon that ur lyf his leve hath lauht,
   Ur bodi lith bounden bi the wowe,
Ur richesses alle from us ben raft,
   In clottes colde ur corse is throwe.
Wher are thi frendes ho wol the knowe?
   Let seo he wol thi soule releve.

Raught, stretched.	*Ifere*, together.
Meve, go.	*Buske* . . . *bere*, go . . . bier.
Yarked yare, ready prepared.	*Rede*, counsel.
Sunne . . . *forfare*, sin . . . destroy.	*Lauht*, taken.
Wowe, wall.	*Throwe*, thrown.

I rede the, mon, ar thou ly lowe,
Beo redi ay to take thi leve.

14th Century.

TRUTH

BALADE DE BON CONSEYL

Flee fro the prees, and dwelle with sothfastnesse,
Suffyce unto thy good, though it be smal;
For hord hath hate, and climbing tikelnesse,
Prees hath envye, and wele blent overal;
Savour no more than thee bihove shal;
Werk wel thy-self, that other folk canst rede;
And trouthe shal delivere, hit is no drede.

10 Tempeste thee noght al croked to redresse,
In trust of hir that turneth as a bal:
Gret reste stant in litel besinesse;
And eek be war to sporne ageyn an al;
Stryve noght, as doth the crokke with the wal.
Daunte thy-self, that dauntest otheres dede;
And trouthe shal delivere, hit is no drede.

That thee is sent, receyve in buxumnesse,
The wrastling for this worlde axeth a fal.
Her nis non hoom, her nis but wildernesse:
20 Forth, pilgrim, forth! Forth, beste, out of thy stal!
Know thy contree, look up, thank God of al;
Hold the hye wey, and lat thy gost thee lede:
And trouthe shal delivere, hit is no drede.

Prees, throng.
Wele blent, wealth blinds.
Tempeste, violently trouble.
Daunte, subdue.

Tikelnesse, unstableness.
Savour, have appetite for.
Sporne, kick.

Envoy

Therfore, thou Vache, leve thyn old wrecchednesse
Unto the worlde; leve now to be thral;
Crye him mercy, that of his hy goodnesse
Made thee of noght, and in especial
Draw unto him, and pray in general
For thee, and eek for other, hevenlich mede;
And trouthe shal delivere, hit is no drede.

Geoffrey Chaucer

BALLADE

Hyd, Absolon, thy gilte tresses clere;
Ester, ley thou thy meknesse al a-doun;
10 Hyd, Jonathas, al thy frendly manere;
Penalopee, and Marcia Catoun,
Mak of your wyfhod no comparisoun;
Hyde ye your beautes, Isoude and Eleyne,
My lady cometh, that al this may disteyne.

Thy faire body, lat it nat appere,
Lavyne; and thou, Lucresse of Rome toun,
And Polixene, that boghten love so dere,
And Cleopatre, with al thy passioun,
Hyde ye your trouthe of love and your renoun;
20 And thou, Tisbe, that hast of love swich peyne;
My lady cometh, that al this may disteyne.

Herro, Dido, Laudomia, alle y-fere,
And Phyllis, hanging for thy Demophoun,
And Canace, espyed by thy chere,

Vache, Sir Philip la Vache.
Disteyne, bedim, dull.
Espyed by thy chere, recognized by thy sad countenance.

Ysiphile, betraysed with Jasoun,
Maketh of your trouthe neyther boost ne soun;
Nor Ypermistre or Adriane, ye tweyne;
My lady cometh, that al this may disteyne.

Geoffrey Chaucer

THE COMPLEYNT OF CHAUCER TO HIS PURSE

To you, my purse, and to noon other wyght
    Compleyne I, for ye be my lady dere!
I am so sorry now that ye been light;
    For, certes, but ye make me hevy chere,
    Me were as leef be leyd upon my bere,
10 For whiche unto your mercy thus I crye,—
Beth hevy ageyn, or elles mot I dye!

Now voucheth sauf this day or hit be nyght,
    That I of you the blisful soun may here,
Or see your colour lyk the sonne bright,
    That of yelownesse hadde never pere.
    Ye be my lyf! ye be myn hertes stere!
Quene of comfort and of good companye!
Beth hevy ageyn, or elles mot I dye.

Now, purse, that be to me my lyves light
20   And saveour, as doun in this worlde here,
    Out of this toune help me through your myght,
    Syn that ye wole not been my tresorere;
    For I am shave as nye as is a frere.
But yet I pray unto your curtesye,
Beth hevy ageyn, or elles mot I dye!

Hevy chere, heavy appearance.
Soun, sound.
Stere, rudder.

L'Envoye De Chaucer

O conquerour of Brutes Albioun,
Which that by lyne and free eleccioun
    Ben verray kyng, this song to you I sende,
    And ye that mowen al myn harm amende,
Have mynde upon my supplicacioun!

Geoffrey Chaucer

SONG

    Adam lay ibounden,
        Bounden in a bond;
    Four thousand winter
        Thoght he not too long;
10 And all was for an appil,
        An appil that he tok,
    As clerkes finden
        Writen in here book.
    Ne hadde the appil take ben,
        The appil taken ben,
    Ne hadde never our lady
        A ben hevene quene.
    Blessed be the time
        That appil take was.
20 Therefore we moun singen
        Deo Gracias.

Early 15th Century.

A CAROL

Noel, el, el, el, el,
I thanke it a maiden every del.

Conquerour, etc. Henry IV, who in 1399 had just ascended
the throne of Brutus' Albion.   *Mowen,* may.
Here, their.   *Moun,* may.

The first day whan Crist was borne,
There sprang a rose out of a thorne,
To save mankind that was forlorne,
    I thanke it a maiden every del.

In an oxstall the child was found;
In pore clothing the child was wound;
He sofered many a dedly wound.
    I thanke it a maiden every del.

A garlond of thornes on his hed was sett;
10 A scharp spere to his hart was smet;
The Jewes seiden 'Tak thee that!'
    I thanke it a maiden every del.

The Jewes deden cryen her parlement;
On the day of jugement
They werren aferd they shuld hem schent.
    I thanke it a maiden every del.

To the peler he was bounden;
To his hart a spere was stunggen;
For us he sofered a dedly wounden.
20   I thanke it a maiden every del.
                        15th Century.

MALORY'S MORTE D'ARTHUR

IF WE are right in supposing the compiler of Le Morte
D'arthur to have been a Sir Thomas Malory of Warwick-
shire, who fought in France in the train of an Earl of
Warwick, who served in parliament after succeeding to his

family estate, and who died in 1470, we may reasonably guess that the old knight turned to the work during the fifteen years of imprisonment with which he ended his days. It was finished, he wrote at the end, in 1469. Probably Malory had no notion of achieving literary fame, but only of making a convenient summary of Arthurian stories for his own use. It was his good fortune to write at a time when English was taking on its modern characteristics, so that his romance has always been read without difficulty; and it was his luck that William Caxton, the pioneer among English printers, brought out an edition of the book in 1485, thus giving it a wider public than it could have had under the old conditions of manuscript production.

Yet the Morte D'arthur deserves the fame it has won, for it presents the completest collection of stories about Arthur ever put in a single book, and it presents them in noble and resonant prose. What Malory did was to work through a vast series of prose romances in French, summarizing, arranging, and translating as suited his purpose, but always with the end in view of showing the whole life of Arthur. He also had by him certain English romances in verse, which he used along with his French sources. He was thus much more than a translator, for he made out of very disorderly materials a book that is not without a plan, though a sufficiently complex one, and a book of abiding charm.

THE CHOOSING OF ARTHUR

BOOK I. CHAPTER IV-VII.

And then he fell passing sore sick, so that three days and three nights he was speechless: wherefore all the barons made great sorrow, and asked Merlin what counsel were best. There is none other remedy, said Merlin, but God will have his will. But look ye all barons be before King Uther to-morn, and God and I shall make him to speak. So on the morn all the barons, with Merlin, came tofore the king. Then Merlin said aloud unto King Uther, Sir, shall 10 your son Arthur be king after your days, of this

And then he, King Uther.

realm with all the appurtenance? Then Uther Pendragon turned him, and said in hearing of them all,
I give him God's blessing and mine, and bid him pray
for my soul, and righteously and worshipfully that
he claim the crown, upon forfeiture of my blessing;
and therewith he yielded up the ghost, and then
was he interred as longed to a king. Wherefore
the queen, fair Igraine, made great sorrow, and all
the barons.

10   Then stood the realm in great jeopardy long while,
for every lord that was mighty of men made him
strong, and many weened to have been king. Then
Merlin went to the Archbishop of Canterbury, and
counselled him for to send for all the lords of the
realm, and all the gentlemen of arms, that they should
to London come by Christmas, upon pain of cursing;
and for this cause, that Jesus, that was born on that
night, that he would of his great mercy show some
miracle, as he was come to be king of mankind, for
20 to show some miracle who should be rightwise king
of this realm. So the Archbishop, by the advice of
Merlin, sent for all the lords and gentlemen of arms
that they should come by Christmas even unto London. And many of them made them clean of their
life, that their prayer might be the more acceptable
unto God.

So in the greatest church of London, whether it
were Paul's or not the French book maketh no mention, all the estates were long or day in the church
30 for to pray. And when matins and the first mass
was done, there was seen in the churchyard, against
the high altar, a great stone four square, like unto
a marble stone, and in midst thereof was like an
anvil of steel a foot on high, and therein stuck a

Clean of their life, made confession.
Estates, ranks or orders of society.

fair sword, naked by the point, and letters there
were written in gold about the sword that said
thus: Whoso pulleth out this sword of this stone and
anvil, is rightwise king born of all England. Then
the people marvelled, and told it to the Archbishop.
I command, said the Archbishop, that ye keep you
within your church, and pray unto God still; that
no man touch the sword till the high mass be all done.
So when all masses were done, all the lords went to
10 behold the stone and the sword. And when they
saw the scripture, some assayed; such as would have
been king. But none might stir the sword nor move
it. He is not here, said the Archbishop, that shall
achieve the sword, but doubt not God will make
him known. But this is my counsel, said the Archbishop, that we let purvey ten knights, men of good
fame, and they to keep this sword. So it was ordained, and then there was made a cry, for every man
should assay that would, for to win the sword.
20 And upon New Year's Day the barons let make
a jousts and a tournament, that all knights that
would joust or tourney there might play, and all
this was ordained for to keep the lords together and
the commons, for the Archbishop trusted that God
would make him known that should win the sword.
So upon New Year's Day, when the service was
done, the barons rode unto the field, some to joust
and some to tourney, and so it happened that Sir
Ector, that had great livelihood about London, rode
30 unto the jousts, and with him rode Sir Kay his
son, and young Arthur that was his nourished
brother; and Sir Kay was made knight at All Hal-
lowmass afore.
So as they rode to the jousts-ward, Sir Kay lost
his sword, for he had left it at his father's lodging,

Assayed, tried.   *Purvey*, provide.   *Nourished*, foster.

and so he prayed young Arthur for to ride for his
sword. I will well, said Arthur, and rode fast after
the sword, and when he came home, the lady and
all were out to see the jousting. Then was Arthur
wroth, and said to himself, I will ride to the churchyard, and take the sword with me that sticketh in
the stone, for my brother Sir Kay shall not be without a sword this day. So when he came to the
churchyard, Sir Arthur alit and tied his horse to the
10 stile, and so he went to the tent, and found no
knights there, for they were at the jousting; and so
he handled the sword by the handles, and lightly and
fiercely pulled it out of the stone, and took his horse
and rode his way until he came to his brother Sir
Kay, and delivered him the sword.

And as soon as Sir Kay saw the sword, he wist
well it was the sword of the stone, and so he rode
to his father Sir Ector, and said: Sir, lo here is the
sword of the stone, wherefore I must be king of
20 this land. When Sir Ector beheld the sword, he
returned again and came to the church, and there
they alit all three, and went into the church. And
anon he made Sir Kay to swear upon a book how he
came to that sword. Sir, said Sir Kay, by my
brother Arthur, for he brought it to me. How gat
ye this sword? said Sir Ector to Arthur. Sir, I will
tell you. When I came home for my brother's sword,
I found nobody at home to deliver me his sword,
and so I thought my brother Sir Kay should not be
30 swordless, and so I came hither eagerly and pulled
it out of the stone without any pain. Found ye any
knights about this sword? said Sir Ector. Nay, said
Arthur. Now, said Sir Ector to Arthur, I understand ye must be king of this land. Wherefore I,
said Arthur, and for what cause? Sir, said Ector,
for God will have it so, for there should never man

have drawn out this sword, but he that shall be
rightwise king of this land. Now let me see whether
ye can put the sword there as it was, and pull it out
again. That is no mastery, said Arthur, and so he
put it in the stone, wherewithal Sir Ector assayed
to pull out the sword and failed. Now assay, said
Sir Ector unto Sir Kay. And anon he pulled at the
sword with all his might, but it would not be.

Now shall ye assay, said Sir Ector to Arthur. I
10 will well, said Arthur, and pulled it out easily. And
therewithal Sir Ector kneeled down to the earth, and
Sir Kay. Alas, said Arthur, my own dear father
and brother, why kneel ye to me? Nay, nay, my
lord Arthur, it is not so; I was never your father
nor of your blood, but I wot well ye are of an higher
blood than I weened ye were. And then Sir Ector
told him all, how he was betaken him for to nourish
him, and by whose commandment, and by Merlin's
deliverance.

20   Then Arthur made great dole when he understood
that Sir Ector was not his father. Sir, said Ector
unto Arthur, will ye be my good and gracious lord
when ye are king? Else were I to blame, said
Arthur, for ye are the man in the world that I am
most beholden to, and my good lady and mother
your wife, that as well as her own hath fostered
me and kept. And if ever it be God's will that I
be king as ye say, ye shall desire of me what I may
do, and I shall not fail you. God forbid I should
30 fail you. Sir, said Sir Ector, I will ask no more of
you, but that ye will make my son, your foster
brother, Sir Kay, seneschal of all your lands. That
shall be done, said Arthur, and more, by the faith

Rightwise, true, real.   *Mastery,* task.
Betaken, entrusted.   *Dole,* lamentation.

of my body, that never man shall have that office but he, while he and I live.

Therewithal they went unto the Archbishop, and told him how the sword was achieved, and by whom; and on Twelfth-day all the barons came thither, and to assay to take the sword, who that would assay. But there afore them all, there might none take it out but Arthur. Wherefore there were many lords wroth, and said it was a great shame unto them all 10 and the realm, to be overgoverned with a boy of no high blood born. And so they fell out at that time that it was put off till Candlemas, and then all the barons should meet there again; but always the ten knights were ordained to watch the sword day and night, and so they set a pavilion over the stone and the sword, and five always watched.

So at Candlemas many more great lords came thither for to have won the sword, but there might none prevail. And right as Arthur did at Christmas, 20 he did at Candlemas, and pulled out the sword easily, whereof the barons were sore aggrieved and put it off in delay till the high feast of Easter. And as Arthur sped afore, so did he at Easter, yet there were some of the great lords had indignation that Arthur should be king, and put it off in a delay till the feast of Pentecost. Then the Archbishop of Canterbury by Merlin's providence let purvey then of the best knights that they might get, and such knights as Uther Pendragon loved best and most 30 trusted in his days. And such knights were put about Sir Arthur as Sir Baudwin of Britain, Sir Kay, Sir Ulfius, Sir Barsias. All these with many other were always about Arthur, day and night, till the feast of Pentecost.

And at the feast of Pentecost all manner of men

Candlemas, Epiphany.　　　　　*Providence,* arrangement.

assayed to pull at the sword that would assay, but none might prevail but Arthur, and pulled it out afore all the lords and commons that were there. Wherefore all the commons cried at once, We will have Arthur unto our king; we will put him no more in delay, for we all see that it is God's will that he shall be our king, and who that holdeth against it, we will slay him. And therewith all they kneeled at once, both rich and poor, and cried Arthur
10 mercy because they had delayed him so long, and Arthur forgave them, and took the sword between both his hands, and offered it upon the altar, where the Archbishop was, and so was he made knight of the best man that was there. And so anon was the coronation made. And there was he sworn unto his lords and the commons for to be a true king, to stand with true justice from thenceforth the days of his life.

LAUNCELOT AND THE GRAIL CASTLE

BOOK XVII. CHAPTERS XIII-XV

Now saith the history, that when Launcelot was
20 come to the water of Mortoise, as it is rehearsed before, he was in great peril, and so he laid him down and slept, and took the adventure that God would send him.

So when he was asleep, there came a vision unto him and said: Launcelot, arise up and take thine armour, and enter into the first ship that thou shalt find. And when he heard these words, he started up and saw great clearness about him. And then he lifted up his hand and blessed him, and so took
30 his arms and made him ready; and so by adventure

Of the best man, by the best man.

he came by a strand, and found a ship the which was without sail or oar. And as soon as he was within the ship there, he felt the most sweetness that ever he felt, and he was fulfilled with all thing that he thought on or desired. Then he said: Fair sweet Father, Jesu Christ, I wot not in what joy I am, for this joy passeth all earthly joys that ever I was in. And so in this joy he laid him down to the ship's board, and slept till day.

10 And when he awoke, he found there a fair bed, and therein lying a gentlewoman dead, the which was Sir Percivale's sister. And as Launcelot devised her, he espied in her right hand a writ, the which he read, the which told him all the adventures that ye have heard tofore, and of what lineage she was come. So with this gentlewoman Sir Launcelot was a month and more. If ye would ask how he lived, He that fed the people of Israel with manna in the desert, so was he fed; for every day when he had 20 said his prayers, he was sustained with the grace of the Holy Ghost.

So on a night he went to play him by the water side, for he was somewhat weary of the ship. And then he listened and heard an horse come, and one riding upon him. And when he came nigh, he seemed a knight. And so he let him pass, and went thereas the ship was; and there he alit, and took the saddle and the bridle and put the horse from him, and went into the ship. And then Launcelot 30 dressed unto him, and said: Ye be welcome. And he answered and saluted him again, and asked him: What is your name? for much my heart giveth unto you. Truly, said he, my name is Launcelot du Lake. Sir, said he, then be ye welcome, for ye

Devised, looked at.   *Dressed,* went.
Giveth unto you, is moved towards you.

were the beginner of me in this world. Ah, said
he, are ye Galahad? Yea, forsooth, said he; and
so he kneeled down and asked him his blessing,
and after took off his helm and kissed him.
And there was great joy between them, for there
is no tongue can tell the joy that they made either
of other, and many a friendly word spoken between,
as kin would, the which is no need here to be rehearsed. And there everyeach told other of their
10 adventures and marvels that were fallen to them
in many journeys sith that they departed from the
court. Anon, as Galahad saw the gentlewoman dead
in the bed, he knew her well enough, and told great
worship of her, that she was the best maid living,
and it was great pity of her death. But when
Launcelot heard how the marvellous sword was gotten, and who made it, and all the marvels rehearsed
afore, then he prayed Galahad, his son, that he would
show him the sword, and so he did; and anon he
20 kissed the pommel, and the hilts, and the scabbard.
Truly, said Launcelot, never erst knew I of so high
adventures done, and so marvellous and strange.
So dwelt Launcelot and Galahad within that ship
half a year, and served God daily and nightly with
all their power; and often they arrived in isles far
from folk, where there repaired none but wild beasts,
and there they found many strange adventures and
perilous, which they brought to an end; but for
those adventures were with wild beasts, and not in
30 the quest of the Sangreal, therefore the tale maketh
here no mention thereof, for it would be too long
to tell of all those adventures that befell them.
So after, on a Monday, it befell that they arrived
in the edge of a forest tofore a cross; and then saw
they a knight armed all in white, and was richly
horsed, and led in his right hand a white horse; and

so he came to the ship, and saluted the two knights
on the High Lord's behalf, and said: Galahad, sir,
ye have been long enough with your father. Come
out of the ship, and start upon this horse, and go
where the adventures shall lead thee in the quest
of the Sangreal. Then he went to his father and
kissed him sweetly, and said: Fair sweet father, I
wot not when I shall see you more till I see the
body of Jesu Christ. I pray you, said Launcelot,
10 pray ye to the High Father that He hold me in His
service. And so he took his horse, and there they
heard a voice that said: Think for to do well, for the
one shall never see the other before the dreadful day
of doom. Now, son Galahad, said Launcelot, syne
we shall depart, and never see other, I pray to the
High Father to conserve me and you both. Sir, said
Galahad, no prayer availeth so much as yours. And
therewith Galahad entered into the forest.

And the wind arose, and drove Launcelot more
20 than a month throughout the sea, where he slept
but little, but prayed to God that he might see some
tidings of the Sangreal. So it befell on a night, at
midnight, he arrived afore a castle, on the back side,
which was rich and fair, and there was a postern
opened toward the sea, and was open without any
keeping, save two lions kept the entry; and the
moon shone clear. Anon Sir Launcelot heard a
voice that said: Launcelot, go out of this ship and
enter into the castle, where thou shalt see a great
30 part of thy desire.

Then he ran to his arms, and so armed him, and
so went to the gate and saw the lions. Then set
he hand to his sword and drew it. Then there came
a dwarf suddenly, and smote him on the arm so
sore that the sword fell out of his hand. Then heard

Syne, since.

he a voice say: O man of evil faith and poor belief, wherefore trowest thou more on thy harness than in thy Maker, for He might more avail thee than thine armour, in whose service that thou art set. Then said Launcelot: Fair Father Jesu Christ, I thank thee of Thy great mercy that Thou reprovest me of my misdeeds; now see I well that ye hold me for your servant. Then took he again his sword and put it up in his sheath, and made a cross in his forehead, and came to the lions, and they made semblant to do him harm. Notwithstanding, he passed by them without hurt, and entered into the castle to the chief fortress, and there were they all at rest.

Then Launcelot entered in so armed, for he found no gate nor door but it was open. And at the last he found a chamber whereof the door was shut, and he set his hand thereto to have opened it, but he might not. Then he enforced him mickle to undo the door. Then he listened and heard a voice which sang so sweetly that it seemed none earthly thing; and him thought the voice said: Joy and honour be to the Father of Heaven. Then Launcelot kneeled down tofore the chamber, for well wist he that there was the Sangreal within that chamber. Then said he: Fair sweet Father, Jesu Christ, if ever I did thing that pleased Thee, Lord for Thy pity never have me not in despite for my sins done aforetime, and that Thou show me something of that I seek. And with that he saw the chamber door open, and there came out a great clearness, that the house was as bright as all the torches of the world had been there. So came he to the chamber door, and would have entered. And anon a voice said to him: Flee, Launcelot, and enter not, for thou oughtest not to

Trowest, trustest.　　　　　　*Made semblant,* threatened.
Enforced him mickle, tried hard.

do it; and if thou enter, thou shalt forthink it.   Then he withdrew him aback right heavy.

Then looked he up in the middes of the chamber, and saw a table of silver and the holy vessel, covered with red samite, and many angels about it, whereof one held a candle of wax burning, and the other held a cross, and the ornaments of an altar. And before the holy vessel he saw a good man clothed as a priest.   And it seemed that he was at
10 the sacring of the mass.   And it seemed to Launcelot that above the priest's hands were three men, whereof the two put the youngest by likeness between the priest's hands; and so he lifted it up right high, and it seemed to show so to the people.   And then Launcelot marvelled not a little, for him thought the priest was so greatly charged of the figure that him seemed that he should fall to the earth.   And when he saw none about him that would help him, then came he to the door a great pace, and said: Fair
20 Father Jesu Christ, ne take it for no sin though I help the good man which hath great need of help. Right so entered he into the chamber, and came toward the table of silver; and when he came nigh he felt a breath, that him thought it was intermedled with fire, which smote him so sore in the visage that him thought it brent his visage; and therewith he fell to the earth, and had no power to arise, as he that was so araged, that had lost the power of his body, and his hearing, and his seeing.   Then felt he
30 many hands about him, which took him up and bare him out of the chamber door without any amending of his swoon, and left him there, seeming dead to all people.

Forthink, repent.   *Heavy,* troubled.   *Sacring,* consecration.
Charged of, burdened with.   *Intermedled,* mingled.
Brent, burned.   *Araged,* enraged.

So upon the morrow when it was fair day, they within were arisen, and found Launcelot lying afore the chamber door. All they marvelled how that he came in, and so they looked upon him, and felt his pulse to wit whether there were any life in him; and so they found life in him, but he might not stand nor stir no member that he had. And so they took him by every part of the body, and bare him into a chamber, and laid him in a rich bed far from all 10 folk; and so he lay four days. Then the one said he was on live, and the other said, Nay. In the name of God, said an old man, for I do you verily to wit he is not dead, but he is so full of life as the mightiest of you all; and therefore I counsel you that he be well kept till God send him life again.

ARTHUR'S LAST BATTLE AND DEATH

BOOK XXI. CHAPTERS IV-VII

Then were they condescended that King Arthur and Sir Mordred should meet betwixt both their hosts, and everyeach of them should bring fourteen persons; and they came with this word unto 20 Arthur. Then said he: I am glad that this is done, and so he went into the field. And when Arthur should depart, he warned all his host that an they see any sword drawn: Look ye come on fiercely, and slay that traitor, Sir Mordred, for I in no wise trust him. In likewise Sir Mordred warned his host that: An ye see any sword drawn, look that ye come on fiercely, and so slay all that ever before you standeth; for in no wise I will not trust for this treaty, for I know well my father will be avenged on me. And 30 so they met as their appointment was, and so they

Condescended, pleased to agree.

were agreed and accorded thoroughly; and wine was fetched, and they drank.

Right soon came an adder out of a little heath bush, and it stung a knight on the foot. And when the knight felt him stung, he looked down and saw the adder, and then he drew his sword to slay the adder, and thought of none other harm. And when the host on both parties saw that sword drawn, then they blew beaums, trumpets, and horns, and shouted
10 grimly. And so both hosts dressed them together. And King Arthur took his horse, and said: Alas this unhappy day! and so rode to his party. And Sir Mordred in likewise.

And never was there seen a more dolefuller battle in no Christian land; for there was but rushing and riding, foining and striking, and many a grim word was there spoken either to other, and many a deadly stroke. But ever King Arthur rode throughout the battle of Sir Mordred many times, and did full
20 nobly as a noble king should, and at all times he fainted never; and Sir Mordred that day put him in devoir, and in great peril. And thus they fought all the long day, and never stinted till the noble knights were laid to the cold earth; and ever they fought still till it was near night, and by that time was there an hundred thousand laid dead upon the down.

Then was Arthur wood wroth out of measure, when he saw his people so slain from him. Then
30 the king looked about him, and then was he ware, of all his host and of all his good knights, were left no more on live but two knights; that one was Sir Lucan de Butler, and his brother Sir Bedivere, and

---

Beaums, trumpets.   *Dressed them,* arranged themselves.
Foining, thrusting.   *Battle,* forces.
Devoir, hard effort.   *Wood,* mad.

they were full sore wounded. Jesu mercy, said the king, where are all my noble knights become? Alas that ever I should see this doleful day! For now, said Arthur, I am come to mine end. But would to God that I wist where were that traitor Sir Mordred, that hath caused all this mischief!

Then was King Arthur ware where Sir Mordred leaned upon his sword among a great heap of dead men. Now give me my spear, said Arthur unto
10 Sir Lucan, for yonder I have espied the traitor that all this woe hath wrought. Sir, let him be, said Sir Lucan, for he is unhappy; and if ye pass this unhappy day, ye shall be right well revenged upon him. Good lord, remember ye of your night's dream, and what the spirit of Sir Gawain told you this night, yet God of his great goodness hath preserved you hitherto. Therefore, for God's sake, my lord, leave off by this, for blessed be God, ye have won the field, for here we be three on live, and with Sir Mordred
20 is none on live; and if ye leave off now, this wicked day of destiny is past. Tide me death, betide me life, saith the king, now I see him yonder alone he shall never escape mine hands, for at a better avail shall I never have him. God speed you well, said Sir Bedivere.

Then the king gat his spear in both his hands, and ran toward Sir Mordred, crying: Traitor, now is thy death day come. And when Sir Mordred heard Sir Arthur, he ran until him with his sword drawn in
30 his hand. And there King Arthur smote Sir Mordred under the shield, with a foin of his spear, throughout the body, more than a fathom. And when Sir Mordred felt that he had his death wound, he thrust himself with the might that he had up to the bur of King Arthur's spear. And right so he

Bur, leather protector on shaft of spear below the grip.

smote his father Arthur, with his sword holden in
both his hands, on the side of the head, that the
sword pierced the helmet and the brain pan, and
therewithal Sir Mordred fell stark dead to the earth.

And the noble Arthur fell in a swoon to the earth,
and there he swooned ofttimes. And Sir Lucan de
Butler and Sir Bedivere ofttimes heaved him up.
And so weakly they led him betwixt them both to a
little chapel not far from the seaside. And when
10 the king was there, he thought him well eased. Then
heard they people cry in the field. Now go thou,
Sir Lucan, said the king, and do me to wit what
betokens that noise in the field. So Sir Lucan departed, for he was grievously wounded in many
places. And so as he yede, he saw and hearkened by
the moonlight, how that pillers and robbers were
come into the field, to pill and rob many a full noble
knight of brooches and beads, of many a good ring,
and of many a rich jewel; and who that were not
20 dead all out, there they slew them for their harness
and their riches. When Sir Lucan understood this
work, he came to the king as soon as he might, and
told him all what he had heard and seen. Therefore
by my rede, said Sir Lucan, it is best that we bring
you to some town. I would it were so, said the king,
but I may not stand, mine head works so. Ah, Sir
Launcelot, said King Arthur, this day have I sore
missed thee. Alas, that ever I was against thee,
for now have I my death, whereof Sir Gawain me
30 warned in my dream.

Then Sir Lucan took up the king the one part,
and Sir Bedivere the other part, and in the lifting
the king swooned; and Sir Lucan fell in a swoon
with the lift, that the part of his guts fell out of his

Yede, went.
Dead all out, dead outright.

Pillers, pillagers.
Rede, advice.

body, and therewith the noble knight's heart brast. And when the king awoke, he beheld Sir Lucan, how he lay foaming at the mouth, and part of his guts lay at his feet. Alas, said the king, this is to me a full heavy sight, to see this noble duke so die for my sake, for he would have holpen me that had more need of help than I. Alas, he would not complain him, his heart was so set to help me! Now Jesu have mercy upon his soul!

10 Then Sir Bedivere wept for the death of his brother. Leave this mourning and weeping, said the king, for all this will not avail me, for wit thou well an I might live myself, the death of Sir Lucan would grieve me evermore; but my time hieth fast, said the king. Therefore, said Arthur unto Sir Bedivere, take thou Excalibur, my good sword, and go with it to yonder water side; and when thou comest there, I charge thee throw my sword in that water, and come again and tell me what thou there seest. My 20 lord, said Bedivere, your commandment shall be done, and lightly bring you word again.

. So Sir Bedivere departed, and by the way he beheld that noble sword, that the pommel and the haft was all of precious stones; and then he said to himself: If I throw this rich sword in the water, thereof shall never come good, but harm and loss. And then Sir Bedivere hid Excalibur under a tree. And so, as soon as he might, he came again unto the king, and said he had been at the water, and had 30 thrown the sword in the water. What saw thou there? said the king. Sir, he said, I saw nothing but waves and winds. That is untruly said of thee, said the king. Therefore go thou lightly again, and do my commandment; as thou art to me lief and dear, spare not, but throw it in.

Brast, burst.

Then Sir Bevidere returned again, and took the sword in his hand; and then him thought sin and shame to throw away that noble sword, and so eft he hid the sword, and returned again, and told to the king that he had been at the water, and done his commandment. What saw thou there? said the king. Sir, he said, I saw nothing but the waters wappe and waves wanne. Ah, traitor untrue, said King Arthur, now hast thou betrayed me twice. Who 10 would have weened that thou that hast been to me so lief and dear? and thou art named a noble knight, and would betray me for the richness of the sword. But now go again lightly, for thy long tarrying putteth me in great jeopardy of my life, for I have taken cold. And but if thou do now as I bid thee, if ever I may see thee, I shall slay thee with mine own hands; for thou wouldst for my rich sword see me dead.

Then Sir Bedivere departed, and went to the 20 sword, and lightly took it up, and went to the water side; and there he bound the girdle about the hilts, and then he threw the sword as far into the water as he might; and there came an arm and an hand above the water and met it, and caught it, and so shook it thrice and brandished, and then vanished away the hand with the sword in the water. So Sir Bedivere came again to the king and told him what he saw. Alas, said the king, help me hence, for I dread me I have tarried over long.

30 Then Sir Bedivere took the king upon his back, and so went with him to that water side. And when they were at the water side, even fast by the bank hoved a little barge with many fair ladies in it, and among them all was a queen, and all they had black hoods, and all they wept and shrieked when they saw

Eft, again.   *Wappe . . . wanne,* lap . . . wash.

King Arthur. Now put me into the barge, said the king, and so he did softly. And there received him three queens with great mourning; and so they set them down, and in one of their laps King Arthur laid his head. And then that queen said: Ah, dear brother, why have ye tarried so long from me? Alas, this wound on your head hath caught overmuch cold. And so then they rowed from the land, and Sir Bedivere beheld all those ladies go from
10 him. Then Sir Bedivere cried: Ah, my lord Arthur, what shall become of me, now ye go from me and leave me here alone among mine enemies? Comfort thyself, said the king, and do as well as thou mayest, for in me is no trust for to trust in; for I will into the vale of Avilion to heal me of my grievous wound. And if thou hear never more of me, pray for my soul. But ever the queens and ladies wept and shrieked, that it was pity to hear.

And as soon as Sir Bedivere had lost the sight
20 of the barge, he wept and wailed, and so took the forest; and so he went all that night, and in the morning he was ware, betwixt two holts hoar, of a chapel and an hermitage. Then was Sir Bedivere glad, and thither he went; and when he came into the chapel, he saw where lay an hermit grovelling on all four there fast by a tomb was new graven. When the hermit saw Sir Bedivere, he knew him well, for he was but little tofore Bishop of Canterbury, that Sir Mordred flemed. Sir, said Bedivere, what man
30 is there interred that ye pray so fast for? Fair son, said the hermit, I wot not verily, but by my deeming. But this night, at midnight, here came a number of ladies, and brought hither a dead corpse, and prayed me to bury him; and here they offered an hundred

Holts hoar, grey copses.   *Flemed,* banished.
Deeming, judging.

tapers, and they gave me an hundred besants. Alas, said Sir Bedivere, that was my lord King Arthur, that here lieth buried in this chapel.

Then Sir Bedivere swooned; and when he awoke, he prayed the hermit he might abide with him still there, to live with fasting and prayers. For from hence will I never go, said Sir Bedivere, by my will, but all the days of my life here to pray for my lord Arthur. Ye are welcome to me, said the hermit, for 10 I know you better than ye ween that I do. Ye are the bold Bedivere, and the full noble duke, Sir Lucàn de Butler, was your brother. Then Sir Bedivere told the hermit all as ye have heard tofore. So there bode Sir Bedivere with the hermit that was tofore Bishop of Canterbury, and there Sir Bedivere put upon him poor clothes, and served the hermit full lowly in fasting and in prayers.

Thus of Arthur I find never more written in books that are authorized, nor more of the very certainty of 20 his death heard I never read. But thus was he led away in a ship, wherein were three queens. That one was King Arthur's sister, Queen Morgan le Fay; the other was the Queen of North Wales; the third was the Queen of the Waste Lands. Also there was Ninive the chief lady of the lake, that had wedded Pelleas, the good knight. And this lady had done much for King Arthur, for she would never suffer Sir Pelleas to be in no place where he should be in danger of his life; and so he lived to the utter- 30 most of his days with her in great rest. More of the death of King Arthur could I never find, but that the ladies brought him to his burials; and such one was buried there that the hermit bare witness, that sometime was Bishop of Canterbury. But yet the hermit knew not in certain that he was verily the

Besants, gold coins.

body of King Arthur; for this tale, Sir Bedivere, knight of the table round, made it to be written. Yet some men say in many parts of England that King Arthur is not dead, but had by the will of our Lord Jesu into another place; and men say that he shall come again, and he shall win the holy cross. I will not say it shall be so, but rather I will say, here in this world he changed his life. But many men say that there is written upon his tomb this verse:
10 *Hic jacet Arthurus, Rex quondam, Rexque futurus.* Thus leave I here Sir Bedivere with the hermit, that dwelled that time in a chapel beside Glastonbury, and there was his hermitage. And so they lived in their prayers, and fastings, and great abstinence.

POPULAR BALLADS

BALLADS are properly included in a volume of selections from mediæval literature, but not because of the language in which they are written, since the texts of comparatively few are older than the eighteenth century. We know, however, that the ballad as a metrical and narrative form is at least as old as the thirteenth century, when an admirable specimen was copied in a manuscript; and we can be equally sure that many of the ballads sung by country folk in modern times had their origin long centuries ago.

A ballad is a story that is sung. Ballads therefore belong to the domain of folk-music quite as much as they do to what we may call folk-literature. Not every folk-song is a ballad, because a ballad always tells a story; but every true ballad is a folk-song. In manner and form, moreover, ballads have characteristics so well-marked that they are easily distinguishable from other narrative verse. In the first place, the story is told quite impersonally and without

Had . . . into another place, taken elsewhere.

comment. Sympathy is aroused by the handling of the incident itself, not at all by the intervention of the story-teller. No more poignant expression of maternal longing has ever been found than that of *The Wife of Usher's Well*, yet nothing was ever balder. The story, furthermore, is always narrated as if it were something from the immediate past, not as something remote and distant. In a very real sense, a ballad is rather the event itself than an account of the event, which is why dialogue is such an important feature. The story is more than half dramatized. Sometimes, as in *Edward,* the entire poem is made up of speech and reply, without one word of explanation. This method of narration results in the amazing and admirable brevity by which so many of the best ballads are marked. The theme of *The Bonny Earl of Murray* would serve for a novel. The condensation is sometimes carried so far, to be sure, that a ballad must be read twice before the sequence of events is plain, but even in such cases vividness of presentation compensates for momentary bewilderment. Sometimes a central fact is implied rather than stated, as in *Sir Patrick Spence,* with superb effect. Keats, it should be remembered, imitated this quality of ballads successfully, in *La Belle Dame Sans Merci.* Equally characteristic of them is the method by which the story progresses by means of what Professor Gummere called "incremental repetition." In a simple case, like that of *Edward,* the mother's questions and comments, with the son's replies, lead to the terrible revelation at the end. The importance of this device of repeating a formula and yet varying it cannot be over-emphasized.

Since ballads are songs as well as stories, and always have been sung, it is quite certain that their exquisite and subtle rhythms have resulted from adaptation of words to music. Ever since Bishop Percy published the *Reliques of Ancient English Poetry* in 1765, our poets have been learning from ballads certain secrets of their craft. It is impossible to account for these beauties of rhythmic effect except by supposing that ballad-singers—who have always been ballad-makers, as I shall show—have heard in their ears and felt in their blood the beat of the music to which they have chanted.

Ballad-singers, I have just said, have always been ballad-makers. All ballads have been orally transmitted, taught by one generation to the next; and all have been changed for better or worse as they have been sung. This is perhaps the most important fact to remember about them. Widely different versions of the same ballad have been found, some good and some bad in the literary sense. Furthermore, two versions may have the same stanza phrased quite differently, and each beautiful in its own way. This must mean that by slow degrees, and quite unconsciously, singers have made changes for the better as well as for the worse. When traditional taste in music and verse has been good, these changes have been in the direction of effectiveness of narrative, beauty of phrase, and loveliness of rhythm. At other times the same ballads have fallen upon evil days, which is why one finds rhymed doggerel cheek by jowl with noble poetry. It seems clear that some ballads have begun life very simply in the excitement of popular festivals, and to the beat of the dance. We know that primitive folk have no self-consciousness about verse-making, and are willing to contribute their share if a leader starts to poetize some event of common experience. *Babylon,* for example, seems still to bear the traces of such an origin. Other ballads, it is equally clear, must have been the work of individuals. Whatever their beginnings, however, all true ballads have been submitted to the same process of reshaping and rephrasing by those who have sung them; and without this process they would certainly lack the qualities that make them one of the most precious heritages of our race.

BABYLON; OR, THE BONNIE BANKS O FORDIE

THERE were three ladies lived in a bower,
   Eh vow bonnie
And they went out to pull a flower,
   On the bonnie banks o Fordie

They hadna pu'ed a flower but ane,
When up started to them a banisht man.

He's taen the first sister by her hand,
And he's turned her round and made her stand.

"It's whether will ye be a rank robber's wife,
Or will ye die by my wee pen-knife?"

"It's I'll not be a rank robber's wife,
But I'll rather die by your wee pen-knife."

He's killed this may, and he's laid her by,
For to bear the red rose company.

He's taken the second ane by the hand,
And he's turned her round and made her stand.

"It's whether will ye be a rank robber's wife,
10 Or will ye die by my wee pen-knife?"

"I'll not be a rank robber's wife,
But I'll rather die by your wee pen-knife."

He's killed this may, and he's laid her by,
For to bear the red rose company.

He's taken the youngest ane by the hand,
And he's turned her round and made her stand.

Says, "Will ye be a rank robber's wife,
Or will ye die by my wee pen-knife?"

"I'll not be a rank robber's wife,
20 Nor will I die by your wee pen-knife.

"For I hae a brother in this wood,
And gin ye kill me, it's he'll kill thee."

"What's thy brother's name? come tell to me."
"My brother's name is Baby Lon."

May, maid.   *Hae*, have.   *Gin*, if.

"O sister, sister, what have I done!
O have I done this ill to thee!

"O since I've done this evil deed,
Good sall never be seen o me."

He's taken out his wee pen-knife,
And he's twyned himsel o his ain sweet life.

EDWARD

"WHY dois your brand sae drap wi bluid,
             Edward, Edward,
Why dois your brand sae drap wi bluid,
10   And why sae sad gang yee O?"
"O I hae killed my hauke sae guid,
             Mither, mither,
O I hae killed my hauke sae guid,
  And I had nae mair bot hee O."

"Your haukis bluid was nevir sae reid,
             Edward, Edward,
Your haukis bluid was nevir sae reid,
  My deir son I tell thee O."
"O I hae killed my reid-roan steid,
20   Mither, mither,
O I hae killed my reid-roan steid,
  That erst was sae fair and frie O."

"Your steid was auld, and ye hae gat mair,
             Edward, Edward,
Your steid was auld, and ye hae gat mair,
  Sum other dule ye drie O."

Twyned, deprived.
Gang, go.   *Dule,* sorrow.   *Drie,* suffer.

"O I hae killed my fadir deir,
                    Mither, mither,
O I hae killed my fadir deir,
    Alas, and wae is mee O !"

"And whatten penance wul ye drie for that,
                    Edward, Edward,
And whatten penance will ye drie for that?
    My deir son, now tell me O."
"Ile set my feit in yonder boat,
10   Mither, mither,
Ile set my feit in yonder boat,
    And Ile fare ovir the sea O."

"And what wul ye doe wi your towirs and your ha,
                    Edward, Edward?
And what wul you doe wi your towirs and your ha,
    That were sae fair to see O?"
"Ile let thame stand tul they doun fa,
                    Mither, mither,
Ile let thame stand tul they down fa,
20 For here nevir mair maun I bee O."

"And what wul ye leive to your bairns and your
        wife,
                    Edward, Edward?
And what wul ye leive to your bairns and your wife,
    Whan ye gang ovir the sea O?"
"The warldis room, late them beg thrae life,
                    Mither, mither,
The warldis room, late them beg thrae life,
    For thame nevir mair wul I see O."

30 "And what wul ye leive to your ain mither deir,
                    Edward, Edward?

Bairns, children.

And what wul ye leive to your ain mither deir?
  My deir son, now tell me O."
"The curse of hell frae me sall ye beir,
          Mither, mither,
The curse of hell frae me sall ye beir,
  Sic counseils ye gave to me O."

THE MAID FREED FROM THE GALLOWS

"O good Lord Judge, and sweet Lord Judge,
  Peace for a little while!
Methinks I see my own father,
10   Come riding by the stile.

"Oh father, oh father, a little of your gold,
  And likewise of your fee!
To keep my body from yonder grave,
  And my neck from the gallows-tree."

"None of my gold now you shall have,
  Nor likewise of my fee;
For I am come to see you hangd,
  And hanged you shall be."

"Oh good Lord Judge, and sweet Lord Judge,
20   Peace for a little while!
Methinks I see my own mother,
  Come riding by the stile.

"Oh mother, oh mother, a little of your gold,
  And likewise of your fee,
To keep my body from yonder grave,
  And my neck from the gallows-tree!"
  Sic, such.

"None of my gold now shall you have,
Nor likewise of my fee;
For I am come to see you hangd,
And hanged you shall be."

"Oh good Lord Judge, and sweet Lord Judge,
Peace for a little while!
Methinks I see my own brother,
Come riding by the stile.

"Oh brother, oh brother, a little of your gold,
10   And likewise of your fee,
To keep my body from yonder grave,
And my neck from the gallows-tree!"

"None of my gold now shall you have,
Nor likewise of my fee;
For I am come to see you hangd,
And hanged you shall be."

"Oh good Lord Judge, and sweet Lord Judge,
Peace for a little while!
Methinks I see my own sister,
20   Come riding by the stile.

"Oh sister, oh sister, a little of your gold,
And likewise of your fee,
To keep my body from yonder grave,
And my neck from the gallows-tree!"

"None of my gold now shall you have,
Nor likewise of my fee;
For I am come to see you hangd,
And hanged you shall be."

"Oh good Lord Judge, and sweet Lord Judge,
    Peace for a little while!
Methinks I see my own true-love,
    Come riding by the stile.

"Oh true-love, oh true-love, a little of your gold,
    And likewise of your fee,
To save my body from yonder grave,
    And my neck from the gallows-tree."

"Some of my gold now you shall have,
10   And likewise of my fee,
For I am come to see you saved,
    And saved you shall be."

LORD RANDAL

"O where ha you been, Lord Randal, my son?
And where ha you been, my handsome young man?"
"I ha been at the greenwood; mother, mak my bed
        soon,
For I'm wearied wi' hunting, and fain wad lie
    down."

"An wha met ye there, Lord Randal, my son?
An wha met you there, my handsome young man?"
"O I met wi my true-love; mother, mak my bed
        soon,
20 For I'm wearied wi huntin, an fain wad lie down."

"And what did she give you, Lord Randal, my son?
And what did she give you, my handsome young
        man?"
"Eels fried in a pan; mother, mak my bed soon,
For I'm wearied wi huntin, and fain wad lie down."

"And wha gat your leavins, Lord Randal, my son?
And wha gat your leavins, my handsom young
    man?"
"My hawks and my hounds; mother, mak my bed
    soon,
For I'm wearied wi hunting, and fain wad lie down."

"And what becam of them, Lord Randal, my son?
And what becam of them, my handsome young
    man?"
"They stretched their legs out an died; mother,
    mak my bed soon,
For I'm wearied wi huntin, and fain wad lie down."

"O I fear you are poisoned, Lord Randal, my son!
10 I fear you are poisoned, my handsome young man!"
"O yes, I am poisoned; mother, mak my bed soon,
For I'm sick at the heart, and I fain wad lie down."

"What d'ye leave to your mother, Lord Randal, my
    son?
What d'ye leave to your mother, my handsome young
    man?"
"Four and twenty milk kye; mother, mak my bed
    soon,
For I'm sick at the heart, and I fain wad lie down."

"What d'ye leave to your sister, Lord Randal, my
    son?
What d'ye leave to your sister, my handsome young
    man?"
"My gold and my silver; mother, mak my bed soon,
20 For I'm sick at the heart, an I fain wad lie down."
    Kye, cows.

"What d'ye leave to your brother, Lord Randal, my
    son?
What d'ye leave to your brother, my handsome young
    man?"
"My houses and my lands; mother, mak my bed
    soon,
For I'm sick at the heart, and I fain wad lie down."

"What d'ye leave to your true-love, Lord Randal,
    my son?
What d'ye leave to your true-love, my handsome
    young man?"
"I leave her hell and fire; mother, mak my bed soon,
For I'm sick at the heart, and I fain wad lie down."

JOHNIE COCK

JOHNY he has risen up i the morn,
10   Calls for water to wash his hands;
But little knew he that his bloody hounds
   Were bound in iron bands.
   Were bound in iron bands.

Johny's mother has gotten word o that,
   And care-bed she has taen:
"O Johny, for my benison,
   I beg you'l stay at hame;
For the wine so red, and the well baken bread,
   My Johny shall want nane.

20 "There are seven forsters at Pickeram Side,
   At Pickeram where they dwell,
And for a drop of thy heart's bluid
   They wad ride the fords of hell."
   Benison, blessing.

Johny he's gotten word of that,
  And he's turnd wondrous keen;
He's put off the red scarlett,
  And he's put on the Lincoln green.

With a sheaf of arrows by his side,
  And a bent bow in his hand,
He's mounted on a prancing steed,
  And he has ridden fast oer the strand.

He's up i Braidhouplee, and down i Bradyslee,
10 And under a buss o broom,
And there he found a good dun deer,
  Feeding in a buss of ling.

Johny shot, and the dun deer lap,
  And she lap wondrous wide,
Until they came to the wan water,
  And he stemd her of her pride.

He 'as taen out the little pen-knife,
  'Twas full three quarters long,
And he has taen out of that dun deer
20 The liver bot and the tongue.

They eat of the flesh, and they drank of the blood,
  And the blood it was so sweet,
Which caused Johny and his bloody hounds
  To fall in a deep sleep.

By then came an old palmer,
  And an ill death may he die!
For he's away to Pickram Side,
  As fast as he can drie.

Buss, bush.   *Ling,* furze.   *Can drie,* is able.

"What news, what news?" says the Seven Forsters,
  "What news have ye brought to me?"
"I have noe news," the palmer said,
  "But what I saw with my eye.

"High up i Bradyslee, low down i Bradisslee,
  And under a buss of scroggs,
O there I spied a well-wight man,
  Sleeping among his dogs.

"His coat it was of Light Lincolm,
10 And his breeches of the same,
His shoes of the American leather,
  And gold buckles tying them."

Up bespake the Seven Forsters,
  Up bespake they ane and a':
"O that is Johny o Cockleys Well,
  And near him we will draw."

O the first y stroke that they gae him,
  They struck him off by the knee;
Then up bespake his sister's son:
20 "O the next 'll gar him die!"

"O some they count ye well-wight men,
  But I do count ye nane;
For you might well ha wakend me,
  And askd gin I wad be taen.

"The wildest wolf in aw this wood
  Wad not ha done so by me;
She'd ha wet her foot ith wan water,

Scroggs, undergrowth.   *Gar,* make.
Gae, gave.

And sprinkled it oer my brae,
And if that wad not ha wakend me,
She wad ha gone and let me be.

"O bows of yew, if ye be true,
In London, where ye were bought,
Fingers five, get up belive,
Manhuid shall fail me nought."

He has killd the Seven Forsters,
He has killd them all but ane,
10 And that wan scarce to Pickeram Side,
To carry the bode-words hame.

"Is there never a boy in a' this wood
That will tell what I can say;
That will go to Cockleys Well,
Tell my mither to fetch me away?"

There was a boy into that wood,
That carried the tidings away,
And many ae was the well-wight man
At the fetching o Johny away.

THOMAS RYMER AND THE QUEEN OF ELFLAND

20 TRUE THOMAS lay oer yond grassy bank,
And he beheld a ladie gay,
A ladie that was brisk and bold,
Come riding oer the fernie brae.

Her skirt was of the grass-green silk,
Her mantel of the velvet fine,

Brae, brow.   *Brae,* hillside.

At ilka tett of her horse's mane
Hung fifty silver bells and nine.

True Thomas he took off his hat,
And bowed him low down till his knee:
"All hail, thou mighty Queen of Heaven!
For your peer on earth I never did see."

"O no, O no, True Thomas," she says,
"That name does not belong to me;
I am but the queen of fair Elfland,
10 And I'm come here for to visit thee.

"But ye maun go wi me now, Thomas,
True Thomas, ye maun go wi me,
For ye maun serve me seven years,
Thro weel or wae as may chance to be."

She turned about her milk-white steed,
And took True Thomas up behind,
And aye wheneer her bridle rang,
The steed flew swifter than the wind.

For forty days and forty nights
20 He wade thro red blude to the knee,
And he saw neither sun nor moon,
But heard the roaring of the sea.

O they rade on, and further on,
Until they came to a garden green:
"Light down, light down, ye ladie free,
Some of that fruit let me pull to thee."

"O no, O no, True Thomas," she says,
"That fruit maun not be touched by thee,

Tett, lock.　　　　　　*Maun,* must.

For a' the plagues that are in hell
    Light on the fruit of this countrie.

"But I have a loaf here in my lap,
    Likewise a bottle of claret wine,
And now ere we go farther on,
    We'll rest a while, and ye may dine."

When he had eaten and drunk his fill,
    "Lay down your head upon my knee,"
The lady sayd, "ere we climb yon hill,
10   And I will show you fairlies three.

"O see not ye yon narrow road,
    So thick beset wi thorns and briers?
That is the path of righteousness,
    Tho after it but few enquires.

"And see not ye that braid braid road,
    That lies across yon lillie leven?
That is the path of wickedness,
    Tho some call it the road to heaven.

"And see not ye that bonnie road,
20   Which winds about the fernie brae?
That is the road to fair Elfland,
    Whe[re] you and I this night maun gae.

"But Thomas, ye maun hold your tongue,
    Whatever you may hear or see,
For gin ae word you should chance to speak,
    You will neer get back to your ain countrie."

He has gotten a coat of the even cloth,
    And a pair of shoes of velvet green,

Fairlies, marvels.   *Braid,* broad.
Lillie leven, lovely glade.   *Even cloth,* smooth cloth.

And till seven years were past and gone
True Thomas on earth was never seen.

THE WIFE OF USHER'S WELL

THERE lived a wife at Usher's Well,
    And a wealthy wife was she;
She had three stout and stalwart sons,
    And sent them oer the sea.

They hadna been a week from her,
    A week but barely ane,
Whan word came to the carline wife
10   That her three sons were gane.

They hadna been a week from her,
    A week but barely three,
When word came to the carlin wife
    That her sons she'd never see.

"I wish the wind may never cease,
    Nor fashes in the flood,
Till my three sons come hame to me,
    In earthly flesh and blood."

It fell about the Martinmass,
20   When nights are lang and mirk,
The carlin wife's three sons came hame,
    And their hats were o the birk.

It neither grew in syke nor ditch,
    Nor yet in ony sheugh;
But at the gates o Paradise,
    That birk grew fair eneugh.

    .   .   .   .   .

Carline wife, old woman.   *Fashes,* troubles.
Birk, birch.   *Syke,* trench.   *Sheugh,* ditch.

"Blow up the fire, my maidens,
    Bring water from the well;
For a' my house shall feast this night,
    Since my three sons are well."

And she has made to them a bed,
    She's made it large and wide,
And she's taen her mantle her about,
    Sat down at the bed-side.

    ′   .   .   .   .   .   .

Up then crew the red, red cock,
10   And up and crew the gray;
The eldest to the youngest said,
    " 'Tis time we were away."

The cock he hadna crawd but once,
    And clappd his wings at a',
When the youngest to the eldest said,
    "Brother, we must awa.

"The cock doth craw, the day doth daw
    The channerin worm doth chide;
Gin we be mist out o our place,
20   A sair pain we maun bide.

"Faer ye weel, my mother dear!
    Fareweel to barn and byre!
And fare ye weel, the bonny lass
    That kindles my mother's fire!"

THE DÆMON LOVER

"O WHERE have you been, my long, long love,
    This long seven years and mair?"

Channerin, fretting.   *Byre,* cow-shed.

"O I'm come to seek my former vows
Ye granted me before."

"O hold your tongue of your former vows,
For they will breed sad strife;
O hold your tongue of your former vows,
For I am become a wife."

He turned him right and round about,
And the tear blinded his ee:
"I wad never hae trodden on Irish ground,
10   If it had not been for thee.

"I might hae had a king's daughter,
Far, far beyond the sea;
I might have had a king's daughter,
Had it not been for love o thee."

"If ye might have had a king's daughter,
Yersel ye had to blame;
Ye might have had taken the king's daughter,
For ye kend that I was nane.

"If I was to leave my husband dear,
20   And my two babes also,
O what have you to take me to,
If with you I should go?"

"I hae seven ships upon the sea—
The eighth brought me to land—
With four-and-twenty bold mariners,
And music on every hand."

She has taken up her two little babes,
Kissd them baith cheek and chin:
Kend, knew.

"O fair ye weel, my ain two babes,
　For I'll never see you again."

She set her foot upon the ship,
　No mariners could she behold;
But the sails were o the taffetie,
　And the masts o the beaten gold.

She had not sailed a league, a league,
　A league but barely three,
When dismal grew his countenance,
10　And drumlie grew his ee.

They had not saild a league, a league,
　A league but barely three,
Until she espied his cloven foot,
　And she wept right bitterlie.

"O hold your tongue of your weeping," says he,
　"Of your weeping now let me be;
I will shew you how the lilies grow
　On the banks of Italy."

"O what hills are yon, yon pleasant hills,
20　That the sun shines sweetly on?"
"O yon are the hills of heaven," he said,
　"Where you will never win."

"O whaten a mountain is yon," she said,
　"All so dreary wi frost and snow?"
"O yon is the mountain of hell," he cried,
　"Where you and I will go."

He strack the tap-mast wi his hand,
　The fore-mast wi his knee,
　　Drumlie, gloomy.

And he brake that gallant ship in twain,
And sank her in the sea.

THE THREE RAVENS

THERE were three rauens sat on a tree,
   Downe a downe, hay down, hay downe
There were three rauens sat on a tree,
   With a downe
There were three rauens sat on a tree,
They were as blacke as they might be.
   With a downe derrie, derrie, derrie, downe, downe.

10 The one of them said to his mate,
"Where shall we our breakefast take?"

"Downe in yonder greene field,
There lies a knight slain vnder his shield.

"His hounds they lie downe at his feete,
So well they can their master keepe.

"His haukes they flie so eagerly,
There's no fowle dare him come nie."

Downe there comes a fallow doe,
As great with yong as she might goe.

20 She lift vp his bloudy hed,
And kist his wounds that were so red.

She got him vp vpon her backe,
And carried him to earthen lake.

She buried him before the prime,
She was dead herselfe ere euen-song time.

God send euery gentleman,
Such haukes, such hounds, and such a leman.

HUGH OF LINCOLN

Four and twenty bonny boys
    Were playing at the ba',
And by it came him sweet Sir Hugh,
    And he play'd oer them a'.

He kick'd the ba' with his right foot,
    And catch'd it wi' his knee,
And throuch-and-thro' the Jew's window
10   He gar'd the bonny ba' flee.

He's doen him to the Jew's castell,
    And walk'd it round about;
And there he saw the Jew's daughter,
    At the window looking out.

"Throw down the ba', ye Jew's daughter,
    Throw down the ba' to me!"
"Never a bit," says the Jew's daughter,
    Till up to me come ye."

"How will I come up? How can I come up?
20   How can I come to thee?
For as ye did to my auld father,
    The same ye'll do to me."

She's gane till her father's garden,
    And pu'd an apple red and green;
'T was a' to wyle him, sweet Sir Hugh,
    And to entice him in.

Gar'd, made.   *Leman*, love.

She's led him in through ae dark door,
    And so has she thro' nine;
She's laid him on a dressing-table,
    And stickit him like a swine.

And first came out the thick, thick blood,
    And syne came out the thin,
And syne came out the bonny heart's blood;
    There was nae mair within.

She's row'd him in a cake o' lead,
10   Bade him lie still and sleep;
She's thrown him in Our Lady's draw-well,
    Was fifty fathom deep.

When bells were rung, and mass was sung,
    And a' the bairns came hame,
When every lady gat hame her son,
    The Lady Maisry gat nane.

She's ta'en her mantle her about,
    Her coffer by the hand,
And she's gane out to seek her son,
20   And wander'd o'er the land.

She's doen her to the Jew's castell,
    Where a' were fast asleep:
"Gin ye be there, my sweet Sir Hugh,
    I pray you to me speak."

She's doen her to the Jew's garden,
    Thought he had been gathering fruit:
"Gin ye be there, my sweet Sir Hugh,
    I pray you to me speak."

Syne, then.   *Row'd,* rolled.   *Coffer,* box.

She near'd Our Lady's deep draw-well,
  Was fifty fathom deep:
"Whare'er ye be, my sweet Sir Hugh,
  I pray you to me speak."

"Gae hame, gae hame, my mither dear,
  Prepare my winding sheet;
And, at the back o' merry Lincoln,
  The morn I will you meet."

Now Lady Maisry is gane hame;
10 Made him a winding sheet;
And, at the back o' merry Lincoln,
  The dead corpse did her meet.

And a' the bells o' merry Lincoln
  Without men's hands were rung;
And a' the books o' merry Lincoln
  Were read without man's tongue;
And ne'er was such a burial
  Sin Adam's days begun.

CHILDE WATERS

Childe Watters in his stable stoode,
20 And stroaket his milke-white steede;
To him came a ffaire young ladye
  As ere did weare womans weede.

Saies, "Christ you saue, good Chyld Waters!"
  Sayes, "Christ you saue and see!
My girdle of gold, which was too longe,
  Is now to short ffor mee.

Sin, since.

"And all is with one chyld of yours,
   I ffeele sturre att my side;
My gowne of greene, it is to strayght;
   Before it was to wide."

"If the child be mine, Faire Ellen," he sayd,
   "Be mine, as you tell mee,
Take you Cheshire and Lancashire both,
   Take them your owne to bee.

"If the child be mine, Ffaire Ellen," he said,
10   "Be mine, as you doe sweare,
Take you Cheshire and Lancashire both,
   And make that child your heyre."

Shee saies, "I had rather haue one kisse,
   Child Waters, of thy mouth,
Then I wold haue Cheshire and Lancashire both,
   That lyes by north and south.

"And I had rather haue a twinkling,
   Child Waters, of your eye,
Then I wold haue Cheshire and Lancashire both,
20   To take them mine oune to bee."

"To-morrow, Ellen, I must forth ryde
   Soe ffarr into the north countrye;
The ffairest lady that I can ffind,
   Ellen, must goe with mee."
"And euer I pray you, Child Watters,
   Your ffootpage let me bee!"

"If you will my ffootpage be, Ellen,
   As you doe tell itt mee,
Then you must cutt your gownne of greene
30   An inche aboue your knee.

"Soe must you doe your yellow lockes,
  Another inch aboue your eye;
You must tell noe man what is my name;
  My ffootpage then you shall bee."

All this long day Child Waters rode,
  Shee ran bare ffoote by his side;
Yett was he neuer soe curteous a knight
  To say, Ellen, will you ryde?

But all this day Child Waters rode,
10 Shee ran barffoote thorow the broome;
Yett he was neuer soe curteous a knight
  As to say, Put on youre shoone.

"Ride softlye," shee said, "Child Watters;
  Why doe you ryde soe ffast?
The child which is no mans but yours
  My bodye itt will burst."

He sayes, "Sees thou yonder water, Ellen,
  That fflowes from banke to brim?"
"I trust to God, Child Waters," shee said,
20 "You will neuer see mee swime."

But when shee came to the waters side,
  Shee sayled to the chinne:
"Except the lord of heauen be my speed,
  Now must I learne to swime."

The salt waters bare vp Ellens clothes,
  Our Ladye bare vpp her chinne,
And Child Waters was a woe man, good Lord,
  To ssee Faire Ellen swime.

And when shee ouer the water was,
  Shee then came to his knee:
He said, "Come hither, Ffaire Ellen,
  Loe yonder what I see!

"Seest thou not yonder hall, Ellen?
  Of redd gold shine the yates;
There's four and twenty ffayre ladyes,
  The ffairest is my wordlye make.

"Seest thou not yonder hall, Ellen?
10 Of redd gold shineth the tower;
There is four and twenty ffaire ladyes,
  The fairest is my paramoure."

"I doe see the hall now, Child Waters,
  That of redd gold shineth the yates;
God giue good then of youre selfe,
  And of your wordlye make!

"I doe see the hall now, Child Waters,
  That of redd gold shineth the tower;
God giue good then of your selfe,
20 And of your paramoure!"

There were four and twenty ladyes,
  Were playing att the ball,
And Ellen, was the ffairest ladye,
  Must bring his steed to the stall.

There were four and twenty faire ladyes
  Was playing att the chesse;
And Ellen, shee was the ffairest ladye,
  Must bring his horsse to grasse.

Yates, gates.   *Wordlye make,* earthly mate.

And then bespake Child Waters sister,
  And these were the words said shee:
"You haue the prettyest ffootpage, brother,
  That euer I saw with mine eye;

"But that his belly it is soe bigg,
  His girdle goes wonderous hye;
And euer I pray you, Child Waters,
  Let him goe into the chamber with mee."

"It is more meete for a little ffootpage,
10 That has run through mosse and mire,
To take his supper vpon his knee
  And sitt downe by the kitchin fyer,
Than to goe into the chamber with any ladye
  That weares soe rich attyre."

But when the had supped euery one,
  To bedd they took the way;
He sayd, "Come hither, my little footpage,
  Harken what I doe say.

"And goe thee downe into yonder towne,
20 And low into the street;
The ffairest ladye that thou can find,
  Hyer her in mine armes to sleepe,
And take her vp in thine armes two,
  For filinge of her ffeete."

Ellen is gone into the towne,
  And low into the streete;
The fairest ladye that shee cold find,
  Shee hyred in his armes to sleepe,
And tooke her in her armes two,
30 For filinge of her ffeete.

Mosse, bog.   *Filinge,* defiling.

"I pray you now, good Child Waters,
   That I may creepe in att your bedds feete;
For there is noe place about this house
   Where I may say a sleepe."

This night and itt droue on affterward
   Till itt was neere the day:
He sayd, "Rise vp, my litle ffoote-page,
   And giue my steed corne and hay;
And soe doe thou the good blacke oates,
10   That he may carry me the better away."

And vp then rose Ffaire Ellen,
   And gaue his steed corne and hay,
And soe shee did and the good blacke oates,
   That he might carry him the better away.

Shee layned her backe to the manger side,
   And greuiouslye did groane;
And that beheard his mother deere,
   And heard her make her moane.

Shee said, "Rise vp, thou Child Waters,
20   I thinke thou art a cursed man;
For yonder is a ghost in thy stable,
   That greuiouslye doth groane,
Or else some woman laboures of child,
   Shee is soe woe begone."

But vp then rose Child Waters,
   And did on his shirt of silke;
Then he put on his other clothes
   On his body as white as milke.
Say a sleepe, try to sleep.

And when he came to the stable-dore,
  Full still that hee did stand,
That hee might heare now Faire Ellen,
  How shee made her monand.

Shee said, "Lullabye, my owne deere child!
  Lullabye, deere child, deere!
I wold thy father were a king,
  Thy mother layd on a beere!"

"Peace now," he said, "good Faire Ellen,
10 And be of good cheere, I thee pray,
And the bridall and the churching both,
  They shall bee vpon one day."

SIR PATRICK SPENCE

THE king sits in Dumferling toune,
  Drinking the blude-reid wine:
"O whar will I get guid sailor,
  To sail this schip of mine?"

Up and spak an eldern knicht,
  Sat at the kings richt kne:
"Sir Patrick Spence is the best sailor
20   That sails upon the se."

The king has written a braid letter,
  And signd it wi his hand,
And sent it to Sir Patrick Spence,
  Was walking on the sand.

The first line that Sir Patrick red,
  A loud lauch lauched he;

Monand, moaning.
Braid letter, either long, or on a broad sheet.

The next line that Sir Patrick red,
  The teir blinded his ee.

"O wha is this has don this deid,
  This ill deid don to me,
To send me out this time o' the yeir,
  To sail upon the se?

"Mak hast, mak haste, my mirry men all,
  Our guid schip sails the morne."
"O say na sae, my master deir,
  For I feir a deadlie storme.

"Late late yestreen I saw the new moone
  Wi the auld moone in her arme,
And I feir, I feir, my deir master,
  That we will cum to harme."

O our Scots nobles wer richt laith
  To weet their cork-heild schoone;
Bot lang owre a' the play wer playd,
  Thair hats they swam aboone.

O lang, lang may their ladies sit,
  Wi thair fans into their hand,
Or eir they se Sir Patrick Spence
  Cum sailing to the land.

O lang, lang may the ladies stand,
  Wi thair gold kems in their hair,
Waiting for thair ain deir lords,
  For they'll se thame na mair.

Haf owre, haf owre to Aberdour,
  It's fiftie fadom deip,

Laith, loath.   *Kems,* combs.

And thair lies guid Sir Patrick Spence,
Wi the Scots lords at his feit.

YOUNG WATERS

ABOUT Yule, when the wind blew cule,
    And the round tables began,
A there is cum to our king's court
    Mony a well-favord man.

The queen luikt owre the castle-wa,
    Beheld baith dale and down,
And there she saw Young Waters
10   Cum riding to the town.

His footmen they did rin before,
    His horsemen rade behind;
And mantel of the burning gowd
    Did keip him frae the wind.

Gowden-graithd his horse before,
    And siller-shod behind;
The horse Young Waters rade upon
    Was fleeter than the wind.

Out then spack a wylie lord,
20   Unto the queen said he,
"O tell me wha's the fairest face
    Rides in the company?"

"I've sene lord, and I've sene laird,
    And knights of high degree,
Bot a fairer face than Young Waters
    Mine eyne did never see."

Gowd, gold.   *Gowden-graithd,* harnessed with gold.
Laird, landowner below degree of knight.

Out then spack the jealous king,
  And an angry man was he:
"O if he had bin twice as fair,
  You micht have excepted me."

"You're neither laird nor lord," she says,
  "Bot the king that wears the crown;
There is not a knight in fair Scotland
  But to thee maun bow down."

For a' that she coud do or say,
  Appeas'd he wad nae bee,
Bot for the words which she had said,
  Young Waters he maun die.

They hae taen Young Waters,
  And put fetters to his feet;
They hae taen Young Waters,
  And thrown him in dungeon deep.

"Aft I have ridden thro Stirling town
  In the wind bot and the weit;
But I neir rade thro Stirling town
  Wi fetters at my feet.

"Aft I have ridden thro Stirling town
  In the wind bot and the rain;
Bot I neir rade thro Stirling town
  Neir to return again."

They hae taen to the heiding-hill
  His young son in his craddle,
And they hae taen to the heiding-hill
  His horse bot and his saddle.

Maun, must.

They hae taen to the heiding-hill
His lady fair to see,
And for the words the queen had spoke
Young Waters he did die.

THE BONNY EARL OF MURRAY

Ye Highlands, and ye Lawlands,
Oh where have you been?
They have slain the Earl of Murray,
And they layd him on the green.

"Now wae be to thee, Huntly!
And wherefore did you sae?
I bade you bring him wi you,
But forbade you him to slay."

He was a braw gallant,
And he rid at the ring;
And the bonny Earl of Murray,
Oh he might have been a king!

He was a braw gallant,
And he playd at the ba;
And the bonny Earl of Murray
Was the flower amang them a'.

He was a braw gallant,
And he playd at the glove;
And the bonny Earl of Murray,
Oh he was the Queen's love!

Heiding-hill, hill for executions.
Braw, handsome.
At the ring, in the game of riding to lance a suspended ring.

Oh lang will his lady
    Look oer the castle Down,
Eer she see the Earl of Murray
    Come sounding thro the town!
Eer she, etc.

MARY HAMILTON

WORD's gane to the kitchen,
    And word's gane to the ha,
That Marie Hamilton gangs wi bairn
    To the hichest Stewart of a'.

10 He's courted her in the kitchen,
    He's courted her in the ha,
He's courted her in the laigh cellar,
    And that was warst of a'.

She's tyed it in her apron
    And she's thrown it in the sea;
Says, Sink ye, swim ye, bonny wee babe!
    You'l neer get mair o me.

Down then cam the auld queen,
    Goud tassels tying her hair:
20 "O Marie, where's the bonny wee babe
    That I heard greet sae sair?"

"There was never a babe intill my room,
    As little designs to be;
It was but a touch o my sair side,
    Come oer my fair bodie."

Hichest, highest.   *Sair*, sore.
Laigh, low.   *Intill*, in.

"O Marie, put on your robes o black,
  Or else your robes o brown,
For ye maun gang wi me the night,
  To see fair Edinbro town."

"I winna put on my robes o black,
  Nor yet my robes o brown;
But I'll put on my robes o white,
  To shine through Edinbro town."

When she gaed up the Cannogate,
10 She laughd loud laughters three;
But when she cam down the Cannogate
  The tear blinded her ee.

When she gaed up the Parliament stair,
  The heel cam aff her shee;
And lang or she cam down again
  She was condemnd to dee.

When she cam down the Cannogate,
  The Cannogate sae free,
Many a ladie lookd oer her window,
20 Weeping for this ladie.

"Ye need nae weep for me," she says,
  "Ye need nae weep for me;
For had I not slain mine own sweet babe,
  This death I wadna dee.

"Bring me a bottle of wine," she says,
  "The best that eer ye hae,
That I may drink to my weil-wishers,
  And they may drink to me.

Gaed, went.   *Shee*, shoe.

"Here's a health to the jolly sailors,
 That sail upon the main;
Let them never let on to my father and mother
 But what I'm coming hame.

"Here's a health to the jolly sailors,
 That sail upon the sea;
Let them never let on to my father and mother
 That I cam here to dee.

"Oh little did my mother think,
10 The day she cradled me,
What lands I was to travel through,
 What death I was to dee.

"Oh little did my father think,
 The day he held up me,
What lands I was to travel through,
 What death I was to dee.

"Last night I washd the queen's feet,
 And gently laid her down;
And a' the thanks I've gotten the nicht
20 To be hangd in Edinbro town!

"Last nicht there was four Maries,
 The nicht there'l be but three;
There was Marie Seton, and Marie Beton,
 And Marie Carmichael, and me."

CHEVY CHASE

God prosper long our noble king,
 our liffes and saftyes all!
A woefull hunting once there did
 in Cheuy Chase befall.

To dríue the deere with hound and horne
  Erle Pearcy took the way:
The child may rue *that* is vnborne
  the hunting of *that* day!

The stout Erle of Northumberland
  a vow to God did make
His pleasure in the Scottish woods
  three sommers days to take,

The cheefest harts in Cheuy C[h]ase
10 to kill and beare away:
These tydings to Erle Douglas came
  in Scottland, where he lay.

Who sent Erle Pearcy present word
  he would prevent his sport;
The English erle, not fearing that,
  did to the woods resort,

With fifteen hundred bowmen bold,
  all chosen men of might,
Who knew ffull well in time of neede
20 to ayme their shafts arright.

The gallant greyhound[s] swiftly ran
  to chase the fallow deere;
On Munday they began to hunt,
  ere daylight did appeare.

And long before high noone the had
  a hundred fat buckes slaine;
Then hauing dined, the drouyers went
  to rouze the deare againe.

The bowmen mustered on the hills,
   well able to endure;
Theire backsids all with speciall care
   that day were guarded sure.

The hounds ran swiftly through the woods
   the nimble deere to take,
That with their cryes the hills and dales
   an eccho shrill did make.

Lord Pearcy to the querry went
10   to veiw the tender deere;
Quoth he, "Erle Douglas promised once
   this day to meete me heere;

"But if I thought he wold not come,
   noe longer wold I stay."
With *that* a braue younge gentlman
   thus to the erle did say:

"Loe, yonder doth Erle Douglas come,
   hys men in armour bright;
Full twenty hundred Scottish speres
20   all marching in our sight.

"All men of pleasant Tiuydale,
   fast by the riuer Tweede:"
"O ceaze your sportts!" Erle Pearcy said,
   "and take your bowes with speede.

"And now with me, my countrymen,
   your courage forth advance!
For there was neuer champion yett,
   in Scottland nor in Ffrance,
     Querry, place where dead deer were collected.

"*That* eu*er* did on horsbacke come,
    [but], and if my hap it were,
I durst encounter man for man,
    with him to break a spere."

Erle Douglas on his milke-white steede,
    most like a baron bold,
Rode formost of his company,
    whose armor shone like gold.

"Shew me," sayd hee, "whose men you bee
10   *tha*t hunt soe boldly heere,
*Tha*t without my consent doe chase
    and kill my fallow deere."

The first man *that* did answer make
    was noble Pearcy hee,
Who sayd, "Wee list not to declare
    nor shew whose men wee bee;

"Yett wee will spend our deerest blood
    thy cheefest harts to slay."
Then Douglas swore a solempne oathe,
20   and thus in rage did say:

"Ere thus I will outbraued bee,
    one of vs tow shall dye;
I know thee well, an erle thou art;
    Lord Pearcy, soe am I.

"But trust me, Pearcye, pittye it were,
    amd great offence, to kill
Then any of these our guiltlesse men,
    for they haue done none ill.

"Let thou and I the battell trye,
　　and set our men aside:"
"Accurst bee [he!]" Erle Pearcye sayd,
　　"by whome it is denyed."

Then stept a gallant squire forth—
　　Witherington was his name—
Who said, "I wold not haue it told
　　to Henery our *king,* for shame,

10　"*That* ere my captaine fought on foote,
　　and I stand looking on.
You bee two Erles," q*uoth* Witherington,
　　"and I a squier alone;

"I'le doe the best *that* doe I may,
　　while I haue power to stand;
While I haue power to weeld my sword,
　　I'le fight *with* hart and hand."

Our English archers bent thier bowes;
　　their harts were good and trew;
Att the first flight of arrowes sent,
20　full foure score Scotts the slew.

To driue the deere *with* hound and horne,
　　Dauglas bade on the bent;
Two captaines moued *with* mickle might,
　　their speres to shiuers went.

They closed full fast on eu*er*ye side,
　　noe slacknes there was found,
But many a gallant gentleman
　　lay gasping on the ground.

Bent, field covered with coarse grass.　　　　*Mickle,* great.

O Christ! it was great greeue to see
how eche man chose his spere,
And how the blood out of their brests
did gush like water cleare.

At last these two stout erles did meet,
like captaines of great might;
Like lyons woode they layd on lode;
the made a cruell fight.

The fought vntill they both did sweat,
10 with swords of tempered steele,
Till blood downe their cheekes like raine
the trickling downe did feele.

"O yeeld thee, Pearcye!" Douglas sayd,
"And in faith I will thee bringe
Where thou shall high advanced bee
by Iames our Scottish king.

"Thy ransome I will freely giue,
and this report of thee,
Thou art the most couragious knight
20 [that ever I did see.]"

"Noe, Douglas!" quoth Erle Percy then,
"thy profer I doe scorne;
I will not yeelde to any Scott
that euer yett was borne!"

With that there came an arrow keene,
out of an English bow,
Which stroke Erle Douglas on the brest
a deepe and deadlye blow.

Greeue, grief.   *Layd on lode,* fought fiercely.

Who neuer sayd more words than these;
  "Fight on, my merry men all!
For why, my life is att [an] end,
  lord Pearcy sees my fall."

Then leauing liffe, Erle Pearcy tooke
  the dead man by the hand;
Who said, "Erle Dowglas, for thy life,
  wold I had lost my land!

"O Christ! my verry hart doth bleed
10 for sorrow for thy sake,
For sure, a more redoubted knight
  mischance cold neuer take."

A knight amongst the Scotts there was
  which saw Erle Douglas dye,
Who streight in hart did vow revenge
  vpon the Lord Pearcye.

Sir Hugh Mountgomerye was he called,
  who, with a spere full bright,
Well mounted on a gallant steed,
20 ran feircly through the fight,

And past the English archers all,
  without all dread or feare,
And through Erle Percyes body then
  he thrust his hatfull spere.

With such a vehement force and might
  his body he did gore,
The staff ran through the other side
  a large cloth-yard and more.

Thus did both those nobles dye,
30 whose courage none cold staine;

An English archer then perceiued
the noble erle was slaine.

He had [a] good bow in his hand,
made of a trusty tree;
An arrow of a cloth-yard long
to the hard head haled hee.

Against Sir Hugh Mountgomerye
his shaft full right he sett;
The grey-goose winge *that* was there-on
10   in his harts bloode was wett.

This fight from breake of day did last
till setting of the sun,
For when the rung the euening-bell
the battele scarse was done.

With stout Erle Percy there was slaine
Sir Iohn of Egerton,
Sir Robert Harcliffe and Sir William,
Sir Iames, that bold barron.

And with Sir George and Sir Iames,
20   both knights of good account,
Good Sir Raphe Rebbye there was slaine,
whose prowesse did surmount.

For Witherington needs must I wayle
as one in dolefull dumpes,
For when his leggs were smitten of,
he fought vpon his stumpes.

And with Erle Dowglas there was slaine
Sir Hugh Mountgomerye,

Haled, thrust.

And Sir Charles Morrell, *that* from feelde
  one foote wold neu*er* flee;

Sir Roger Heuer of Harcliffe tow,
  his sisters sonne was hee;
Sir David Lambwell, well esteemed,
  but saved he cold not bee.

And the Lord Maxwell, in like case,
  with Douglas he did dye;
Of twenty hundred Scottish speeres,
10 scarce fifty-fiue did flye.

Of fifteen hundred Englishmen
  went home but fifty-three;
The rest in Cheuy Chase were slaine,
  vnder the greenwoode tree.

Next day did many widdowes come
  their husbands to bewayle;
They washt their wounds in brinish teares,
  but all wold not pr*e*vayle.

Theyr bodyes, bathed in purple blood,
20 the bore with them away;
They kist them dead a thousand times
  ere the were cladd in clay.

The newes was brought to Eddenborrow,
  where Scottlands k*i*ng did rayne,
*Tha*t braue Erle Douglas soddainlye
  was with an arrow slaine.

"O heauy newes!" K*i*ng Iames can say;
  "Scottland may wittenesse bee
Can say, said.

I haue not any cap*taine* more
of such account as hee."

Like tydings to K*ing* Henery came,
wi*t*hin as short a space,
*Tha*t Pearcy of Northumberland
was slaine in Cheuy Chase.

"Now God be wi*t*h him!" said our k*ing,*
"sith it will noe better bee;
I trust I haue within my realme
10   fiue hundred as good as hee.

"Yett shall not Scotts nor Scottland say
but I will vengeance take,
And be revenged on them all
for braue Erle Percyes sake."

This vow the k*ing* did well p*er*forme
after on Humble-downe;
In one day fifty k*nigh*ts were slayne,
wi*t*h lords of great renowne.

And of the rest, of small account,
20   did many hundreds dye:
Thus endeth the hunting in Cheuy Chase,
made by the Erle Pearcye.

God saue our k*ing,* and blesse this land
wi*t*h plentye, ioy, and peace,
And grant hencforth *tha*t foule debate
twixt noble men may ceaze!

ROBIN HOOD AND GUY OF GISBORNE

WHEN shawes beene sheene, and shradds full fayre,
 And leeues both large and longe,
Itt is merry, walking in the fayre fforrest,
 To heare the small birds songe.

The woodweele sang, and wold not cease,
 Amongst the leaues a lyne:
And it is by two wight yeomen,
 By deare God, *that* I meane.

. . . .

"Me thought they did mee beate and binde,
10 And tooke my bow mee froe;
If I bee Robin a-liue in this lande,
 I 'le be wrocken on both them towe."

"Sweauens are swift, m*a*ster," qu*o*th Iohn
 "As the wind *tha*t blowes ore a hill;
Ffor if itt be neu*er* soe lowde this night,
 To-morrow it may be still."

"Buske yee, bowne yee, my merry men all.
 Ffor Iohn shall goe w*i*th mee;
For I 'le goe seeke yond wight yeomen
20 In greenwood where the bee."

The cast on their gowne of greene,
 A shooting gone are they,
Vntill they came to the merry greenwood,
 Where they had gladdest bee;

Shawes beene sheene, woods are bright. *Shradds,* thickets.
Woodweele, woodlark. *A lyne,* probably alone.
Wrocken, avenged. Robin is relating a dream.
Sweauens, dreams.
Buske yee, bowne yee, hasten. make ready.
Wight, sturdy.

There were the ware of [a] wight yeoman,
   His body leaned to a tree.

A sword and a dagger he wore by his side,
   Had beene many a mans bane,
And he was cladd in his capull-hyde,
   Topp, and tayle, and mayne.

"Stand you still, *master*," qu*o*th Litle Iohn,
   "Vnder this trusty tree,
And I will goe to yond wight yeoman,
10   To know his meaning trulye."

"A, Iohn, by me thou setts noe store,
   And *that*'s a ffarley thinge;
How offt send I my men beffore,
   And tarry my-selfe behinde?

"It is noe cunning a knaue to ken,
   And a man but heare him speake;
And itt were not for bursting of my bowe,
   Iohn, I wold thy head breake."

But often words they breeden bale,
20   *Tha*t p*a*rted Robin and Iohn;
Iohn is gone to Barn[e]sdale,
   The gates he knowes eche one.

And when hee came to Barnesdale,
   Great heauinesse there hee hadd;
He ffound two of his fellowes
   Were slaine both in a slade,

Capull-hyde, horse hide.   *Ffarley,* marvellous.
And a man, if a man.   *Bale,* trouble.
Gates, roads.   *Slade,* valley.

And Scarlett a ffoote flyinge was,
  Ouer stockes and stone,
For the sheriffe with seuen score men
  Fast after him is gone.

"Yett one shoote I'le shoote," sayes Litle Iohn,
  "With Crist his might and mayne;
I'le make yond fellow *that* flyes soe fast
  To be both glad and ffaine."

Iohn bent vp a good veiwe bow,
10 And ffetteled him to shoote;
The bow was made of a tender boughe,
  And fell downe to his foote.

"Woe worth thee, wicked wood," sayd Litle Iohn,
  "*That* ere thou grew on a tree!
Ffor this day thou art my bale,
  My boote when thou shold bee!"

This shoote it was but looselye shott,
  The arrowe flew in vaine,
And it mett one of the sheriffes men;
20 Good *William* a Trent was slaine.

It had beene better for *William* a Trent
  To hange vpon a gallowe
Then for to lye in the greenwoode,
  There slaine with an arrowe.

And it is sayd, when men be mett,
  Six can doe more then three:
And they haue tane Litle Iohn,
  And bound him ffast to a tree.

Veiwe, yew.   *Ffetteled*, made ready.   *Boote*, help.

"Thou shalt be drawen by dale and downe," quoth
    the sheriffe,
  "And hanged hye on a hill";
"But thou may ffayle," quoth Litle Iohn,
  "If itt be Christs owne will."

Let vs leaue talking of Litle Iohn,
  For hee is bound fast to a tree,
And talke of Guy and Robin Hood,
  In the green woode where they bee.

How these two yeomen together they **mett,**
10 Vnder the leaues of lyne,
To see what marchandise they made
  Euen at that same time.

"Good morrow, good fellow," quoth Sir Guy;
  "Good morrow, good ffellow," quoth hee;
"Methinkes by this bow thou beares in thy hand,
  A good archer thou seems to bee."

"I am wilfull of my way," quoth Sir Guye,
  "And of my morning tyde":
"I'le lead thee through the wood," quoth Robin,
20 "Good ffellow, I'le be thy guide."

"I seeke an outlaw," quoth Sir Guye,
  "Men call him Robin Hood;
I had rather meet with him vpon a day
  Then forty pound of golde."

"If you tow mett, itt wold be seene whether were
    better
  Afore yee did part awaye;

Lyne, lime-tree, linden.   *Wilfull of my way,* lost.

Let vs some other pastime find,
   Good ffellow, I thee pray.

"Let vs some other masteryes make,
   And wee will walke in the woods euen;
Wee may chance mee[t] with Robin Hoode
   Att some vnsett steven."

They cutt them downe the summer shroggs
   Which grew both vnder a bryar,
And sett them three score rood in twinn,
10   To shoote the prickes full neare.

"Leade on, good ffellow," sayd Sir Guye,
   "Lead on, I doe bidd thee":
"Nay, by my faith," quoth Robin Hood,
   "The leader thou shalt bee."

The first good shoot that Robin ledd
   Did not shoote an inch the pricke ffroe;
Guy was an archer good enoughe,
   But he cold neere shoote soe.

The second shoote Sir Guy shott,
20   He shott within the garlande;
But Robin Hoode shott it better then hee,
   For he cloue the good pricke-wande.

"Gods blessing on thy heart!" sayes Guye,
   "Goode ffellow, thy shooting is goode;
For an thy hart be as good as thy hands,
   Thou were better then Robin Hood.

Masteryes, feats of skill.
Vnsett steven, time not arranged.
Summer shroggs, shoots of that year's growth.
In twinn, apart.
Prickes, marks.

"Tell me thy name, good ffellow," quoth Guy
  "Vnder the leaues of lyne":
"Nay, by my faith," quoth good Robin,
  "Till thou haue told me thine."

"I dwell by dale and downe," quoth Guye,
  "And I haue done many a curst turne;
And he *that* calles me by my right name
  Calles me Guye of good Gysborne."

"My dwelling is in the wood," sayes Robin;
10 "By thee I set right nought;
My name is Robin Hood of Barnesdale,
  A ffellow thou has long sought."

He *that* had neither beene a kithe nor kin
  Might haue seene a full fayre sight,
To see how together these yeomen went,
  With blades both browne and bright.

To haue seene how these yeomen together foug[ht],
  Two howers of a sum*m*ers day;
Itt was neither Guy nor Robin Hood
20 *That* ffettled them to flye away.

Robin was reacheles on a roote,
  And stumbled at *that* tyde,
And Guy was quicke and nimble withall,
  And hitt him ore the left side.

"Ah, deere Lady!" sayd Robin Hoode,
  "Thou art both mother and may!
I thinke it was neu*er* mans destinye
  To dye before his day."

Curst turne, spiteful job.   *Browne,* shining.
Reacheles, reckless, careless. *May,* maid.

Robin thought on Our Lady deere,
And soone leapt vp againe,
And thus he came with an awkwarde stroke;
Good Sir Guy hee has slayne.

He tooke Sir Guys head by the hayre,
And sticked itt on his bowes end:
"Thou hast beene traytor all thy liffe,
Which thing must haue an ende."

Robin pulled forth an Irish kniffe,
10   And nicked Sir Guy in the fface,
That hee was neuer on a woman borne
Cold tell who Sir Guye was.

Saies, "Lye there, lye there, good Sir Guye,
And with me be not wrothe;
If thou haue had the worse stroakes at my hand,
Thou shalt haue the better cloathe."

Robin did off his gowne of greene,
Sir Guy hee did it throwe;
And hee put on that capull-hyde,
20   That cladd him topp to toe.

"The bowe, the arrowes, and litle horne,
And with me now I'le beare;
Ffor now I will goe to Barn[e]sdale,
To see how my men doe ffare."

Robin sett Guyes horne to his mouth,
A lowd blast in it he did blow;
That beheard the sheriffe of Nottingham,
As he leaned vnder a lowe.

Awkwarde, backhanded.   *Lowe,* hill.

"Hearken! hearken!" sayd the sheriffe,
  "I heard noe tydings but good;
For yonder I heare Sir Guyes horne **blowe,**
  For he hath slaine Robin Hoode.

"For yonder I heare Sir Guyes horne **blow,**
  Itt blowes soe well in tyde,
For yonder comes *tha*t wighty yeoman,
  Cladd in his capull-hyde.

"Come hither, thou good Sir Guy,
10   Aske of mee what thou wilt haue":
"I'le none of thy gold," sayes Robin **Hood,**
  "Nor I'le none of itt haue.

"But now I haue slaine the m*aster*," he **sayd,**
  "Let me goe strike the knaue;
This is all the reward I aske,
  Nor noe other will I haue."

"Thou art a madman," said the shiriffe,
  "Thou sholdest haue had a knights ffee;
Seeing thy asking [hath] beene soe badd,
20   Well granted it shall be."

But Litle Iohn heard his m*aster* speake,
  Well he knew *tha*t was his steuen;
"Now shall I be loset," qu*o*th Litle Iohn,
  "With Christs might in heauen."

But Robin hee hyed him towards Litle Iohn,
  Hee thoughte hee wold loose him beliue;
The sheriffe and all his companye
  Fast after him did driue.

> *Knights ffee,* knight's stipend, *i.e.,* have been a knight.
> *Steuen,* voice.   *Loset,* released.

"Stand abacke! stand abacke!" sayd Robin;
　　"Why draw you mee soe neere?
Itt was neu*er* the vse in our countrye
　　One's shrift another shold heere."

But Robin pulled forth an Irysh kniffe,
　　And losed Iohn hand and ffoote,
And gaue him S*ir* Guyes bow in his hand,
　　And bade it be his boote.

But Iohn tooke Guyes bow in his hand—
10　　His arrowes were rawstye by the roote—;
The sherriffe saw Litle Iohn draw a bow
　　And ffettle him to shoote.

Towards his house in Nottingam
　　He ffled full fast away,
And soe did all his companye,
　　Not one behind did stay.

But he cold neither soe fast goe,
　　Nor away soe fast runn,
But Litle Iohn, *with* an arrow broade,
20　　Did cleaue his heart in twinn.

THE LOCHMABEN HARPER

Heard ye eer of the silly blind harper,
　　That long livd in Lochmaben town,
How he wad gang to fair England,
　　　To steal King Henry's Wanton Brown?
　　　Sing, Faden dilly and faden dilly
　　　Sing, Faden dilly and deedle dan

Shrift, confession.
Rawstye by the roote, rusty at the end.
Silly, harmless, innocent.

But first he gaed to his gude wife,
    Wi a' the speed that he coud thole;
"This wark," quo he, "will never work
    Without a mare that has a foal."

Quo she, "Thou has a gude gray mare,
    That'al rin oer hills baith law and hie;
Gae tak the gray mare in thy hand,
    And leave the foal at hame wi me.

"And tak a halter in thy hose,
10   And o thy purpose dinna fail;
But wap it oer the Wanton's nose,
    And tie it to the gray mare's tail.

"Syne ca her out at yon back geate,
    Oer moss and muir and ilka dale;
For she'll neer let the Wanton bite
    Till she come hame to her ain foal."

So he is up to England gane,
    Even as fast as he can hie,
Till he came to King Henry's geate;
20   And wha was there but King Henry?

"Come in," quo he, "thou silly blind harper,
    And of thy harping let me hear;"
"O, by my sooth," quo the silly blind harper,
    "I'd rather hae stabling for my mare."

The king he looks oer his left shoulder,
    And says unto his stable-groom,
"Gae tak the silly poor harper's mare,
    And tie her side my Wanton Brown."

Thole, be capable of.   *Wap,* fasten.
Moss and muir, bog and moor.

And ay he harpit, and ay he carpit,
　Till a' the lords had fitted the floor;
They thought the music was sae sweet,
　And they forgot the stable-door.

And ay he harpit, and ay he carpit,
　Till a' the nobles were sound asleep;
Then quietly he took aff his shoon,
　And safly down the stair did creep.

Syne to the stable-door he hies,
10　Wi tread as light as light coud be,
And when he opned and gaed in,
　There he fand thirty gude steads and three.

He took the halter frae his hose,
　And of his purpose did na fail;
He slipt it oer the Wanton's nose,
　And tied it to his gray mare's tail.

He ca'd her out at yon back geate,
　Oer moss and muir and ilka dale,
And she loot neer the Wanton bite,
20　But held her still gaun at her tail.

The gray mare was right swift o fit,
　And did na fail to find the way,
For she was at Lochmaben geate
　Fu lang three hours ere 't was day.

When she came to the harper's door,
　There she gave mony a nicher and sneer;
"Rise," quo the wife, "thou lazey lass,
　Let in thy master and his mare."

Carpit, sang or chanted.　*Fitted*, footed.　*Safly*, softly.
Nicher and sneer, snicker and snort.

Then up she rose, pat on her claes,
　　And lookit out through the lock-hole;
"O, by my sooth," then quoth the lass,
　　"Our mare has gotten a braw big foal!"

"Come had thy peace, thou foolish lass,
　　The moon's but glancing in thy eye;
I'll wad my hail fee against a groat,
　　It's bigger than eer our foal will be."

The neighbours too that heard the noise
10　Cried to the wife to put hir in;
"By my sooth," then quo the wife,
　　"She's better than ever he rade on."

But on the morn, at fair day light,
　　Whan they had ended a' thier chear,
King Henry's Wanton Brown was stawn,
　　And eke the poor old harper's mare.

"Allace! allace!" says the silly blind harper,
　　"Allace, allace, that I came here!
In Scotland I've tint a braw cowte-foal,
20　In England they've stawn my gude gray mare."

"Come had thy tongue, thou silly blind harper,
　　And of thy allacing let me be;
For thou shalt get a better mare,
　　And weel paid shall thy cowte-foal be."

JOCK O THE SIDE

"Now Liddisdale has ridden a raid,
　　But I wat they had better staid at hame;

Wad my hail fee, wager my whole property.
Braw, fine.　　　　　　*Come had,* come hold.

For Mitchel o Winfield he is dead,
    And my son Johnie is prisner tane."
        With my fa ding diddle, la la dow diddle.

For Mangerton House auld Downie is gane;
    Her coats she has kilted up to her knee,
And down the water wi speed she rins,
    While tears in spaits fa fast frae her eie.

Then up and bespake the lord Mangerton:
    "What news, what news, sister Downie, to me?"
10 "Bad news, bad news, my lord Mangerton;
    Mitchel is killd, and tane they hae my son Johnie."

"Neer fear, sister Downie," quo Mangerton;
    "I hae yokes of oxen four and twentie,
My barns, my byres, and my faulds, a' weel filld,
    And I'll part wi them a' ere Johnie shall die.

"Three men I'll take to set him free,
    Weel harnessd a' wi best o steel;
The English rogues may hear, and drie
    The weight o their braid swords to feel.

20 "The Laird's Jock ane, the Laird's Wat twa,
    Oh, Hobie Noble, thou ane maun be;
Thy coat is blue, thou has been true,
    Since England banishd thee, to me."

Now Hobie was an English man,
    In Bewcastle-dale was bred and born;
But his misdeeds they were sae great,
    They banishd him neer to return.

Spaits, floods.
Byres, cow-houses.
Drie . . . to feel, come to feel.

Lord Mangerton them orders gave,
  "Your horses the wrang way maun a' be shod;
Like gentlemen ye must not seem,
  But look like corn-caugers gawn ae road.

"Your armour gude ye maunna shaw,
  Nor ance appear like men o weir;
As country lads be all arrayd,
  Wi branks and brecham on ilk mare."

Sae now a' their horses are shod the wrang way,
10 And Hobie has mounted his grey sae fine,
Jock his lively bay, Wat's on his white horse behind,
  And on they rode for the water o Tyne.

At the Choler-ford they a' light down,
  And there, wi the help o the light o the moon,
A tree they cut, wi fifteen naggs upo ilk side,
  To climb up the wa o Newcastle town.

But when they cam to Newcastle town,
  And were alighted at the wa,
They fand their tree three ells oer laigh,
20 They fand their stick baith short and sma.

Then up and spake the Laird's ain Jock,
  "There's naething for 't, the gates we maun
    force;"
But when they came the gates unto,
  A proud porter withstood baith men and horse.

His neck in twa I wat they hae wrung,
  Wi hand or foot he neer playd paw;

Corn-caugers, grain dealers.   Weir, war.
Branks, makeshift bridle.   Brecham, rough pack-saddle.
Naggs, notches.   Laigh, low.   Playd paw, stirred again.

His life and his keys at anes they hae tane,
    And cast his body ahind the wa.

Now soon they reach Newcastle jail,
    And to the prisner thus they call:
"Sleips thou, wakes thou, Jock o the Side?
    Or is thou wearied o thy thrall?"

Jock answers thus, wi dolefu tone:
    "Aft, aft I wake, I seldom sleip;
But wha's this kens my name sae weel,
10   And thus to hear my waes does seik?"

Then up and spake the good Laird's Jock,
    "Neer fear ye now, my billie," quo he;
"For here's the Laird's Jock, the Laird's Wat,
    And Hobie Noble, come to set thee free."

"Oh, had thy tongue, and speak nae mair,
    And o thy tawk now let me be!
For if a' Liddisdale were here the night,
    The morn's the day that I maun die.

"Full fifteen stane o Spanish iron
20   They hae laid a' right sair on me;
Wi locks and keys I am fast bound
    Into this dungeon mirk and drearie."

"Fear ye no that," quo the Laird's Jock;
    "A faint heart neer wan a fair ladie;
Work thou within, we'll work without,
    And I'll be bound we set thee free."

The first strong dore that they came at,
    They loosed it without a key;

Thrall, imprisonment.   *Kens,* knows.

The next chaind dore that they cam at,
　　They gard it a' in flinders flee.

The prisner now, upo his back,
　　The Laird's Jock 's gotten up fu hie;
And down the stair him, irons and a',
　　Wi nae sma speed and joy brings he.

"Now, Jock, I wat," quo Hobie Noble,
　　"Part o the weight ye may lay on me;"
"I wat weel no," quo the Laird's Jock,
10　　"I count him lighter than a flee."

Sae out at the gates they a' are gane,
　　The prisner 's set on horseback hie;
And now wi speed they 've tane the gate,
　　While ilk ane jokes fu wantonlie.

"O Jock, sae winsomely 's ye ride,
　　Wi baith your feet upo ae side!
Sae weel's ye're harnessd, and sae trig!
　　In troth ye sit like ony bride."

The night, tho wat, they didna mind,
20　　But hied them on fu mirrilie,
Until they cam to Cholerford brae,
　　Where the water ran like mountains hie.

But when they came to Cholerford,
　　There they met with an auld man;
Says, "Honest man, will the water ride?
　　Tell us in haste, if that ye can."

Gard . . . flinders flee, made it fly to pieces.
Tane the gate, took the road.
Tho wat, though wet.　　　　　　*Brae,* river bank.
Will the water ride, can one ford the stream.

"I wat weel no," quo the good auld man;
  "Here I hae livd this threty yeirs and three,
And I neer yet saw the Tyne sae big,
  Nor rinning ance sae like a sea."

Then up and spake the Laird's saft Wat,
  The greatest coward in the company;
"Now halt, now halt, we needna try't;
  The day is comd we a' maun die!"

"Poor faint-hearted thief!" quo the Laird's Jock,
10 "There'll nae man die but he that's fie;
I'll lead ye a' right safely through;
  Lift ye the prisner on ahint me."

Sae now the water they a' hae tane,
  By anes and twas they a' swam through;
"Here are we a' safe," says the Laird's Jock,
  "And, poor faint Wat, what think ye now?"

They scarce the ither side had won,
  When twenty men they saw pursue;
Frae Newcastle town they had been sent,
20 A' English lads, right good and true.

But when the land-sergeant the water saw,
  "It winna ride, my lads," quo he;
Then out he cries, "Ye the prisner may take,
  But leave the irons, I pray, to me."

"I wat weel no," cryd the Laird's Jock,
  "I'll keep them a', shoon to my mare they'll be;
My good grey mare, for I am sure,
  She's bought them a' fu dear frae thee."

He that's fie, he that's doomed.
Land-sergeant, officer of Border patrol.   *Shoon,* shoes.

Sae now they're away for Liddisdale,
　　Een as fast as they coud them hie;
The prisner's brought to his ain fire-side,
　　And there o's airns they make him free.

"Now, Jock, my billie," quo a' the three,
　　"The day was comd thou was to die;
But thou's as weel at thy ain fire-side,
　　Now sitting, I think, tween thee and me."

They hae gard fill up ae punch-bowl,
10　And after it they maun hae anither,
And thus the night they a' hae spent,
　　Just as they had been brither and brither.

THE BRAES OF YARROW

"I dreamed a dreary dream this night,
　　That fills my heart wi sorrow;
I dreamed I was pouing the heather green
　　Upon the braes of Yarrow.

"O true-luve mine, stay still and dine,
　　As ye ha done before, O;"
"O I'll be hame by hours nine,
20　And frae the braes of Yarrow."

"I dreamed a dreary dream this night,
　　That fills my heart wi sorrow;
I dreamed my luve came headless hame,
　　O frae the braes of Yarrow!

"O true-luve mine, stay still and dine,
　　As ye ha done before, O;"

Billie, comrade.

"O I'll be hame by hours nine,
  And frae the braes of Yarrow."

"O are ye going to hawke," she says,
  "As ye ha done before, O?
Or are ye going to weild your brand,
  Upon the braes of Yarrow?"

"O I am not going to hawke," he says,
  "As I have done before, O,
But for to meet your brother Jhon,
10   Upon the braes of Yarrow."

As he gade down yon dowy den,
  Sorrow went him before, O;
Nine well-wight men lay waiting him,
  Upon the braes of Yarrow.

"I have your sister to my wife,
  Ye think me an unmeet marrow;
But yet one foot will I never flee
  Now frae the braes of Yarrow."

Than four he killd and five did wound,
20   That was an unmeet marrow!
And he had weel nigh wan the day
  Upon the braes of Yarrow.

Bot a cowardly loon came him behind,
  Our Lady lend him sorrow!
And wi a rappier pierced his heart,
  And laid him low on Yarrow.

Now Douglas to his sister's gane,
  Wi meikle dule and sorrow:

Dowy den, gloomy narrow valley.
Well-wight, stalwart.   Unmeet marrow, unsuitable mate.

"Gae to your luve, sister," he says,
  "He's sleeping sound on Yarrow."

As she went down yon dowy den,
  Sorrow went her before, O;
She saw her true-love lying slain
  Upon the braes of Yarrow.

She swoond thrice upon his breist
  That was her dearest marrow;
Said, "Ever alace and wae the day
10 Thou wentst frae me to Yarrow!"

She kist his mouth, she kaimed his hair,
  As she had done before, O;
She wiped the blood that trickled doun
  Upon the braes of Yarrow

Her hair it was three quarters lang,
  It hang baith side and yellow;
She tied it round her white hause-bane,
  And tint her life on Yarrow.

THE UNQUIET GRAVE

"The wind doth blow today, my love,
20 And a few small drops of rain;
I never had but one true-love,
  In cold grave she was lain.

"I'll do as much for my true-love
  As any young man may;
I'll sit and mourn all at her grave
  For a twelvemonth and a day."

Hause-bane, neck.

The twelvemonth and a day being up,
  The dead began to speak:
"Oh who sits weeping on my grave,
  And will not let me sleep?"

" 'Tis I, my love, sits on your grave,
  And will not let you sleep;
For I crave one kiss of your clay-cold lips,
  And that is all I seek."

"You crave one kiss of my clay-cold lips;
10   But my breath smells earthy strong;
If you have one kiss of my clay-cold lips,
  Your time will not be long.

" 'Tis down in yonder garden green,
  Love, where we used to walk,
The finest flower that ere was seen
  Is withered to a stalk.

"The stalk is withered dry, my love,
  So will our hearts decay;
So make yourself content, my love,
20   Till God calls you away."

LADY ISABEL AND THE ELF-KNIGHT

Fair lady Isabel sits in her bower sewing,
  Aye as the gowans grow gay
There she heard an elf-knight blawing his horn.
  The first morning in May.

"If I had yon horn that I hear blawing,
And yon elf-knight to sleep in my bosom."
  Gowans, daisies.

This maiden had scarcely these words spoken,
Till in at her window the elf-knight has luppen.

"It's a very strange matter, fair maiden," said he,
"I canna blaw my horn but ye call on me.

"But will ye go to yon greenwood side?
If ye canna gang, I will cause you to ride."

He leapt on a horse, and she on another,
And they rode on to the greenwood together.

"Light down, light down, lady Isabel," said he,
10 "We are come to the place where ye are to die."

"Hae mercy, hae mercy, kind sir, on me,
Till ance my dear father and mother I see."

"Seven king's-daughters here hae I slain,
And ye shall be the eight o them."

"O sit down a while, lay your head on my knee,
That we may hae some rest before that I die."

She stroak'd him sae fast, the nearer he did creep,
Wi a sma charm she lulld him fast asleep.

Wi his ain sword-belt sae fast as she ban him,
20 Wi his ain dag-durk sae sair as she dang him.

"If seven king's-daughters here ye hae slain,
Lye ye here, a husband to them a'."

Ban, bound.
Dag-durk, dagger.
Dang, struck.

THE TWA SISTERS

There was twa sisters in a bowr,
　　Edinburgh, Edinburgh
There was twa sisters in a bowr,
　　Stirling for ay
There was twa sisters in a bowr,
There came a knight to be their wooer.
　　Bonny Saint Johnston stands upon Tay.

He courted the eldest wi glove an ring,
But he lovd the youngest above a' thing.

10 He courted the eldest wi brotch an knife,
But lovd the youngest as his life.

The eldest she was vexed sair,
An much envi'd her sister fair.

Into her bowr she could not rest,
Wi grief an spite she almos brast.

Upon a morning fair an clear,
She cried upon her sister dear:

"O sister, come to yon sea stran,
An see our father's ships come to lan."

20 She's taen her by the milk-white han,
An led her down to yon sea stran.

The youngest stood upon a stane,
The eldest came an threw her in.

She tooke her by the middle sma,
An dashd her bonny back to the jaw.

"O sister, sister, tak my han,
An Ise mack you heir to a' my lan.

"O sister, sister, tak my middle,
An yes get my goud an my gouden girdle.

"O sister, sister, save my life,
An I swear Ise never be nae man's wife."

"Foul fa the han that I should tacke,
10 It twin'd me an my wardles make.

"Your cherry cheeks an yellow hair,
Gars me gae maiden evermair."

Sometimes she sank, an sometimes she swam,
Till she came down yon bonny mill-dam.

O out it came the miller's son,
An saw the fair maid swimmin in.

"O father, father, draw your dam,
Here's either a mermaid or a swan."

The miller quickly drew the dam,
20 An there he found a drownd woman.

You couldna see her yellow hair
For gold and pearle that were so rare.

You couldna see her middle sma
For gouden girdle that was sae braw.

Jaw, wave.
Yes, you will.
Wardles make, earthly mate.

You couldna see her fingers white
For gouden rings that was sae gryte.

And by there came a harper fine,
That harped to the king at dine.

When he did look that lady upon,
He sighd and made a heavy moan.

He's taen three locks o her yallow hair,
An wi them strung his harp sae fair.

The first tune he did play and sing,
10 Was, "Farewell to my father the king."

The nextin tune that he playd syne,
Was, "Farewell to my mother the queen."

The lasten tune that he playd then,
Was, "Wae to my sister, fair Ellen."

ALLISON GROSS

O Allison Gross, that lives in yon towr,
  The ugliest witch i the north country,
Has trysted me ae day up till her bowr,
  An monny fair speech she made to me.

She stroaked my head, an she kembed my hair,
20   An she set me down saftly on her knee;
Says, "Gin ye will be my lemman so true,
  Sae monny braw things as I would you gi."

She showd me a mantle o red scarlet,
  Wi gouden flowrs an fringes fine;
  Gryte, large.

Says, "Gin ye will be my lemman so true,
 This goodly gift it sal be thine."

"Awa, awa, ye ugly witch,
 Haud far awa, an lat me be;
I never will be your lemman sae true,
 An I wish I were out o your company."

She neist brought a sark o the saftest silk,
 Well wrought wi pearles about the ban;
Says, "Gin you will be my ain true love,
10 This goodly gift you sal comman."

She showd me a cup of the good red gold,
 Well set wi jewls sae fair to see;
Says, "Gin you will be my lemman sae true,
 This goodly gift I will you gi."

"Awa, awa, ye ugly witch,
 Had far awa, and lat me be;
For I woudna ance kiss your ugly mouth
 For a' the gifts that ye coud gi."

She's turnd her right and roun about,
20 An thrice she blaw on a grass-green horn,
An she sware by the meen and the stars abeen,
 That she'd gar me rue the day I was born.

Then out has she taen a silver wand,
 And she's turned her three times roun an roun;
She's mutterd sich words till my strength it faild,
 An I fell down senceless upon the groun.

She's turnd me into an ugly worm,
 And gard me toddle about the tree;

Ban, edge, hem. *Meen,* moon. *Abeen,* above.

An ay, on ilka Saturdays night,
  My sister Maisry came to me.

Wi silver bason an silver kemb,
  To kemb my heady upon her knee;
But or I had kissd her ugly mouth,
  I'd rather a toddled about the tree.

But as it fell out on last Hallow-even,
  When the seely court was ridin by,
The queen lighted down on a gowany bank,
10 Nae far frae the tree when I wont to lye.

She took me up in her milk-white han,
  An she's stroakd me three times oer her knee;
She chang'd me again to my ain proper shape,
  An I nae mair maun toddle about the tree.

TAM LIN

"O I forbid you, maidens a',
  That wear gowd on your hair,
To come or gae by Carterhaugh,
  For young Tam Lin is there.

"There's nane that gaes by Carterhaugh
20 But they leave him a wad,
Either their rings, or green mantles,
  Or else their maidenhead."

Janet has kilted her green kirtle
  A little aboon her knee,

Seely court, fairy court, which rides on Hallowe'en.
Aboon her bree, over her brow.
Wad, pledge, security.

And she has broded her yellow hair
  A little aboon her bree,
And she's awa to Carterhaugh,
  As fast as she can hie.

When she came to Carterhaugh,
  Tam Lin was at the well,
And there she fand his steed standing,
  But away was himsel.

She had na pu'd a double rose,
10 A rose but only twa,
Till up then started young Tam Lin,
  Says, "Lady, thou's pu nae mae.

"Why pu's thou the rose, Janet,
  And why breaks thou the wand?
Or why comes thou to Carterhaugh
  Withouten my command?"

"Carterhaugh, it is my ain,
  My daddie gave it me;
I'll come and gang by Carterhaugh,
20 And ask nae leave at thee."

Janet has kilted her green kirtle
  A little aboon her knee,
And she has snooded her yellow hair
  A little aboon her bree,
And she is to her father's ha,
  As fast as she can hie.

Four and twenty ladies fair
  Were playing at the ba,

Aboon her bree, over her brow.
Wand, twig.   *Snooded,* filleted.

And out then cam the fair Janet,
  Ance the flower amang them a'.

Four and twenty ladies fair
  Were playing at the chess,
And out then cam the fair Janet,
  As green as onie glass.

Out then spak an auld grey knight,
  Lay oer the castle wa,
And says, "Alas, fair Janet, for thee
10 But we'll be blamed a'."

"Haud your tongue, ye auld-fac'd knight,
  Some ill death may ye die!
Father my bairn on whom I will,
  I'll father nane on thee."

Out then spak her father dear,
  And he spak meek and mild;
"And ever alas, sweet Janet," he says,
  "I think thou gaes wi child."

"If that I gae wi child, father,
20 Mysel maun bear the blame;
There's neer a laird about your ha
  Shall get the bairn's name.

"If my love were an earthly knight,
  As he's an elfin grey,
I wad na gie my ain true-love
  For nae lord that ye hae.

"The steed that my true-love rides on
  Is lighter than the wind;

Wi siller he is shod before,
  Wi burning gowd behind."

Janet has kilted her green kirtle
  A little aboon her knee,
And she has snooded her yellow hair
  A little aboon her bree,
And she's awa to Carterhaugh,
  As fast as she can hie.

When she cam to Carterhaugh,
10 Tam Lin was at the well,
And there she fand his steed standing,
  But away was himsel.

She had na pu'd a double rose,
  A rose but only twa,
Till up then started young Tam Lin,
  Says, "Lady, thou pu's nae mae.

"Why pu's thou the rose, Janet,
  Amang the groves sae green,
And a' to kill the bonie babe
20 That we gat us between?"

"O tell me, tell me, Tam Lin," she says,
  "For's sake that died on tree,
If eer ye was in holy chapel,
  Or christendom did see?"

"Roxbrugh he was my grandfather,
  Took me with him to bide,
And ance it fell upon a day
  That wae did me betide.

Christendom, christening.

"And ance it fell upon a day,
  A cauld day and a snell,
When we were frae the hunting come,
  That frae my horse I fell;
The Queen o Fairies she caught me,
  In yon green hill to dwell.

"And pleasant is the fairy land,
  But, an eerie tale to tell,
Ay at the end of seven years
10 We pay a tiend to hell;
I am sae fair and fu o flesh,
  I'm feard it be mysel.

"But the night is Halloween, lady,
  The morn is Hallowday;
Then win me, win me, an ye will,
  For weel I wat ye may.

"Just at the mirk and midnight hour
  The fairy folk will ride,
And they that wad their true-love win,
20 At Miles Cross they maun bide."

"But how shall I thee ken, Tam Lin,
  Or how my true-love know,
Among sae mony unco knights
  The like I never saw?"

"O first let pass the black, lady,
  And syne let pass the brown,
But quickly run to the milk-white steed,
  Pu ye his rider down.

Snell, sharp.
Tiend, tithe, tenth part.
Unco, strange.

"For I'll ride on the milk-white steed,
    And ay nearest the town;
Because I was an earthly knight
    They gie me that renown.

"My right hand will be glovd, lady,
    My left hand will be bare,
Cockt up shall my bonnet be,
    And kaimd down shall my hair,
And thae's the takens I gie thee,
10   Nae doubt I will be there.

"They'll turn me in your arms, lady,
    Into an esk and adder;
But hold me fast, and fear me not,
    I am your bairn's father.

"They'll turn me to a bear sae grim,
    And then a lion bold;
But hold me fast, and fear me not,
    As ye shall love your child.

"Again they'll turn me in your arms
20   To a red het gaud of airn;
But hold me fast, and fear me not,
    I'll do to you nae harm.

"And last they'll turn me in your arms
    Into the burning gleed;
Then throw me into well water,
    O throw me in wi speed.

"And then I'll be your ain true-love,
    I'll turn a naked knight;

Esk, newt or lizard, considered venomous.
Het gaud of airn, hot bar of iron.   *Gleed,* glowing coal.

Then cover me wi your green mantle,
  And cover me out o sight."

Gloomy, gloomy was the night,
  And eerie was the way,
As fair Jenny in her green mantle
  To Miles Cross she did gae.

About the middle o the night
  She heard the bridles ring;
This lady was as glad at that
10 As any earthly thing.

First she let the black pass by,
  And syne she let the brown;
But quickly she ran to the milk-white steed,
  And pu'd the rider down.

Sae weel she minded whae he did say,
  And young Tam Lin did win;
Syne coverd him wi her green mantle,
  As blythe's a bird in spring.

Out then spak the Queen o Fairies,
20 Out of a bush o broom:
"Them that has gotten young Tam Lin
  Has gotten a stately groom."

Out then spak the Queen o Fairies,
And an angry woman was she:
"Shame betide her ill-far'd face,
  And an ill death may she die,
For she's taen awa the boniest knight
  In a' my companie.

"But had I kend, Tam Lin," she says,
  "What now this night I see,
I wad hae taen out thy twa grey een,
  And put in twa een o tree."

SAINT STEPHEN AND HEROD

Seynt Stevene was a clerk in kyng Herowdes halle,
And servyd him of bred and cloth, as every kyng
  befalle.

Stevyn out of kechone cam, wyth boris hed on honde;
He saw a sterre was fayr and bryght over Bedlem
  stonde.

He kyst adoun the boris hed and went in to the
  halle:
10 "I forsak the, kyng Herowdes, and thi werkes alle.

"I forsak the, kyng Herowdes, and thi werkes alle;
Ther is a chyld in Bedlem born is beter than we alle."

"Quat eylyt the, Stevene? quat is the befalle?
Lakkyt the eyther mete or drynk in kyng Herowdes
  halle?"

"Lakit me neyther mete ne drynk in kyng Herowdes
  halle;
Ther is a chyld in Bedlem born is beter than we alle."

"Quat eylyt the, Stevyn? art thu wod, or thu gyn-
  nyst to brede?
Lakkyt the eyther gold or fe, or ony ryche wede?"

Eylyt, aileth.   Wod, mad.
Brede, have insane fancies.   Gold or fe, gold or wage.
Wede, clothing.

"Lakyt me neyther gold ne fe, ne non ryche wede;
Ther is a chyld in Bedlem born xal helpyn us at our
    nede."

"That is al so soth, Stevyn, al so soth, iwys,
As this capoun crowe xal that lyth here in myn
    dysh."

That word was not so sone seyd, that word in that
    halle,
The capoun crew *Christus natus est!* among the
    lordes alle.

"Rysyt up, myn turmentowres, be to and al be on,
And ledyt Stevyn out of this town, and stonyt hym
    wyth ston!"

Tokyn he Stevene, and stonyd hym in the way,
10 And therfore is his evyn on Crystes owyn day.

THE CHERRY-TREE CAROL

Joseph was an old man,
    and an old man was he,
When he wedded Mary,
    in the land of Galilee.

Joseph and Mary walked
    through an orchard good,
Where was cherries and berries,
    so red as any blood.

Joseph and Mary walked
20   through an orchard green,

Iwys, indeed, truly.   *Tokyn he,* they took.
Be to and al be on, in pairs and singly.
His evyn, his vigil, which falls on Christmas.

Where was berries and cherries,
  as thick as might be seen.

O then bespoke Mary,
  so meek and so mild:
"Pluck me one cherry, Joseph,
  for I am with child."

O then bespoke Joseph,
  with words most unkind:
"Let him pluck thee a cherry
  that brought thee with child."

O then bespoke the babe,
  within his mother's womb:
"Bow down then the tallest tree,
  for my mother to have some."

Then bowed down the highest tree
  unto his mother's hand;
Then she cried, "See, Joseph,
  I have cherries at command."

O then bespake Joseph:
  "I have done Mary wrong;
But cheer up, my dearest,
  and be not cast down."

Then Mary plucked a cherry,
  as red as the blood,
Then Mary went home
  with her heavy load.

Then Mary took her babe,
  and sat him on her knee,

Saying, "My dear son, tell me
    what this world will be."

"O I shall be as dead, mother,
    as the stones in the wall;
O the stones in the streets, mother,
    shall mourn for me all.

"Upon Easter-day, mother,
    my uprising shall be;
O the sun and the moon, mother,
10   shall both rise with me."

BONNIE GEORGE CAMPBELL

Hie upon Hielands,
    and laigh upon Tay,
Bonnie George Campbell
    rode out on a day.

He saddled, he bridled,
    and gallant rode he,
And hame cam his guid horse,
    but never cam he.

Out cam his mother dear,
20   greeting fu sair,
And out cam his bonnie bryde,
    riving her hair.

"The meadow lies green,
    the corn is unshorn,
But bonnie George Campbell
    will never return."

Saddled and bridled
and booted rode he,
A plume in his helmet,
a sword at his knee.

But toom cam his saddle,
all bloody to see,
Oh, hame cam his guid horse,
but never cam he!

Toom, empty.

NOTES

NOTES

The following notes are intended as a supplement to those interspersed with the text, not as a substitute for them. Although the editor trusts that they may not be found necessary to an intelligent reading of the selections, he hopes that they will be useful. In so far as they are explanatory, they deal for the most part with matters of literary construction and the like, which could not well be discussed in foot-notes. The opportunity has also been taken to supply brief suggestive bibliographies.

OLD ENGLISH LITERATURE

The student who knows no Old English but who wishes to learn more about pre-Conquest literature may read with profit the admirable translations in J. D. Spaeth's *Old English Poetry* (Princeton Univ. Press), 1921, where he will find also much illuminating comment. For the prose, Cook and Tinker, *Select Translations from Old English Prose* (Ginn), 1908, may be commended. The best general survey of the literature remains that of B. ten Brink, *Early English Literature,* translated by H. M. Kennedy. Stopford Brooke, *History of Early English Literature,* 1892, and *English Literature from the Beginning to the Norman Conquest,* 1898, may be read for his stimulating aesthetic criticism, though his knowledge and judgment are often at fault. Excellent books dealing with the Middle English period as well are W. P. Ker, *English Literature: Mediaeval* (Home University Library), C. S. Baldwin, *Introduction to English Medieval Literature,* 1914, and W. W. Lawrence, *Medieval Story,* 2nd ed. 1926. For the history of the period, see C. Oman, *England before the Norman Conquest,* 1913. For the life of the Germanic tribes, see F. B. Gummere, *Germanic Origins,* 1892.

BEOWULF

Apart from the translation by Professor Spaeth of about two thirds of the poem, the student will find the best translation the one in verse by F. B. Gummere, *The Oldest English Epic* (Macmillan), 1909, to which are appended versions of other heroic poems. The most satisfactory prose translation is that of C. B. Tinker, 2nd ed. 1910. The best editions of the original text are those by Wyatt and Chambers, 1920, and F. Klaeber, 1922, which contain much valuable illustrative material. Indispensable to an adequate knowledge of the poem is W. W. Lawrence, *Beowulf and the Epic Tradition*, 1928. To be recommended also is H. M. Chadwick, *The Heroic Age*, 1912. For the relations between heroic poetry and later narrative verse, see W. P. Ker, *Epic and Romance*, 1897, and W. M. Dixon, *English Epic and Heroic Poetry*, 1912.

The main story that lies behind the poem of *Beowulf* was perhaps brought to northern England by belated colonists in the sixth century. At all events, real events that took place in that century are imbedded in it, and they are wholly Continental. Of this much we can be reasonably sure: somewhere in the northern lands tradition wove about the person of a purely fictitious Beowulf a web of high adventure. He was made a great king of the Geats, somewhat as Arthur in later centuries was made a great king of the Britons; he was endowed with supernatural powers and made the ideal hero of his race. Probably some of his exploits had earlier been told of a vaguely remembered demi-god called Beowa, whom the Angles would have known before their migration across the North Sea. The story, somewhat as we have it, must certainly have been known in England for a considerable time before the author of *Beowulf* took it in hand. The names show this, as do certain changes wrought in the legends themselves, which can be checked by reference to Continental versions of the tales. Whether the English poet had lays to work with, or only oral tradition, we have no means whatever of knowing. All we can say is that he made from heroic material of diverse origin an epic in which the point of view is that of christianized Anglia at the end of the seventh century. He was a Christian, but he had not forgotten the traditions of an older day. His pictures of court life, as well as of adventure, idealize the life of the past times but are based on knowledge of his own.

P. 10. The Danes occupied, in the sixth century, an ill-defined region, of which the island of Zealand in Denmark was the centre. This was the country from which the Angles had migrated earlier. Of all the tribes left on the Continent, the Danes seem to have been closest to the inhabitants of northern England. There is reason to believe that Hrothgar was a real king, though his magnificence is of course purely imaginary.

P. 11, 1. 11. *Hart he named it,* or Heorot, probably because adorned with stags' antlers on the gables.

Pp. 11-13. The monster Grendel, half man and half beast, is a strange combination of pagan superstitions and Old Testament lore.

P. 13. Hygelac's kinsman, Beowulf, is represented as the son of Ecgtheow, who had married a princess of the Geats. The Geats probably lived in what is now Sweden. Hygelac was certainly a real king, who made an unsuccessful raid on the Franks about 516. He was succeeded by his son Heardred, after whom Beowulf obtained the throne.

Pp. 14 ff. The stately dignity of Beowulf's reception should be noted. Something like these would have been the manners at a Northumbrian court in the poet's time. It is doubtful whether they would have been so good in sixth century Denmark. Throughout the poem, indeed, the manners pictured are less primitive than the events of the story would lead us to expect.

Pp. 34-35. Hrothgar's account of Grendel's mere is one of the best examples in Old English poetry of what may be called impressionistic description. In such passages, which are of frequent occurrence, clearness of visualization is sacrificed to emotional appeal, very much as it is in some modern romantic poetry. The same method, applied to passages of action, accounts for what we may term the stuttering effect of much narrative verse in Old English. But what is lost in clarity is gained in vividness and intensity of feeling.

P. 50, 1. 25. *Nægling.* Names for swords are common in heroic legend. Unferth had given Beowulf the sword called Hrunting (see p. 42) ; Balmung is the name of Sigurd's sword in the *Nibelungenlied,* and Miming of Siegfried's in the *Thidrekssaga.* The last was made by Weland the Smith. Nor is Beowulf's unfortunate tendency to have swords fail him at need (p. 38) altogether unexampled. Similar overpowering strength was attributed to Sigurd and Offa.

P. 51, 11. 29-30 *the work of giants.* It should be remembered that even in the eighth century stone buildings were uncommon among northern peoples. The ruins of

Roman work were marvels to them, as is shown by numerous references like this one.

CYNEWULF

For an account of Old English poetry on Christian themes, see A. J. Barnouw, *Anglo-Saxon Christian Poetry,* translated by Louise Dudley, 1914.

AN ADVENT HYMN

Pp. 57-58. This passage is from Christ, vv. 378-415. The best edition of the poem is that by A. S. Cook, 1900. For a prose translation of all the Cynewulfian poetry, see C. W. Kennedy, *The Poems of Cynewulf,* 1910, which also contains a valuable introduction.

CONSTANTINE'S VISION

Pp. 58-63. This passage from *Elene* occurs at the beginning of the poem and includes vv. 1-147. The best edition is that of A. S. Cook, *The Old English Elene, Phœnix, and Physiologus,* 1919. For some account of the adaptation of such material in Old English, see the editor's *Saints' Legends,* 1916, pp. 55-93. The poem proceeds with the story of the adventures of Queen Helena, who goes to Jerusalem at her son's command to recover the true cross.

THE WANDERER

Pp. 63-66. The translation of this noble poem is from J. D. Spaeth, *Old English Poetry,* 1921, pp. 140-144. The text may be found in any Old English reader.

MIDDLE ENGLISH LITERATURE

See W. H. Schofield, *English Literature from the Norman Conquest to Chaucer,* 1906, as well the following, which have a wider scope: W. P. Ker, *English Literature: Mediaeval* (Home University Library), C. S. Baldwin, *Introduction to English Medieval Literature,* 1914, W. W. Lawrence, *Medieval Story,* 2nd ed. 1926.

THE VISION OF PIERS PLOWMAN

Pp. 67-78. The edition of W. W. Skeat in two volumes (1886) contains all three versions of the poem.

P. 68, 1. 5. A. H. Bright, in *New Light on Piers Plow-man*, 1928, argues plausibly for the identification of a certain valley in the Malvern Hills as the one the author had in mind.

P. 69, 1. 10. *Qui loquitur turpiloquium*, he who utters obscenity, which is not a quotation from St. Paul, as a careless reading of the text might make one think.

L. 15. *knaves of Robert*, a common term for thievish vagabonds in the fourteenth century.

L. 26. *the friars.* See Chaucer's sketch, pp. 161-163.

P. 70, 1. 5. *a pardoner.* See Chaucer's Pardoner, pp. 176-178, 202-221.

L. 21. *time of the pestilence*, probably the Black Death of 1348-9.

P. 71, 1. 16. *Dieu vous save*, the refrain of a popular song, significantly in French.

THE PEARL

Pp. 80-85. There are editions of the poem by C. G. Osgood, 1906, and Sir I. Gollanz, revised 1921. Translations by Gollanz in the edition named, and by G. G. Coulton, 1906.

SIR GAWAIN AND THE GREEN KNIGHT

Pp. 85-152. The poem is now available in an excellent edition by J. R. R. Tolkien and E. V. Gordon, 1925. The reader should observe how carefully the author has arranged his material. The division of the romance into four parts is not arbitrary, for each part represents a different stage of the narrative and contributes to the organic symmetry of the whole. Even the hunting scenes in the third part, with detail so exact that it would have satisfied any fourteenth century hunting knight, though they seem a little overwrought to us, are justified by the way they balance the encounters between Gawain and Bercilak's wife. Chaucer himself never wrote a narrative more structurally perfect. Similarly, the conversations throughout the poem are admirable not only in the way they preserve the accent of real speech but advance the action. Although the plot is fantastic, the ways of the people involved are the ways of mediaeval lords and ladies, not the movements of puppets. A vein of humor, one should not fail to notice, runs throughout the story, appearing both in conversation and in event. The author had the happy gift of treating serious issues and ideals without pulling a long face. He made excellent use, too, of the possibilities of verse by way of heightening and intensifying his story. The reader of any prose translation must take this important element on trust, but he should not forget it.

Pp. 85-86. The opening stanzas were probably not too seriously intended. To place Arthur in the succession of British kings was the conventional thing to do. "This," the author says in effect, "is to be a tale from the dignified history of our island." He then pictures immediately a very gay young Arthur surrounded by light-hearted courtiers. Notice that he returns to the *Brut* at the end of the poem (p. 152).

Pp. 89-91. One accepts the supernatural here, as throughout the tale, because it is so naturally introduced against a background of reality. The circumstantial detail, moreover, lulls us into credulity.

Pp. 100-105. The arming of Gawain is a careful account of the ritual proper to such occasions. It should be noted that the knight was equipped according to the latest fashion of the fourteenth century. The elaborate comment on the pentangle and its significance serves the same end: to dignify Gawain and emphasize the seriousness of his quest. The effect of this is heightened by the description of his journey, which follows. In the original this latter passage is romantic poetry of a high order.

Pp. 105-114. The description of the castle, as Gawain approaches it, is intentionally a little fantastic. Remember his emotional tension. Once within, however, he is received with perfect courtesy according to the customs of the times. I doubt whether one can get anywhere a better notion than is given here of life in a mediaeval castle.

Pp. 115-138. The reader should not fail to notice, throughout this third part, the undercurrent of apprehension in Gawain's mind. Never was man more sorely tried. He was facing certain death if he kept his appointment with Green Knight; he would be recreant if he did not reach the Green Chapel on the day set, yet he was still in the dark as to how to get there; he must not fail to behave with perfect courtesy to his host's wife, yet he could not in loyalty to his host become entangled with her; he was compelled, withal, to present a gay and untroubled surface to everyone.

Pp. 140-143. Notice how the tension of the scene is increased by the fears of the guide and the roughness of weather and landscape.

P. 152. The baldric of green, as the badge of an order of knighthood, has no connection, so far as is known, with any actual group of knights. The motto at the end of the poem *Hony soyt qui mal pence* is that of the order of the Garter, but the members of it seem never to have worn a green badge.

GEOFFREY CHAUCER

The standard edition of Chaucer is still that by W. W. Skeat in six volumes, 1894. Skeat's condensation of this in one volume, *The Student's Chaucer*, 1900, is on the whole better than the *Globe* edition, 1903, by Pollard, Heath, Liddell, and McCormick. The only really satisfactory edition of any portion of Chaucer's works is the *Troilus and Criseyde* by R. K. Root, 1926. The best manual is *The Poetry of Chaucer*, rev. ed. 1922, by the same scholar, and the best biographical sketch that by J. M. Manly in the introduction to *Canterbury Tales*, 1928 (so called, though important stories are omitted). For appreciative criticism, admirably done, see G. L. Kittredge, *Chaucer and His Poetry*, 1915.

We do not know whence Chaucer derived his plan of using the adventures of a group of pilgrims as a dramatic framework for his collection of tales. Probably the notion came from his own experience and imagination. Boccaccio's *Decameron*, pretty clearly, he had never encountered, though he was familiar with Boccaccio's poems, and adapted two of them for his own purposes. He had already begun *The Legend of Good Women*, we must remember, which is essentially a not too reverent burlesque of the collections of saints' legends popular at the time. The tale within a tale was an old device, which he may have known from such works as the *Seven Sages*. However he came upon it, the plan of the *Canterbury Tales* was a notion of genius, for it permitted the assemblage of people of every degree, much by-play along the road, and a great variety of stories.

The student should practise reading Chaucer aloud, which he can do with a little effort. By observing the following rules he will be able to approximate the correct pronunciation and get at least some notion of the poet's metrical skill.

1. Every syllable is pronounced; and there are no silent letters except final unstressed *e* before another vowel or *h*. The final *e* at the end of a line is sounded.

2. Vowels have the so-called Continental values, as in

Latin, German, or Italian: *a* as in *far*, *e* as in *café*, *i* (*y*) as in *machine*, *o* as in *lone*, *u* as in French *nature*, *ou* as in *group*. Short vowels have the same sounds, more rapidly spoken.

3. Diphthongs: *ai* (or *ay*) and *ei* (or *ey*) as in *vain* or *vein*, *au* (or *aw*) like *ow* in *now*, *oi* (or *oy*) as in *toy*.

4. Consonants as at present, except *ch* like Scotch or German *ch*.

THE PROLOGUE

Pp. 156-157. The *Knight*. A typical figure of more than common experience, for he had made war ("no man farther", l. 20) even beyond the limits of Christian lands. He had been at Alexandria in Egypt in 1365; he had served with the Teutonic Knights of Prussia, who were constantly fighting the barbarians of Lettow (Lithuania) and Ruce (Russia); he had assisted at the siege of Algeciras on the south coast of Spain when it was captured from the Moorish King of Granada (ll. 29-30); he had fought in the Moorish states of Belmarye and Tramissene in northern Africa; he had helped capture Lyeys in Armenia from the Turks about 1367, and Satalye on the coast of Asia Minor fifteen years earlier; he had been on expeditions in the Mediterranean ("the Grete See"), and at fifteen set battles; and he had fought for a time with the Christian lord of Palatye in Anatolia.

Pp. 157-158. The *Squire*. The Knight's court-trained son, ripe for knighthood. His accomplishments are those of the gilded youth of his period. It is interesting to note that his military experience had covered the regions in which Chaucer had served as a soldier in 1359.

P. 158. The *Yeoman*. It pleased the Knight (ll. 11-12) to take no servants with him to Canterbury except his sturdy forester (l. 27) or gamekeeper.

Pp. 159-160. The *Prioress*. The head of an establishment that must at least have aspired to be a retreat for women of good birth. Her name (Madame Wildrose) gives a hint of the gentle irony with which she is treated by Chaucer, as if when she "took pains to ape the courtly manner" (159, ll. 19-20) she did not succeed in being wholly natural. Yet she was lively ("of greet disport"), and so amiable and tender-hearted that one could not fail to like her.

P. 160, ll. 6-8. The set of beads was arranged with one large green bead to every ten smaller ones. A string was commonly composed of fifty small beads for Aves and five large ones for Paternosters.

Pp. 160-161. The *Monk*. A representative specimen of the young man with ability who went into the monastic life as a career. He was already in charge of a branch establishment and was likely to be an abbot before he was through. He was "fair for the maistrye", or very superior, but not interested in the true purposes of monasticism.

P. 160, l. 21. St. Benedict founded the first order of monks in the West in the sixth century. His rule became the basis for all later ones. St. Maur was one of his immediate disciples.

P. 161, l. 5. The Austin or Augustinian Canons made up their rule from the writings of St. Augustine of Hippo. He thus might be said to have given his commands: "As Austin bit".

Pp. 161-163. The *Friar*. One of the good-natured rascals who in the name of religion preyed upon England. The Friars, who had done great good as preachers, teachers, and attendants on the sick and poor during the thirteenth century, became very corrupt in the fourteenth. Chaucer gives an ironic but tolerant picture of a man who was a firm support ("a noble post") to his order, because such a smooth beggar. He could make himself agreeable to all sorts of people, could even unbend and romp like a puppy (163, l. 13), but he cultivated the prosperous rather than the poor. In curious contrast to his robust body is his affected speech (ll. 20-21).

Pp. 163-164. The *Merchant*. It must be remembered that trade had flourished in Chaucer's day, and that merchants had gained in importance. This man knew all about foreign exchange and had opinions about the necessity of a strong naval policy to protect the sea-route between Flanders and England, because he shipped wool that way.

P. 164. The *Clerk*. A humorous but kindly sketch of a young scholar who was carrying on what we should call graduate study. He was to be a priest but had not yet taken full orders and a "living" (l. 15). Chaucer makes a joke of his being a philosopher and yet not using his art to enrich himself by the "philosopher's stone" (ll. 20-21).

P. 165. The *Sergeant of the Law*. Only advocates of the greatest eminence were admitted as sergeants. Chaucer stresses both the successful career and the ability of his Man of Law. So clever was he that complicated legal transfers of property were as easy to him as outright sales, and could not be found invalid (ll. 11-12). Knowing by heart the statutes (l. 19) and legal reports (l. 15), he could write down and compose (l. 17) any sort of document.

Pp. 165-166. The *Franklin*. The rich old country gentleman might well have met the eminent lawyer at the county assizes. White of beard and ruddy of complexion, he pampers himself with food and drink. In the morning he takes wine with bread or cake in it (165, l. 26), and all day his table is set with dainties suitable to the season, though his bread and ale never vary in quality (166, l. 3). He fattens his partridges in a coop and keeps fish ready in a pond (ll. 11-12), seeing to it that his cook does his duty by them.

Pp. 166-167. The *Haberdasher, Carpenter, Weaver, Dyer, and Upholsterer* were dressed in a sort of livery, which members of the same guild or fraternity wore on state occasions. They showed their prosperity by their new and freshly adorned equipment, as well as by the silver-mountings of their girdles and bags. Each was the kind of burgess to sit on the daïs in the guild-hall, or to be elected alderman— an honor pleasing to wives because it permitted them to head the procession on the vigils of feast-days.

P. 167. The *Cook*. It is significant that the Knight and the epicurean Franklin are ready to take their luck at the inns, but that the tradesmen must have a cook of their own.

Pp. 167-168. The *Shipman* came from the West, perhaps from Dartmouth, then a thriving port. Though he knew the ports from the island of Gottland in the Baltic to Finistère, and was as good a sailor as any man from Hull to Cartagena in Spain, he did not scruple to steal wine on the way across from Bordeaux or to make his victims walk the plank (168, l. 4) after a fight at sea.

Pp. 168-169. The *Doctor*, though Chaucer jokes about his fondness for gold, was an orthodox physician. Apart from drugs, he used "natural magic", or scientific practice supposedly founded on nature, to heal his patients. Thus he made images at times when the influence of the planets was right, and by means of observing and treating them worked cures.

Pp. 169-170. The *Wife of Bath* is Chaucer's most amazing comic figure. She cherished her position of respectability in *bourgeois* society, as is shown by her insistence on making her offering at church before anyone else and by the kerchiefs she wore, which were so closely woven ("ful fyne were of ground") that they weighed ten pounds. At the same time, she had a past that included five husbands, not to mention "other company in youth," and she knew "the old dance" of love. Before she tells her story, she gives a long, rambling account of her life to the other pilgrims.

Pp. 170-171. The *Parson.* One of the best pictures of a wise and humble minister of God ever penned.

P. 171, ll. 11-12. From *Matthew* v, 19.

Ll. 21-25. He did not leave his parish in charge of a vicar and run to London to get appointed to a chantry or join a religious fraternity.

P. 172. The *Plowman.* It was not unusual for priests to come from the laboring classes. This farmhand was his brother's equal in goodness, even though an ignorant man. He loved God both when happy and unfortunate (l. 16), and his neighbor as himself. He gave his services freely to the poor, and paid his tithes to the church both with labor and money (l. 22).

Pp. 172-173. The *Miller.* As strong as he is ugly, he shows his strength at wrestling matches and his rascality at his mill.

Pp. 173-174. The *Manciple.* The point made about this steward is that he can cheat a group of the cleverest lawyers of England, and yet not be found out. When he bought provisions, whether for cash or credit, he took good care always to have the better of the bargain (173, ll. 21-23). The inns of court were called "temples" because two of them are on the site of the old establishment of the Knights Templar.

Pp. 174-175. The *Reeve* had risen in the world, having started in life as a carpenter and become business agent of a great estate. There is more than a hint that he was dishonest, though no auditor could prove it (174, l. 16), or anybody else find out that his accounts were not correct (l. 34). Chaucer had had experience as executor of an estate in Norfolk, which is perhaps why he made the Reeve come from that county and called his dapple grey horse Scot, which is still a common name there.

Pp. 175-176. The *Summoner.* Perhaps the most despicable rascal of the lot. His looks and manners were terrifyingly bad; and in spite of knowing a few Latin phrases, like the speech of a jay or a parrot, he was ignorant, as anyone who tested him (176, l. 4) could find out. He would rob a gull (l. 12), yet teach a boon companion not to mind the curse of the archdeacon, who controlled the ecclesiastical court, arguing that archdeacons imposed fines only for the sake of the money they got (ll. 13-18). "A significavit" (l. 22) means a writ of excommunication, which usually began with that word.

Pp. 176-178. The *Pardoner* was either a travelling agent of the Augustinian house of Rounvical, or represented himself to have that authority. He was not necessarily in orders, but peddled "pardons" that cost him a penny apiece, using his unquestioned powers as a "spell-binder" to persuade people to buy indulgences and absolutions from him. With his false relics, like what purported to be the veil of the Virgin (177, l. 23), his singing, and his eloquence, it was not strange that he got more money in a day than a poor priest did in two months (177, l. 29-178, l. 2).

P. 178, ll. 23-26. Chaucer begs his readers not to attribute to his own vulgarity ("vileinye") the words and actions of some of the pilgrims—the realist's apology.

P. 179, ll. 7-10. A humorous apology for not letting the pilgrims tell their stories in the order of their social rating.

Ll. 15-21. The *Host*, who is named Harry Bailly, as we soon learn. An inn-keeper with that name twice represented Southwark in parliament. Chaucer represents him as a jovial big man with a commanding presence, equal to any rich burgess of Cheapside across the river, though Southwark was a small place.

L. 34. "The blessed martyr reward you."

P. 180, ll. 12-13. "We did not have to consult long; it did not seem worth while to deliberate."

Ll. 25-28. The arrangement is that the pilgrim who tells the best stories, in content and amusing quality, shall have a supper at the expense of all when they return to London.

P. 181, l. 21. They rode at a jog-trot.

L. 26. That is: "If what you said last night agrees with what you feel this morning."

THE NUN'S PRIEST'S TALE

Pp. 182-202. Chaucer worked at the *Canterbury Tales* in groups, not straight on from a beginning towards the end. Thus he left at his death ten fragments, the arrangement of which in the manuscripts is much confused. After the Knight, the Miller, and the Reeve have told their stories, the Cook begins a tale that was never completed. At least two groups intervened before the series in which occurs the

Nun's Priest's Tale. The narratives of this series are those
of the Shipman, the Prioress, Chaucer, the Monk, and the
young Priest.

A fable is well made, I take it, when the actors are
equally in character as beasts and as men. Chaucer's fable
has this virtue to a pre-eminent degree. Chauntecleer never
ceases to be a cock, and at the same time he has all the
qualities of the sort of man who reminds one of a cock.
A fable is usually short, pithy, and humorous, as well as
satiric and moralistic. Chaucer has enlarged its scope without sacrificing anything save brevity. Two thirds of the
tale is devoted to an inspired introduction, wherein the whole
character of Chauntecleer is developed dramatically through
a long conversation with his favorite wife. The action, when
it comes, is swift and sure.

P. 182, 1. 25. Sir John was a generic name for poor
priests, like "George" for Pullman porters.

P. 183, ll. 13-19. The widow had little property ("catel")
or income ("rente"), but supported herself by careful man-
agement ("housbondrye") of what God sent her. She lived
in a two-room cottage, consisting of "bower" and "hall". The
sheep "named Malle" was doubtless almost a member of the
family.

P. 184, 1.10. I.e., every hour.

Ll. 13-19. The mock-heroic vein in which the cock is
described appears again on pp. 195 and 199.

Pp. 185-187. Pertelote reveals herself as a practical and
unimaginative housewife. Humor lurks in her appeal to
Cato as an authority, for the proverbs that went under his
name were like the maxims of Poor Richard. The learned
Chauntecleer is naturally impatient with such ignorance, as
he shows by his conclusive and pedantic disquisition on
dreams (pp. 187-193).

P. 185, 1. 1. "My dear one is gone away", which must
have been the refrain of a popular song.

P. 186, ll. 11-13. "Dreams come from over-eating, and
often from vapors arising from the stomach, and from physi-
cal temperaments, when bodily humors are too abundant in
a person."

P. 188, 1. 8. *Oon of the gretteste auctours,* Cicero, perhaps read in a book by Robert Holkot.

P. 189, 1. 24. "no longer would he delay."

P. 190, 1. 14. "And also so racked the inn-keeper."

P. 191, 1. 15. "And of many a confused thought as well."

P. 194, ll. 13-14. That God made the world in March was a notion going back to the Church Fathers.

P. 195, ll. 3-5. A reference to the prose romance of *Lancelot* in French, one of the best-known of the Arthurian cycle.

L. 7. A "col-fox" was probably black.

L. 26. "But what God foreknows must necessarily come to pass."

P. 196, l. 31. *Phisiologus* was a moralizing Latin poem about fabulous creatures.

P. 199, ll. 10-11. King Richard was killed by an arrow ("with shot").

P. 200, ll. 10-31. Note the speed of the verse during the chase. The Flemish were unpopular with the peasantry because they were foreigners and industrialists, whether traders or weavers.

THE PARDONER'S TALE

Pp. 202-221. Preceded by the pathetic *Physician's Tale* of Virginia. To cheer the company the Host turned to the Pardoner, who was riding with his friend the Summoner (see p. 176). As for the Summoner,

> A gerland had he set up-on his heed,
> As greet as it were for an ale-stake;
> A bokeler had he maad him of a cake.

Presumably both of the men were provided with liquor and had already been drinking. So the Pardoner, making his little joke about the ale-stake, leaned over and broke off a bit of his companion's buckler. He then started to think of some "honest thing," and succeeded in pulling out of his befuddled brain the text from 1 Timothy vi, 10. This set him off, with drunken shamelessness, on an account of his scandalous way of life. The discourse, which is roughly in the form of one of his sermons, suggested to him (p. 206) ensamples and brought back to his mind the tale he had to tell. He began it bravely, but after a few lines wandered again into part of a sermon on the Seven Deadly Sins, which did not lack eloquence in spite of its drunken absurdity. The story, when he finally came to it (p. 213), was indeed an exemplum, but an exemplum developed magnificently into one of the best tales of terror ever written. Note that Chaucer set his scene with care to create the proper atmosphere and to make plain his theme, introduced mystery in the unexplained figure of the old man, developed as the main event the arrangements of the three rioters, and restrained himself to a few lines in the crashing irony of the close.

P. 202, l. 24. "I take pains to have a high-sounding manner of speech."

P. 203, l. 23. "That any snake has bitten or stung."

P. 207, l. 10. By swearing by different parts of His body.

P. 208, l. 27. I *Corinthians* vi, 13.

P. 209, l. 7. "How great labor and expense it is to provide for thee!"

Ll. 24-25. Imitating the drunkard's snore reminds the Pardoner that Samson was a total abstainer, a Nazarite.

L. 31. "He can keep no secret, sure enough."

P. 210, ll. 3-4. Because Spanish wines were used to fortify and adulterate the lighter French wines from Rochelle and Bordeaux.

P. 212, ll. 6-7. *Matthew* v, 34, and *Jeremiah* iv. 2.

L. 13. In the Authorized Version this is the third commandment instead of the second, as in the Vulgate.

P. 215, l. 22. *Leviticus* xix, 32.

P. 217, l. 33. "Can you keep a secret?"

THE FRANKLIN'S TALE

Pp. 221-250. The *Squire's Tale,* which precedes this, was left unfinished by Chaucer, but the connecting link had been written. The *Franklin's Tale* itself is the crown of what is called the Marriage Group, in which the relations of men and women are discussed and illustrated from different points of view. Here marital devotion is the theme, accompanied by other loyalties of heart and behavior. Chaucer called the tale a lay, which is a name for short verse romances made popular by Marie de France in the twelfth century.

Pp. 223-227. The Franklin begins his tale with a summary of the relations existing between Arveragus and Dorigen, an understanding of which is essential to the story. Only when they are clear does he picture his first scene, that of the disconsolate lady on the shore of the Channel. In her preoccupation with the rocks we see the dominant note of the action struck at once.

P. 225, l. 7. The position of the planets may cause men to err in action or speech.

L. 27. Penmarch is the name of a village, once a place of some importance, and of a desolate sandy cape skirted by dangerous rocks that forms the southwestern tip of Brittany.

P. 226, ll. 3-4. All his ambition was set on honors gained in fighting.

P. 227, l. 1. "To come and walk about in company."

Ll. 23-25. "Eternal God, Who through Thy providence controllest the world with unerring skill, Ye make nothing in vain, so men say."

L. 33. "It does no good, as far as I can see, but works harm."

P. 228, ll. 6-7. "How then can Ye create such instruments to destroy it?"

P. 229, l. 20. "As to my doom" means "in my judgment."

P. 230, l. 21. "She" is the subject understood.

P. 231, l. 16. "the length of Brittany."

L. 27. "What pleasure can a man have?"

P. 232, l. 7. As if the horizon absorbed the light of the sun.

L. 15. "And on his bare knees."

P. 233, l. 8. "Is to be enlivened and lighted by your fire."

Ll. 15-16. The sun's power would be greatest when in the sign of Leo, its so-called "mansion."

Ll. 26-28. If the moon travelled at the same rate as the sun, it would always be in opposition, and high tide would be perpetual.

P. 234. Suspense of one sort is substituted for another when Arveragus comes home. Dorigen is no longer troubled about the rocks, but Aurelius is.

P. 235, l. 11. "Curious arts" means arts of skill or magic.

Ll. 15-16. "he saw a book of the magic based on nature."

P. 237, ll. 12-15. "No food was lacking that could please them; Aurelius in all his life never saw a house so well provided as this one."

P. 238, l. 11. "And after supper they discussed."

P. 239, ll. 5-9. The sun, which at the summer solstice ("hote declinacioun") shone like burnished gold, was now at the winter solstice ("in Capricorn") and therefore pale.

L. 12. Janus is double-faced.

P. 240, ll. 25-26. "Aurelius, who is still despairingly uncertain whether he shall have his love or fail."

P. 241, l. 21. "You know well what you have promised." Note the extraordinary and delicate courtesy of this entire speech.

P. 242. Dorigen takes the centre of the stage again, when Aurelius has announced the disappearance of the rocks. She must decide whether to keep her word. Notice that Aurelius has made no insistent demand upon her. Like everyone in the story, he behaves well according to the code of courtly love and good manners prevalent in the Middle Ages.

L. 13. "She can scarcely walk because of her terror."

L. 22. "That has coiled me unawares in thy chain."

Ll. 26-27. "yet I should prefer to lose my life than submit to bodily shame."

Pp. 242-245. All these examples of Dorigen's were taken from a work by St. Jerome.

P. 243, ll. 8-9. "They secretly threw themselves into a well and were drowned."

P. 244, l. 26. "They slew themselves on account of the same sort of thing."

P. 245, l. 32. "let sleeping dogs lie."

P. 246, l. 11. "draw a long face."

P. 247, ll. 26-27. "Give up every pledge and every bond that you have heretofore made me."

L. 33. "But let every woman beware of promises."

P. 248, l. 19. Magicians were called philosophers.

P. 250, l. 2. "it is no drede" means "surely."

L. 5. "As if you had just now crept out of the ground," like an insect emerging.

THE SECOND NUN'S TALE

Pp. 250-269. Although Chaucer had placed this poem before the *Canon's Yeoman's Tale,* he had not adapted it, at the time of his death, to its place in the series, as will be seen from the reference on p. 252, l. 22. We know that it had been written before he began the *Canterbury Tales,* for there is a reference to it in the Prologue to the *Legend of Good Women.* There is no evidence whatever, on the other hand, that it was an early work, as has sometimes been carelessly said. It has seldom received its due meed of praise, chiefly, I suspect, because it has been read without reference to its peculiar quality. Although Chaucer called it a translation, in which he followed "the wordes and sentence" of his original, he actually lifted the narrative from mediocre prose to poetry of singular sweetness, with a hymn-like melody that gives it great charm. We should not ask for bold characterization, for dramatic arrangement of event, for humorous comment in a tale so reverentially told, any more than we should look for such qualities in *The Eve of St. Agnes*. Chaucer showed himself the great artist here, as he did elsewhere, precisely by suiting his verse to the subject in hand. He was writing a legend, and he chose for it his favorite rhyme royal stanza, in which he could produce the utmost suavity of tone when he wished. The only liberty he took with his Latin source was to hurry on from the conversion of Valerian and Tiburce to their martyrdom—a notable improvement in the narrative, but not a falsification. Anyone who fails to catch the beauty of the poem had better read it aloud, although this recommendation need not be confined to this one tale.

P. 250, l. 26. "Till a man is caught by a fold of his garment."

P. 252, ll. 25-26. "Give me intelligence and time so to do that I may escape the place that is most dark," i.e. hell.

P. 254, l. 7. "in figuringe" means figuratively.

Ll. 20-21. "Just so men saw spiritually in this noble maiden the great-heartedness of faith."

P. 255, l. 15. St. Cecilia is the patron saint of music.

Ll. 17-18. "Oh Lord, guide my soul and also my body in purity so that I may not be confounded."

P. 257, l. 14. "herde" means shepherd.

P. 258, l. 21. "sote savour" means sweet fragrance.

P. 259, ll. 24-26. "We have been in dreams up to this time certainly, my brother, but now for the first time we dwell in the truth."

P. 261, l. 22. "Men might sensibly fear."

P. 262, l. 3. "That there was another life in which men may live."

L. 17. "To accomplish full remission (of sin) for mankind."

P. 263, l. 16-18. "They rescued from the false faith the torturers, Maximus, and all his followers."

P. 268, l. 18. "but by no kind of chance."

L. 30. "She began to preach to those she had nurtured."

LYRICS

Pp. 269-276. A delightful collection of early lyrical poems is *Early English Lyrics* by E. K. Chambers and F. Sidgwick, 1907. For one kind of song, *Religious Lyrics of the XIVth Century* by C. Brown, 1924, is both exclusive and admirable.

MALORY'S MORTE D'ARTHUR

Pp. 276-297. The best edition of Malory is that by H. O. Sommer, 1889-91. Of editions with modern spelling, that in Everyman's Library is satisfactory.

POPULAR BALLADS

Pp. 297-351. The great collection of ballads by F. J. Child, *English and Scottish Popular Ballads*, 5 vols., 1882-1898, can never be superseded. The one volume edition of this by H. C. Sargent and G. L. Kittredge, 1904, gives at least one version of all but four of the three hundred and five ballads in the larger work and is indispensable. The ballad-lover will like to own also *Popular Ballads of the Olden Time*, by F. Sidgwick, 4 series, 1903-1912. Within the last two decades much has been done to rescue ballad melodies and ballad variants. Of especial interest to American students are such books as C. J. Sharp and O. D. Campbell, *English Folk Songs from the Southern Appalachians*, 1917; J. H. Cox, *Folk-Songs of the South*, 1925; and Reed Smith, *South Carolina Ballads*, 1928. The best book about ballads is F. B. Gummere, *The Popular Ballad*, 1907.

BABYLON

Pp. 299-301. This is a Scottish version, from Motherwell's *Minstrelsy*, 1827.

EDWARD

Pp. 301-303. This is again a Scottish version, from Percy's *Reliques*, 1765.

THE MAID FREED FROM THE GALLOWS

Pp. 303-305. Child II, 346-355, from the Percy Papers. Sent to Bishop Percy from Wye, Kent. Child knew thirteen versions, and various interesting ones have since been collected.

LORD RANDAL

Pp. 305-307. Child I, 157-158, from a manuscript volume lent to Child by Mr. Macmath, of Edinburgh. The version was written out in the nineteenth century. The ballad has remained very popular. Child gathered twenty-five versions, and Sharp records finding twenty versions in England, besides almost as many in America.

JOHNIE COCK

Pp. 307-310. Child III, 3-4, from the Percy Papers. Sent to Percy from Carlisle in 1780. Child found thirteen versions.

THOMAS RYMER

Pp. 310-313. Child I, 323-324, from a Scottish source of 1800.

THE WIFE OF USHER'S WELL

Pp. 313-314. Scott, *Minstrelsy of the Scottish Border*, 1802, II, 111, from a Scottish source.

THE DÆMON LOVER

Pp. 314-317. *Scott, Minstrelsy o the Scottish Border*, 5th ed. 1812, II, 427, from a Scottish source.

THE THREE RAVENS

Pp. 317-318. Child I, 254, from an early seventeenth century English song-book. Variants have recently been found in the South.

HUGH OF LINCOLN

Pp. 318-320. Jamieson, *Popular Ballads and Songs*, 1806, I, 151-154. A Scottish version. Child found twenty-one versions, and numerous variants have been collected since his time.

CHILDE WATERS

Pp. 320-326. Hales and Furnivall, *Bishop Percy's Folio Manuscript*, 1867-68, II, 269. Seventeenth century English.

SIR PATRICK SPENCE

Pp. 326-328. A Scottish version, from Percy's *Reliques*, 1765. Child found eighteen versions.

YOUNG WATERS

Pp. 328-330. Child II, 342-345. A Scottish version, printed ten years before the publication of Percy's *Reliques*.

THE BONNY EARL OF MURRAY

Pp. 330-331. Child III, 448, from a Scottish version printed in 1750.

MARY HAMILTON

Pp. 331-333. Child III, 384-385, Scottish, collected in the earlier part of the nineteenth century. Child found twenty-eight versions.

CHEVY CHASE

Pp. 333-342. Child III, 311-314. This is an inferior version of *The Hunting of the Cheviot*, which is the English ballad corresponding to the Scottish *Battle of Otterburn*. *Chevy Chase* is given here not only because of its great fame, but because it illustrates what was done to old ballads in seventeenth century broadsides.

ROBIN HOOD AND GUY OF GISBORNE

Pp. 343-351. Hales and Furnivall, *Bishop Percy's Folio Manuscript*, II, 227. Seventeenth century English.

THE LOCHMABEN HARPER

P. 351. Child IV, 17-18. From three sources, including copies collected by Burns and Sir Walter Scott.

JOCK O THE SIDE

P. 354. Child III, 479-481. From the late eighteenth century. There is also a version in the Percy Manuscript. One of the very best Border ballads.

THE BRAES OF YARROW

P. 360. Child IV, 164-165. Sent to Bishop Percy. Versions have been found in Maine and the South.

THE UNQUIET GRAVE

P. 362. Child II, 236. Collected in Sussex in the nineteenth century. A great many English versions have been found.

LADY ISABEL AND THE ELF-KNIGHT

P. 363. Child I, 55. A Scottish version of a ballad found in many countries. It has been very popular among American singers.

THE TWA SISTERS

P. 365. Child I, 127, from a Scottish source. Child found twenty-seven variants of the ballad, and more than forty others have since come to light. It has been popular in America.

ALLISON GROSS

P. 367. Child I, 314-315. Only this Scottish version has survived. It is the most effective witch ballad that we have.

TAM LIN

P. 369. Child I, 340-343. This version was found by Robert Burns.

SAINT STEPHEN AND HEROD

P. 376. Child I, 241-242. Known only from a fifteenth century manuscript.

THE CHERRY-TREE CAROL

P. 377. Child II, 2. From the west of England in the nineteenth century. More variants of the ballad have been found in America than in England.

BONNIE GEORGE CAMPBELL

P. 379. Child IV, 143. From a Scottish source. Vies with *The Bonny Earl of Murray* as an example of compression. The story is complete. A stanza from a West Virginia version printed by J. H. Combs, *Folk-Songs du Midi*, 1925, shows how adaptation to local conditions may take place without destroying the effect:

> "My house is not shingled,
>   my barn is not raised,
> My crops are not gathered,
>   and my babe has not come."